The Religious Genius in Rabbi Kook's Thought:
National "Saint"?

REFERENCE LIBRARY OF JEWISH INTELLECTUAL HISTORY

ACADEMIC
STUDIES
PRESS

The Religious Genius
in Rabbi Kook's Thought:
National "Saint"?

Dov SCHWARTZ

Translated by Edward Levin

Library of Congress Cataloging-in-Publication Data:
A bibliographic record for this title is available
from the Library of Congress.

ISBN 978-1-618114-05-1 (cloth)
ISBN 978-1-618114-06-8 (electronic)
ISBN 978-1-618114-11-2 (paper)

Book design by Ivan Grave
On the cover:
    Portrait by Rivka Pick-Landesman (reproduced by the author's permission).

Published by Academic Studies Press in 2014
28 Montfern Avenue
Brighton, MA 02135, USA
press@academicstudiespress.com
www.academicstudiespress.com

Contents

PREFACE

Numerous studies have been written on the thought of Rabbi Abraham Isaac Hakohen Kook. Rabbi Kook combined halakhic, philosophical, and Kabbalistic intuitions, based on many diverse sources, with an exceptional national stance; he also possessed an extraordinary personality. He unquestionably exemplified religious genius.

Most of the works about Rabbi Kook are anchored in historical and philosophical disciplines. The central question the current book addresses is the degree to which Rabbi Kook's writings can prove to be beneficial to the postmodern discourse. I examine this multifaceted issue and highlight the contribution of his writings to this discourse. The book is concerned with religious genius, as such genius emerges from the thought of Rabbi Kook, and discusses at length the traits of the perfect individual according to him. I assume that Rabbi Kook's thought describes religious genius as well as proving his own genius.

The book had its beginnings in an Elijah Interfaith Institute study project on religious genius headed by Dr. Alon Goshen-Gottstein. In addition to Dr. Goshen-Gottstein, the book was also read by Dr. Uriel Barak and Dr. Meir Munitz, who offered valuable comments. My thanks to Professors Menachem Kellner and Daniel Statman for their assistance. Finally, I wish to thank Edward Levin for his important comments.

Chapters Eleven ("Rabbi Kook and the Revolutionary Consciousness of Religious Zionism") and Twelve ("Maimonides in Rabbi Kook's and Religious Zionist Philosophy: Unity vs. Duality") were originally translated by David Louvish and Batya Stein, respectively, and were adapted for this volume.

I would like to thank the Vice President for Research of Bar-Ilan University Professor Benjamin Ehrenberg and the Zerah Warhaftig Institute for the Research of Religious Zionism for their support of this research.

Dov Schwartz

INTRODUCTION

The spirited interest in saints and religious genius associated with the postmodernist experience and its active study can be traced to three main causes, each of which relates in some manner to the instability and fluidity characteristic of this experience:

(1) A moral anchor: the postmodernist questioning of universalism and absolute truth undermines traditional moral conceptions. "Saintliness," in the characteristic sense of the activity of the "saint," is expressed in behavior, and not in abstract moral principles.[1] It therefore makes ethical education possible, despite the lack of accepted moral principles.

(2) Metaphysical dialectics: the modern world focuses on man and his existence, while metaphysics is shunted aside. Since postmodernism emerged from the conflict with modernism, the concept of "man," which was at the center of modernity, is no longer universal and stable. Postmodernism champions the legitimate voice of the different, the Other, and the individual, which at times was allowed no expression by the modern world. Postmodernism explores the boundaries of metaphysics, employing irony and nostalgia.[2] To a certain degree, this nostalgia ensues from the need for certainty, identity, and meaning in a world in which the stability of time has been undermined (the present facing the future, and so forth). "Saintliness" expresses nostalgia for the metaphysical.

(3) The quest for asceticism: additionally, the postmodernist discourse on sexuality, as expressed especially by Foucault, demands an anchor with which one can withstand temptation.[3] The saint presents a way of life that contends with temptations and overcomes them.

---

[1] See, e.g., E. Wyschogrod, *Saints and Postmodernism: Revisioning Moral Philosophy* (Chicago, 1990). See D. Gurevitz, *Postmodernism* (Tel Aviv, 1997), 269 [Hebrew].

[2] See K. Tester, *The Life and Times of Post-modernity* (London, 1993), 54-78.

[3] See G. G. Harpham, *The Ascetic Imperative in Culture and Criticism* (Chicago, 1993), 220-35.

The Western religious world felt no need to provide a historical and realistic definition of saints, as the scientific research of positivist questions does. The saints, at the rise of Western religion, were primarily martyrs, individuals who gave their lives for their faith. The cult of saints gave the flocks of the faithful of the new religions the resolve to endure. The saint was perceived as a figure standing in the background who is present for the believer.[4] Over the course of time, this perception came to include the individual who lived a life of faith, and thereby was devoted to his fellow (healing, miracles, and the like). For example, the first four khalifs, until Ali, were perceived as saints in Islamic literature. Their ways of life were seen as worthy of study and emulation. The uninterrupted tradition of the Western religions contains the unchanging adoration of saints. From time to time the Catholic Church announces the addition of saints to the existing list. According to Catholic doctrine, only God can proclaim saintliness, but the Pope manifests the divine will. Inge defines the saint as follows (the division here is mine):

(A) They [saints] tell us that they have arrived gradually at an unshakable conviction, not based on inference but on immediate experience,

   (1) that God is a Spirit, with whom the human spirit can hold intercourse;

   (2) that in Him meet all that they can imagine of goodness, truth, and beauty;

   (3) that they can see His footprints everywhere in nature;

   (4) and they can feel His presence within them as the very life of their life, so that in proportion as they come to themselves they come to Him.

---

4   See P. Brown, *The Cult of the Saints: Its Rise and Function in Latin Christianity* (Chicago, 1981). On the medieval period, see A. Vauchez, *Sainthood in the Later Middle Ages*, trans. J. Birrell (Cambridge, 1997); C. Ernst, *Manifestations of Sainthood in Islam* (Istanbul, 1993); idem, *Ruzbihan Baqli: Mysticism and the Rhetoric of Sainthood in Persian Sufism* (Richmond, Surrey, 1996); V. Cornell, *Realm of the Saint: Power and Authority in Moroccan Sufism* (Austin, TX, 1998); J. Shatzmiller, "Jews, Pilgrimage, and the Christian Cult of Saints: Benjamin of Tudela and His Contemporaries," in *After Rome's Fall: Narrators and Sources of Early Medieval History*, ed. A. Collander Murray (Toronto, 1998), 337-47; J. Galinsky, "Different Approaches towards the Miracles of Christian Saints in Medieval Rabbinic Literature," in *Ta Shma: Studies in Judaica in Memory of Israel M. Ta-Shma*, ed. A. Reiner et al. (Alon Shevut, 2011), 195-219 [Hebrew].

(B) They [saints] tell us what separates us from Him and from happiness is

    (1) first, self-seeking in all its forms;

    (2) and, secondly, sensuality in all its forms.

That these are the ways of darkness and death, which hide from us the face of God; while the path of the just is like shining light, which shineth more and more unto the perfect day.[5]

According to Inge, a saint is a complex of experience, theological approaches, and practice. In the postmodernist discourse, the saint appears where general moral principles have lost their validity, and the emotive is the only channel for ethical education. The saint lives a life of sensibility, that enables imitation and internalization. The questions that arise in the study of the modern relationship to sainthood are both scholarly-objective and reflective. Some examples of such questions are:

(1) How is saintliness to be defined in the reality of the postmodern world?

(2) Can the attributes of the saint serve as a common basis for multiple religions?

(3) How are the character traits of the saint to be charted in a world in which abstract research is no longer an absolute criterion for truth and consensus?

These questions are the subject of intensive discussion by philosophers and scholars. In this work I will seek to reexamine them indirectly, by the personification of the general arguments on the nature of sainthood in an analysis of the figure of Rabbi Abraham Isaac Hakohen Kook as saint. I will define below the meanings I find in the idea of the "saint," but I will state here that we are engaged in a study of religious genius, namely perfection and the exceptional dimension in his religious inspiration. Saint and religious genius are not identical, since the former is a realistic figure, while the genius tends toward the ideal. In the following discussion, however, we will not distinguish between the two.

Since there is no authoritative proclamation of sainthood in the Jewish world, the basis for the image of the saint is, primarily, acceptance

---

[5]   W. R. Inge, *Christian Mysticism* (London, 1899), 325-26.

by broad circles of the community. The saint is perceived first and foremost as one who gave his life for his faith and community. The paradigm of saints is those who die for *Kiddush Hashem* (literally, the "sanctification of the name of God"), that is, dying a martyr's death when given the choice of conversion or the sword, or when forced to transgress the laws of Judaism (Rabbi Akiva and the other sages killed by the Romans, the German pietists who committed suicide in the Crusades rather than convert, etc.). Another paradigm focuses on a life of *Kiddush Hashem*, that is, those individuals who are seen as selfless, and whose very being and activity are directed in their entirety to the public good. The term *"kedushat ha-hayyim"* (the sanctification of life), coined during the Holocaust, refers to survival in face of the Nazi machinery of destruction.

In the religious Zionist public in Israel, Rabbi Kook is seen as an unquestioned spiritual and altruistic authority. There are differing opinions within this public on the degree to which his praxis is to be followed, and the extent to which his life was a pure model for a religious Zionist life. However, he is unquestionably revered by the entire religious Zionist camp as one who devoted his life to the people as a whole, and to the national rebirth. In the secular camp, he shares a place of honor as one of the founding fathers of Zionism, whose actions changed the standing of the Jewish people in the world. Among the nonreligious, he is profoundly admired for his support of Zionism, in contrast with the majority of Orthodox rabbis. Furthermore, many of his opponents among the non-Zionist Orthodox public unreservedly state that his motives were "holy." I do not intend to discuss the historical parameters that present Rabbi Kook as a saint; rather, I will examine his character traits as a saint through an analysis of the texts that he authored, and the incorporation of those texts in his rich spiritual and cultural world.

Chapter One

METHODOLOGY

Rabbi Abraham Isaac Hakohen Kook lived in a modern world. To a certain extent, he began to experience the undermining of humanism in the First World War.[1] He died in Mandatory Palestine in 1935, and did not live to see the total collapse of normative systems that occurred in the Second World War. Because he did not know the postmodern world, he meets the nostalgic criteria of the saint. As I mentioned above, the figure of the saint in the Christian world begins with official recognition by the Church. That is to say, the element of public recognition is a component of the image of the saint. While originally an official body declared sainthood, beginning in the twentieth century one could also speak of saintliness in the context of consensus—that is, public acceptance. Rabbi Kook is indeed broadly viewed as an exceptional figure. Generations of religious Zionist pupils are educated to follow in his path, and the members of his close circle saw him as a supreme charismatic authority. In the secular public he is perceived as the premier spiritual representative of religious support for the Zionist enterprise.

Another consideration in this context is that the saint, in the Catholic sense, is proclaimed as such only after his passing. Orthodox Jewry in the Diaspora did not acknowledge Rabbi Kook as their spiritual guide during the years of his activity. The evidence shows that even in the 1940s his writings were not commonly known in Europe, although European Jews had heard

---

[1] For Rabbi Kook's life, see A. Rozenak, *Rabbi A. I. Kook* (Jerusalem, 2007) [Hebrew]. Biographies of a hagiographical bent have been written as well, such as Rabbi Judah Leib Maimon (Fishman), *Rabbi Abraham Isaac ha-Kohen Kook* (Jerusalem, 1965) [Hebrew]. It is noteworthy that Rabbi Kook apparently understood the war in a positive manner, since its apocalyptic elements fit into his messianic vision. This is indicated, e.g., in his essay "War," published in his book *Orot*; this topic is worthy of a lengthy discussion.

of him. Rabbi Kook became a saintly figure only after intensive educational work spanning decades, the greater part of which was encouraged by the leaders of state religious education in Israel.[2]

Sources

The saint, with his traits, image, and activity, is a central topic in Rabbi Kook's thought. For our purposes, I define "saint" as a religious personage with characteristics that border on perfect, who possesses an exceptional religious consciousness, and who acts in an altruistic manner for the elevation and redemption of the world. Rabbi Kook added the national dimension to these characteristics, as we will see in Chapter Six. His discussions of the saint clearly tended toward the obsessive, in terms of both his analysis of the characteristics of such a figure and his revealing confessions. In this respect, Rabbi Kook is exceptional in the landscapes of religious Zionist thought and modern Orthodoxy.

The image of Rabbi Kook as religious genius is composed of at least two strata:

(1) Historical activity, constructed from testimonies and evaluations. His activity was based mainly on his connection with the New and Old *Yishuv* (roughly speaking, the New *Yishuv* refers to the Zionist-inspired Jewish community in the Land of Israel, and the Old *Yishuv* refers to the pre-Zionist Jewish community there) on the one hand, and with the Zionist movement and its personages, on the other. Scholarly research has explored the question of the altruistic motives of Rabbi Kook's activity.[3]

(2) Texts: Rabbi Kook barely engaged in methodical writing. His style was generally aphoristic, and was composed of a lengthy series of random paragraphs on various issues. His writings include letters, commentaries, and collections of passages.

The following discussion will be based mainly on textual analysis. I ascribe great importance to the few compositions that are methodical, and

[2] See D. Schwartz, "On Religious Zionist Extremism: Education and Ideology," *Dor le Dor: Studies in the History of Jewish Education in Israel and the Diaspora* (forthcoming) [Hebrew].

[3] See D. Schwartz, "From First Blossoming to Realization: The History of the Religious Zionist Movement and Its Ideas," in *The Religious Zionism: An Era of Changes. Studies in Memory of Zvulun Hammer*, ed. A. Cohen and Y. Harel (Jerusalem, 2004), 40-51 [Hebrew].

that compelled Rabbi Kook to engage in consecutive writing. I especially focus on two works: "*Eder ha-Yakar*" ("The Noble Sum"—from Zechariah 11:13) and "*Ikvei ha-Tzon*" (The Tracks of the Sheep"—from Song of Songs 1:8), both of which were published in 1906, and which were reprinted in a single volume. These essays are infused with the consciousness of the saint and the exemplary individual.

The other sources in Rabbi Kook's writings that are relevant for the religious genius, although not in methodical fashion, fall into two categories:

(1) Revealing personal passages, in which the author attests to his propensities, desires, and visions. The image of the singular individual emerges from within these passages.

(2) Random philosophical passages, which enable us to compose the portrait of the exemplary individual.

Rabbi Kook ascribed great importance to the perception of the *tzaddik* (the spiritual leader of the community) in Hasidism. To a great degree, the figure of the Hasidic *tzaddik* is the starting point for the variegated and rich perception of the saint. The Hasidic influence penetrated as far as the notion of the worth of the *tzaddik*'s eating, which appears from time to time in Rabbi Kook's collections. He found nothing wrong in giving a monetary donation to the *tzaddik*, "in the manner of a gift expressing sublime honor."[4] Rabbi Kook developed a sort of restorative historiographic theory that "Torah scholars" and the "righteous" (*tzaddikim*) were the leadership in ancient times. A series of historical events, first among them the Exile, eroded the standing of those individuals. Hasidism restored the standing of the *tzaddik*: "The recent Hasidism came and strove to rectify this, to restore the living worth of the righteous individual and his unique activity. This notion [of such activity] is both mystic and social, and much attention must be devoted to its positive and negative aspects."[5] The end of this passage teaches of a certain reservation, and Rabbi Kook's conception of the saint is not just another version of the Hasidic *tzaddik*, but a rich and variegated development of the Hasidic figure.

---

[4]   *Kevatzim*, vol. 1, 174.

[5]   *Shemonah Kevatzim* 2:156 (vol. 1, 339).

Phenomenological Methodology

Our discussion will be influenced by methodologies from the phenomenological school of the philosophy of religion that arose at the beginning of the twentieth century in Germany and Austria. Rudolf Otto, Max Scheller, Friedrich Heiler, and Gerardus van der Leeuw each argued in his own way that the religious consciousness must be understood and described from within itself. Psychology, sociology, and politics can aid in understanding the religious mind, but the religious act is understood first and foremost from within religion. They explained holiness and the image of the saint in a similar manner. In the Jewish world, this approach especially influenced Rabbi Joseph B. Soloveitchik[6] and Abraham Joshua Heschel,[7] whose philosophical orientation vastly differs from that of Rabbi Kook. Nonetheless, Rabbi Kook adopted the conception of the existence of a universal religious consciousness, which he called the "holy sentiment [regesh]" or the "general sentiment of religion," connecting to his idea of universal morality.

I use phenomenological methodology as a tool for understanding the image of Rabbi Kook as a "saint" based on his profound religious experience and religious consciousness. I intend to set aside the specific time and place in which he was active, to disregard his leadership of a circle of followers and the thinkers and series of interests that guided him in his activity, and to examine the features of his personality itself in terms of religious genius. I am aware that a study of Rabbi Kook's ideological circles would contribute greatly to an understanding of his conduct as a saint, but in the current book we will focus exclusively on his writings.

From an interpretive aspect, our methodology will be twofold. Rabbi Kook's creative spiritual activity was obviously conducted within a defined conceptual framework. He drew upon Kabbalistic and Hasidic sources, and was influenced by European philosophical approaches such as those of

---

6   See D. Schwartz, *The Philosophy of Rabbi Joseph B. Soloveitchik*, vol. 1: *Religion or Halakha*, trans. B. Stein (Leiden, 2007); vol. 2: *From Phenomenology to Existentialism*, trans. B. Stein (Leiden, 2012).

7   See, e.g., N. Rotenstreich, "On Prophetic Consciousness," *Journal of Religion* 54 (1974): 185-98; D. Schwartz, *Aggadah in the Prism of Phenomenology: A Reexamination of "Heavenly Torah"* (forthcoming).

Kant, Hegel, Schopenhauer, and Bergson. Evaluating Rabbi Kook's thought on the background of its sources will be the platform for our discussion of its meaning. Evaluation is the first interpretive phase; in this book, we will seek to explore the additional significance of Rabbi Kook's thought, namely, as an expression of the "saint." The image of the religious genius is built on a methodical platform and constitutes an additional interpretive stratum.

Systemization

In his examination of the hermeneutic traditions of Western culture, Kepnes distinguished between the "destructive tradition," whose postmodernist representatives are Derrida and Foucault, and the "constructive tradition," represented by Richard Gadamer. The former tradition is concerned with the formational conditions and processes of cultural meanings, while the latter discusses the new possibilities of meaning in cultural products.[8] We cannot examine the deconstructive dimension of Rabbi Kook's teachings by itself. Although it is extremely important to understand the archaeology of the text aided by Freudian, Marxist, and other theories, Rabbi Kook's text involves distinctly constructive dimensions, and the meanings it contains open the way for countless new possibilities.

I have argued on various occasions that Rabbi Kook's writings do not strive for systemization.[9] This is a tremendous collection of passages that may be defined as religious poetry, expressing his religious mood. Rabbi Kook did not refrain from expressing differing, even contradictory, intuitions. His character supports the argument that religious greatness of spirit is not restricted to the confines of method or school. The thought of such an individual is conducted on open and parallel tracks. Specifically for this reason, Rabbi Kook's writings anticipate the postmodernist spirit. We cannot impose only a single interpretive tradition on his writings. Furthermore, the argument that Rabbi Kook did not attempt to formulate

---

8   See S. Kepnes, "Introduction," in *Interpreting Judaism in a Postmodern Age*, ed. S. Kepnes (New York, 1996), 5.

9   See, e.g., D. Schwartz, *Religious Zionism between Logic and Messianism* (Tel Aviv, 1999), 198-233 [Hebrew]; see also J. Garb, "Rabbi Kook—National Thinker or a Mystic Poet," *Daat* 54 (2004): 69-96 [Hebrew].

a defined philosophical method means that we should not search for an underlying textual motif that will explain the text as a whole. Since his writing is usually aphoristic, in that each text is self-sufficient, we must seek its meaning in every subtle motif, citation of biblical verse, and literary ornament that appear in these texts. From the outset, Rabbi Kook did not want to restrict the reading of his writings, and therefore related to them as poetry. He wrote explicitly: "I cannot restrict myself to one topic, to one matter, to a single level, or to a single style. Rather, I must draw upon all styles, all matters, all the levels, everything. If I see a single path that I like and am drawn only to it, afterwards I see how the other ways demand their role of me."[10] In consequence, almost every conceptual passage in his writings takes on a wealth of meanings in different strata. This is how I analyze Rabbi Kook's writings.

Moreover, understanding the traits of the saint require a deconstructive reading of Rabbi Kook's writings. I argue that he planned, from the outset, to enjoy total freedom in his writing—that is, he refused to be subjugated to any one method or approach. The study of the meanings in his writings includes the stratum of personality; such an assumption would seem obvious. We should also note Rabbi Kook's own intuition: he was aware that his personality is a necessary component in the construction of conceptual intuition. He wrote in his letters that

> when a person begins to conduct some study and research, he must always prepare himself, according to his ability, to be close to what is examined; if he can, he should draw so close to the subject that he can sense it from within himself, from his soul, and from the depth of his feelings. Then, if he will not do the most he can, an essential condition will be lacking of the necessary conditions for discovering the truth.[11]

It has already been noted that Rabbi Kook's creative capacity was much greater in the Land of Israel than in the Diaspora.[12] The element of

---

10   *Shemonah Kevatzim* 6:1 (vol. 3, 3). See also ibid., 6:140 (vol. 3, 50).

11   *Igrot ha-Re'ayah*, vol. 1, 94.

12   On the distinction between the Torah of the Diaspora and that of the Land of Israel, see *Igrot*

personality, with its feelings and emotions, fashion ideas. One of the reasons why Rabbi Kook did not succeed in his activity on behalf of Degel Yerushalayim (literally, "Flag of Jerusalem"), the alternative federation led by Torah scholars and those close to them that he wanted to establish in place of the religious Zionist Mizrachi movement, was his unwillingness to remain abroad on behalf of the new movement. That is, not only is the personality involved in meaning, the venue of the writing is of importance, as well.

To return to our deconstructive reading of Rabbi Kook's writings: one of the traditions that Rabbi Kook absorbed was the medieval esoteric tradition of Maimonidean rationalism (see the extensive discussion below, Chapter Twelve). Many fourteenth-century interpreters of Maimonides, by way of example, preferred to explain the nature of his *Guide of the Perplexed* not from its methodical chapters that discuss defined topics (the Creation, Divine Providence, and the like), but rather from his casual references to these topics in chapters that are concerned with entirely different issues.[13] Rabbi Kook was quite familiar with the tradition of the interactive reading of a text, in which "the sky is the limit," and this quite possibly paved the way for the style in which he himself chose to write. He did not, however, absorb this tradition as it was. An example of how Rabbi Kook significantly differed from the medieval rationalist tradition is his deep esteem for aesthetic creativity, while the medieval tradition thought lightly of art and music as an aesthetic experience; this, too, will be discussed below in Chapter Seven.

Basic Characteristics

An initial list of the personality and conceptional motifs that are to be found in Rabbi Kook's character would include the following:

(1) Rationalism: Rabbi Kook was the author of intriguing philosophical and religious ideas;

---

ha-Re'ayah, vol. 1, 112. See, e.g., Y. Cherlow, *The Torah of the Land of Israel in Light of the Teachings of R. Abraham Isaac Hakohen Kook* (Hispin, 1998) [Hebrew].

13   I discussed these questions extensively in my book *Contradiction and Concealment in Medieval Jewish Thought* (Ramat Gan, 2002) [Hebrew].

(2) Mysticism: he possessed the religious consciousness that seeks *unio mystica* with God;

(3) Prophecy: he was charismatic, with the consciousness of a prophet;

(4) Nationalism and altruism: he supported the national idea, against the stance prevalent in the rabbinic circles to which he belonged;

(5) Leadership: he served as the first Chief Rabbi in Mandatory Palestine, and gathered a circle of disciples around him;

(6) Openness and resistance to change: he exhibited openness regarding his cultural sources, but was conservative in many of his halakhic ways;

(7) Dialectics and unification of opposites: he experienced, and formulated, swings between extremes. He was sure that the extremes came from one source.

In each of these categories, however, Rabbi Kook was not unique in his time. Other Orthodox Jewish thinkers, both in the Land of Israel and abroad, also offered conceptional, mystical, and prophetic insights. Additionally, the behavior of some could be understood as exceptionally altruistic. Nevertheless, the combination of all these traits was not commonplace, and explains our view of Rabbi Kook as a "saint."

In his thought, Rabbi Kook anchored the saint in the cosmic reality. That is, all of existence is dependent on the saint for its proper working, on the one hand, and on the other, for its rectification and elevation. The saint is perceived as the one by whose merit material existence endures. Without him, the world would once again be absorbed in the divine light. In Rabbi Kook's terminology, the saint is responsible for the "quantitative" aspect of existence.[14] He creates the merging of the qualitative (the light) with the quantitative. Accordingly, the saint is envisioned as a partner in the act of Creation, whose decisions are accepted by the Master of the Universe. Rabbi Kook enhanced the biblical and midrashic traditions of exceptional individuals, and fully exploited the theurgic element at the basis of Kabbalah. We cannot overestimate the importance of the saint in

---

14   *Shemonah Kevatzim* 7:134 (vol. 3, 200). Although this conception is a fact for Rabbi Kook, it need not serve as a practical program for the saint. In other words, he does not have to trouble himself with the question: "How can the world survive if the spiritual longing is so prevalent?" (*Kevatzim*, vol. 2, 87).

Rabbi Kook's thought, and in this book we will examine the details and meanings of the saint's cosmic responsibility.

Interpretation

An additional note is in order at this juncture. This work is based on the fundamental assumption that the deep infrastructure of Rabbi Kook's thought is Kabbalistic.[15] I argue, however, that many passages in Rabbi Kook's writings were composed, from the outset, with multiple meanings, at times parallel, while in other instances one is built on another. It was axiomatic for Rabbi Kook that the Kabbalah itself requires clarification and a prosaic formulation in modern language (that is, modern Hebrew), for the following reasons:

(1) Esoteric tradition: throughout its history, the Kabbalah was perceived as a teaching transmitted orally from one individual to another, and therefore was not formulated in writing;

(2) Depth: the messages of the Kabbalah are seen to be complicated or hidden, and must be unveiled;

---

[15] This approach was already raised in the important articles by J. Avivi: "History as a Divine Prescription," in *Rabbi Mordechai Breuer Festschrift: Collected Papers in Jewish Studies*, ed. M. Bar-Asher et al. (Jerusalem, 1992), 709-71 [Hebrew]; idem, "The Source of Light: Rabbi Abraham Isaac Hakohen Kook's *Shemonah Kevatzim*," *Tzohar* 1 (2000): 93-111 [Hebrew]. I applied this approach in my analysis of motifs in the thought of Rabbi Kook: see D. Schwartz, *Challenge and Crisis in Rabbi Kook's Circle* (Tel Aviv, 2001), 141-206 [Hebrew]. I will make three minor comments regarding Avivi's first, and fundamental, article, which I used a few times in the writing of the current work:

(1) The comparison of Rabbi Kook with Rabbi Moses Hayyim Luzzatto is illuminating, but in regard to various questions Rabbi Kook cannot be understood without the massive influence of Habad Hasidism, whose terminology he constantly employs. An example of this is the distinction between *Ein-Sof* and His light, which is discussed in depth by J. Ben-Shlomo, "Perfection and Perfectibility in Rabbi Kook's Thought," *Iyyun* 33 (1984): 289-309 [Hebrew]. In his second article, Avivi related to this Hasidic influence.

(2) Avivi's plan for classifying and identifying Rabbi Kook's terminology as a dictionary was daring and important, but it seems that the terms that he classified under Lurianic Kabbalah could also be explained in accordance with the early Kabbalah, such as the Zoharic. Here, as well, Avivi's second article provided balance for his first.

(3) The image of the righteous individual, or saint, is an essential element, one that cannot be disregarded, in Rabbi Kook's formulation of his Kabbalistic approach. The conception of the righteous individual fashions Rabbi Kook's metaphysical approach.

(3) Difficulty: the Kabbalistic teachings are deemed abstract, while formulated in complex symbols.

Rabbi Kook also thought that the need to clarify the Kabbalistic teachings arose in the generation of Redemption, as opposed to previous generations. His mission lay, so he believed, in disseminating the secrets of the Kabbalah to his generation. For him, the revelation of secrets was one of the markers and needs of the process in which the redemption would be realized. He wrote to Rabbi Isaiah Orenstein (1854-1909): "His eminence should know that my entire intent in my notebooks, and in all that I write, is solely to arouse the minds of Torah scholars, old and young, to engage in the study of the inner meaning of the Torah."[16] Rabbi Kook argued in the article "Worship," which he wrote in 1906, that the great and perfect individual is entrusted with the study of the "divine wisdom." He wrote:

> Consequently, the obligation that is imposed on the greatest Torah scholars at present is inestimable, and whoever has the faculty and inclination for sublime spiritual matters should set his study and inquiry mainly in the heights of the divine wisdom, which comprises the aggadah in its entirety, as the outstanding individuals in all the generations cried out continually in this respect, by the scholars in the various and ramified aspects of Kabbalah, Hasidism, philosophy, science, ethical teachings, in all the generations.[17]

Rabbi Kook noted the tradition of the gradual revealing over time of the Kabbalistic secrets to the broad public, to the generation of the "footsteps of the Messiah."[18] Rabbi Kook's antinomian conception (to be discussed in Chapter Eight) is also based on the appeal of engaging in Kabbalah, at the expense of particular halakhic study. An important interpretive element of Rabbi Kook's writings is Kabbalistic.

---

[16] *Igrot ha-Re'ayah*, vol. 1, 41. See N. Gottel, *Mekhutavei Re'ayah: The Circles of R. Avraham Itzhak HaCohen Kook's Correspondents* (Jerusalem: 2000), 97 [Hebrew]. On this issue, see J. Garb, *The Chosen Will Become Herds: Studies in Twentieth-Century Kabbalah*, trans. Y. Berkovits-Murciano (New Haven, 2009), 23-29.

[17] *Eder ha-Yakar*, 143.

[18] *Igrot ha-Re'ayah*, vol. 2, 69.

I therefore maintain that, in large part, Rabbi Kook's writings consist of at least three interpretive layers:

(1) The first layer is Kabbalistic, and usually depicts the process of the Sefirotic emanation, which occurs in the world and in the soul;

(2) The second layer contains the philosophical ideas with which Rabbi Kook occupied himself, from the medieval rationalist orientation to modern Kantian and post-Kantian thought;

(3) The third layer comprises the series of prosaic and literary ideas that he formulated in poetical language, and the ideas that were raised in the historical and nationalist-messianic environment in which Rabbi Kook was active and in which he expressed his thought.

I assume that the characteristics of the saint in Rabbi Kook's thought are woven of a combination of these three layers, and it is in this light that I will relate to his writing and to the wealth of nuances, incorporation of biblical verses, symbols, and motifs that compose it. If we take this assumption to its reasonable conclusion, we find that Rabbi Kook's literary corpus is built for the continuous meeting of writer and reader. The text's meanings are not based solely on the layer of the author's intent; they also incorporate the layer of meaning of the reader, who wants to analyze and internalize the text's contents and messages. The reader himself moves between the different interpretive possibilities, and the results can be formulated as language games. Rabbi Kook's writings assume a great deal of author-reader interaction, and he was also aware of this type of writing from the classical medieval literature (the writings of Judah Halevi, Abraham Ibn Ezra, and Maimonides). Thus, the methodology of phenomenology, which constitutes the object in accordance with the subject and the subjective consciousness, is suitable for a reading of Rabbi Kook's writings.

Chapter Two

THE STATE OF THE RESEARCH

The character of the saint is present in different ways in Rabbi Kook's ideas. He frequently refers in his writings to "those possessing spirituality," the "great noble ones," the "great souls," the "universal souls," the "noble souls," the "great masters of spirituality," "exemplary individuals," and the "great ones of the world" who are active in the messianic era. These are only a few of Rabbi Kook's appellations for the saint. A comparison of these passages with Rabbi Kook's life reveals an inescapable parallelism. Rabbi Kook referred directly to himself and wrote an outline for his spiritual biography, thereby reflecting the religious genius in his personality.

A number of scholars have sensed Rabbi Kook's exceptional personality and used various tools to explore the reasons for this feeling. Most related to the ideas of this great thinker, but wrestled with the question of the nature and genre of his thought (philosopher-Kabbalist; systematical thinker-poet). Any examination of his personality usually occurred by chance. Examples of scholars who adopted this approach are Zvi Yaron, who reviewed some insights of the conception of the righteous individual in Rabbi Kook's thought;[1] Benjamin Ish-Shalom, who noted the balance in the image of the righteous one;[2] and Avinoam Rozenak, whose biography of Rabbi Kook was written within a climate appreciative of Rabbi Kook's personality.[3] We will now survey two approaches that related directly to his image as a religious genius.

---

[1] Z. Yaron, *The Philosophy of Rabbi Kook*, trans. A. Tomaschoff (Jerusalem, 1991), 122-31.

[2] B. Ish-Shalom, *Rav Avraham Itzhak HaCohen Kook: Between Rationalism and Mysticism*, trans. O. Wiskind-Elper (Albany, 1993), 162-66.

[3] See above, Chapter One, n. 1.

Mystic

Semadar Cherlow focused on Rabbi Kook's personality, based on a broad range of testimonies and texts.[4] She explained in her book that she did not intend to present Rabbi Kook's "approach," "method," or "doctrine," but rather sought to sketch his portrait as a mystic. In this aim, she was influenced by the methodology developed in the last decade by scholars of Kabbalah such as Moshe Idel, Yehuda Liebes, Elliot Wolfson, Ron Margolin, Boaz Huss, and Jonathan Garb, which assumes that the character of the mystic is to be taken as part of the understanding of his theoretical and mystical message, and that the reverse holds true, as well. Cherlow paints a sweeping portrait of the exceptional individual and researches its characteristic features. She accepts the primary meaning of Rabbi Kook's writings as Kabbalistic, but argues that this meaning is a basis for the self-image of the righteous individual, the generation's leader, and the redeemer. For example, she challenges Schweid's approach that Rabbi Kook sought to return to the biblical model of prophecy. For her, Rabbi Kook's consciousness is, first and foremost, mystical, as is his circle.

Cherlow presents a narrative, and does not attempt to create a new informative structure. To a great degree, she gives pride of place to experience and consciousness, before the study of contentual and informative message. She writes of her research:

> A new reading of Rabbi Kook's writings reveals a new story. At the center of this new story stands Rabbi Kook's mystical mission as "the tzaddiq is the foundation of the world," following the meaning that the term "tzaddiq" was given by the Kabbalah and Hasidism.[5]

---

[4]   S. Cherlow, *The Tzaddiq Is the Foundation of the World: Rav Kook's Esoteric Mission and Mystical Experience* (Ramat Gan, 2012) [Hebrew]. See also idem, "The Circle of Rav Kook as a Mystical Fraternity," *Tarbiz* 74 (2005): 261-303 [Hebrew]. On Rabbi Kook's circle, see also U. Barak, "New Perspective on Rabbi Kook and His Circle" (PhD diss., Bar-Ilan University, 2009) [Hebrew]; idem, "The Formative Influence of the Description of the First Degree of Prophecy in the *Guide* on the Perception of 'The Beginning of the Redemption' by Rabbi A. I. Kook's Circle," *Daat* 64-66 (2009): 361-415 [Hebrew]; idem, "Can Amalek Be Redeemed? A Comparative Study of the Views of Rabbi Abraham Isaac Kook and Rabbi Jacob Moses Harlap," *Da'at* 73 (2012): xxix-lxix. See also M. Idel, "Rabbi Abraham Abulafia, Gershom Scholem and Rabbi David Ha-Kohen (Ha-Nazir)," in *The Path of the Spirit: The Eliezer Schweid Jubilee Volume*, ed. Y. Amir (*Jerusalem Studies in Jewish Thought* 19; Jerusalem, 2005), 819-34 [Hebrew].

[5]   Cherlow, *The Tzaddiq*, 38.

At times, therefore, she is concerned with the question of the existence of a model of religious consciousness or religious experience common to all religions, adopted by each in accordance with its own special characteristics, or perhaps such a pure model does not exist, and instead different religious consciousnesses exist alongside each other.

In summation, the personality model that she sets forth is mainly that of the righteous individual in the Kabbalistic senses. The importance of Cherlow's discussion for this book lies in the attention it draws to personality and consciousness. Even though this direction was already present in scholarly research (mainly in the hagiographic literature), a bit here and a bit there, Cherlow unquestionably infuses it with greater strength and insight. From now on, any study of Rabbi Kook will have to be based on the findings of her study.

The New Man

An additional course in Rabbi Kook's image was laid in the discussion of the new man in Zionist thought. The Zionist movement sought to create a new Jew, who was totally different from the diasporic (*galuti*—in a disparaging sense) Jew, and Rabbi Kook imparted a clearly religious and messianic dimension to this notion. In another essay, I discussed the image of the new man in religious Zionism and in the thought that it produced, and attempted to chart this model as envisioned by Rabbi Kook.[6] I wrote that many of the traits that Rabbi Kook ascribed to the ideal new man are actually a reflection of his own personality.

The following are the qualities that I listed there, which reflect the new man in accordance with Rabbi Kook's thoughts. These features sketch the image of the saint, some of which will be discussed at length below.

1. The esoteric:
    (1) Mystic: the new man experiences ecstatic ascent to the peak of the reality, and descends in order to lead.[7]

---

6   See D. Schwartz, "Religious Zionism and the Idea of the New Person," *Israel: Studies in Zionism and the State of Israel* 16 (2009), 143-64 [Hebrew]. This question was later examined by Y. Salmon, "The 'New Jew' in the Perception of Religious Zionism," *Israel: Studies in Zionism and the State of Israel* 17 (2010): 246 [Hebrew].

7   "The person ascends to the heavens. He comes to the head, and from there he gazes upon all

(2) Revealing the hidden: the new man uncovers the sublime degrees of the Godhead.[8]

(3) Theurgy: the new man seeks to effect a state of harmony in all the worlds.[9]

(4) Immanence: the new man discerns the divine presence within him.[10]

2. Attitude toward one's surroundings:

(5) Cosmic and national sense: the new man unites with the universe and with the "entire nation."[11]

(6) Involvement: the new man must be sensitive to the generation's spiritual needs.[12]

(7) Family life: the new man sanctifies family life.[13]

(8) Inspiration: the new man possesses the spirit of divine inspiration, which is a stage in the path to prophecy.[14]

(9) Humanism: the new man is characterized by his love of man. "He loves people."[15]

3. Ethos:

(10) Freedom: the new man breaches boundaries, and does not fear the limitations of religious conservatism.[16]

---

the intellective and practical paths of the world, he descends from there to a world full of good and lovingkindness, courage [gevurah], and grandeur, and he tends the flock of the Lord, flocks of people, with love" (Shemonah Kevatzim 1:87 [vol. 1, 27]). This is reminiscent of Plato's metaphor of the cave; on the cave metaphor, see below, Chapter Eight.

8   Shemonah Kevatzim 6:100 (vol. 3, 35).

9   See below, the beginning of Chapter Four.

10   This will be discussed below, in Chapter Three.

11   Shemonah Kevatzim 1:101 (vol. 1, 33-34).

12   This will be discussed below, in Chapter Six.

13   Shemonah Kevatzim 2:37 (vol. 1, 306-7).

14   "The universal basis of the divine spirit is concealed in the great treasury of the supernal souls, that sense the splendor of the secrets of the Torah, and the emanation of the preciousness of the inner nature of the divine service in the majesty of its greatness" (ibid., 3:45 [vol. 2, 29]). I classified prophecy as relating to one's surroundings, because Rabbi Kook's circle frequently emphasized the national significance of prophecy.

15   Ibid., 7:165 (vol. 3, 115).

16   "It [true righteousness] is greater than any instruction, any system of thought, any individual will, any limited choice" (ibid., 4:131 [vol. 2, 182]); "I demand of my soul after every study and

(11) Sanctification of the material: the new man ascribes great worth to material activity and physical health.[17]

(12) Renaissance man: the new man is a polymath; he is not restricted to any one field of creativity, but rather aspires to master them all.[18]

4. Personality:

(13) Intuition: the new man discerns essence through the material envelope.[19]

(14) Austerity and self-negation: the new man has no "self-will at all."[20] He is characterized by his humility,[21] but this is not asceticism.[22]

(15) Self-confirmation: the new man is aware of his abilities and worth.[23]

(16) Dialectic: the new man combines opposing poles.[24]

---

contemplation, after every conception and intellection, that my self be released from those spiritual chains in which the detailed, formal locksmith imprisoned the spirit, to roam about in the world of freedom by means of the essence of the illumination that is concealed in each of those matters that are studied and depicted in their details" (ibid., 8:171 [vol. 3, 300]). See also ibid., 3:820 [vol. 1, 257-58]). On the antinomianism in the figure of the saint, see below, Chapter Eight.

[17] This issue will be discussed at length below, in the beginning of Chapter Five.

[18] *Shemonah Kevatzim* 3:233 (vol. 2, 89); 6:1 (vol. 3, 3).

[19] Ibid., 2:154 (vol. 1, 338), where Rabbi Kook spoke of "those who gaze inward." He further wrote that "the truly great people find within themselves an inner opposition to teaching oneself [*hitlamdut*]" (2:172 [vol. 2, 343]). Intuition, which has emotional aspects, is the manner characteristic of the new man. Rabbi Kook writes: "In my childhood I sensed the stench of the toilet from the prayer houses of the non-Jews, even though they presumably were very clean, and stood within a garden of planted trees" (2:58 [vol. 1, 311]). Consequently, the new man is disgusted by the diasporic experience, despite its distinctly aesthetic aspects.

[20] Ibid., 3:67 (vol. 2, 38). See also 3:182 (vol. 2, 74).

[21] "I hope for true inner humility, which not only will not weaken mental courage and its spiritual joy, the development of its faculties and the addition of its light, it will actually provide a basis for them" (ibid., 6:216 [vol. 3, 84]). See also ibid., 1:689 (vol. 1, 219]).

[22] Rabbi Kook used the argument of the *Kuzari* (3:1) that asceticism was well suited for previous generations, in which there was divine revelation in response to asceticism (*Igrot ha-Re'ayah*, vol. 1, 78).

[23] See *Shemonah Kevatzim* 1:560 (vol. 1, 178); 2:193 (vol. 1, 349); 4:96 (vol. 2, 167). See also Ish-Shalom, *Between Rationalism and Mysticism*, 211-16.

[24] E.g., gradual order as opposed to skipping. See *Shemonah Kevatzim* 1:676 (vol. 1, 216); 5:62-63 (vol. 2, 218); 7:88 (vol. 3, 171). The tension typical of the new man is the contrast between points 14 and 15. Actually, the tension between self-confirmation and self-abnegation is characteristic of mystics. See, e.g., R. C. Zaehner, *Mysticism Sacred and Profane* (Oxford, 1957), 86-88.

(17) Optimism: the new man is characterized by his constant joyfulness.[25]

(18) Psychological unification: the new man's will and thought are unified.[26]

I argued in that article that Rabbi Kook presented a restorative messianic conception. For him, the new man in the messianic era in actuality returns to himself. His "original" self includes these qualities, that during the course of history were heaped up and concealed under epistemological and tangible coverings. The new man no longer remans in isolation; the gap between him and the masses shrinks, and he becomes the paradigm of the entire generation of Redemption. We will extensively discuss these statements in relation to the image of the saint.

Rabbi Kook used these elements to chart the ideal model of the saint. Nonetheless, the new man is one of Redemption, and it is unclear whether all these elements, or their incorporation together, are suitable for the saint, who acts in a worldly and temporal reality. Whatever the answer to this question, in that article I outlined the new man, and indirectly also the personality of the saint.

An Open Reading

The starting point of my exploration of the image of the saint in Rabbi Kook's thought differs from scholarly research up to now in my multidimensional interpretation of his writings. I maintain that a reading of his writings in accordance with a central leitmotif misses both their richness and the author's intent. As I argued above, Rabbi Kook most probably wanted, from the outset, to enable interpretive openness that creates a dialogue with the reader. The result is a mosaic of ideas and open horizons that complement or parallel each other. The image of the saint contains different but concurrent dimensions, clarified by the application of the interpretive principles presented above. In terms of methodology, as was noted above, my starting point is the phenomenology of religion, which assumes the

---

[25]   *Shemonah Kevatzim* 2:189 (vol. 1, 348). See 7:207 (vol. 3, 233-34); 8:195 (vol. 3, 309-10).

[26]   Ibid., 8:114 (vol. 3, p. 279).

existence of independent religious consciousness, experience, and ability. We will examine the expressions of this consciousness in the personality of Rabbi Kook and his environment.

Etymology is not our concern here. Rabbi Kook's innovative language is deserving of a study of its own, as was indicated by the late Menahem Zevi Kaddari.[27] Rabbi Kook generally used the term *"kadosh"* (literally, "holy one"; rendered here as "saint") as synonymous with the perfect or righteous person. Furthermore, most of his uses of *"kedushah"* are adjectival, and do not refer to a specific type. He distinguished only rarely between the *tzaddik* ("righteous one") and the *"kadosh."* For example: "The great righteous ones [*tzaddikim*] must be holy [*kedoshim*], they must cleave to the great light, that satisfies and delights, that sanctifies and purifies, from whose brilliance all the worlds draw."[28] He further declared that the *tzaddik* "continuously bears the sanctity of the world and the sanctity [*kedushah*, in both instances] of life in his soul."[29] Sanctity is perceived as a quality of the righteous one. Thus, Rabbi Kook's style requires a separate examination.

Now we will turn to the characteristics of the exceptional figure, the outstanding individual, and see what, according to Rabbi Kook, makes a person a "saint." It is noteworthy that Rabbi Kook himself did not present the saint as a homogeneous figure. At times he distinguished between different types of saints,[30] and left the reader to decide to which category he himself belonged. The discussions about the perfect and ideal man are an example for the need of interactive reading to interpret Rabbi Kook's words.

---

27 M. Z. Kaddari, "Introduction to an Analysis of the Language of Rabbi Avraham Yitzhak Hacohen Kook," in *A Hundred Years of Religious Zionism*, ed. A. Sagi and D. Schwartz, vol. 1: *Figures and Thought* (Ramat Gan, 2003), 255-60 [Hebrew].

28 *Shemonah Kevatzim* 4:96 (vol. 2, 167).

29 Ibid., 4:130 (vol. 2, 182).

30 See, e.g., ibid., 1:306-307 (vol. 1, 109).

Chapter Three

MORAL GENIUS

Rabbi Kook did not provide any consistent mapping and hierarchy of a typology of saints. The types close to this figure are the "righteous one," the one "of noble soul," and the like. He did, however, establish a firm basis for describing the individual who approaches human perfection, the genius. Genius is not usually a factor in the discussion of saints. Rabbi Kook's personality, however, cannot be comprehended, nor can we project from it the image of the saint, without the concept of genius, and not only in order to draw a dividing line between Rabbi Kook as genius and as saint. The genius reflects a distinct rational dimension that is present in Rabbi Kook's ideas, one that he was loath to abandon when describing the exceptional individual. Moreover, Rabbi Kook turned the genius into a sort of saint by formulating a type not commonly found in the Jewish sources: the moral genius.

The Definition of Genius

Rabbi Kook was probably familiar with the discussion of the figure of the genius in modern thought: one blessed with aptitude not subject to predetermined rules, and all that he produces is original. Kant wrote: "Genius is a *talent* for producing that for which no determinate rule can be given," and added: "consequently that *originality* must be its primary characteristic."[1] Artistic genius is easily revealed. The meeting of the stormy soul and intuitive perception as characteristic of the artist-genius is highlighted in the writings of Schopenhauer and other

---

[1] I. Kant, *Critique of the Power of Judgment*, trans. P. Guyer and E. Matthews (Cambridge, 2000), 186 (emphases in original).

thinkers.[2] Rabbi Kook ascribed great importance to art and music as expressions of spontaneity, on the one hand, and as a means to become aware of realms that cannot be known by scientific and discursive cognition, on the other.

Rabbi Kook depicted the image of the saint in a eulogy that he wrote in memory of his father-in-law, Rabbi Elijah David Rabinowitz-Teomim (1842-1905), or as he was known by his acronym, "the Aderet." In this section I will analyze the eulogy's references to the genius and the righteous individual, and examine their relationship to the saint. In the beginning of his portrayal of the genius we find two concepts that require explanation:

(1) The definition of genius: genius is the combination of two factors, one congenital (a "gift"), and the other acquired ("labor").

(2) The two types of genius: rational-epistemological genius and moral genius.

The opening of his eulogy will be followed by our discussion of these two concepts.

> Genius is connected to the world, by means of a gift and labor.[3] Whether the genius and aptitude of the intellect, or that of morality and justice, either is present only when these two are joined together in the genius soul: God's gift of an extra and wondrous soul,[4] that stores within it a great sum of spiritual traits and sublime power by the essence of its nature [toledatah],[5] with diligence and the loving acceptance of the yoke of labor to develop one's faculties, to realize the concealed property.[6] At times, too, we find excellent geniuses who attained what they are only by much labor and great toil, of wonderful industry [see Jeremiah 1:12]. Whoever casts a penetrating

---

2   See, e.g., S. Zemach, *On the Beautiful: Methods to Explain Beauty and Its Sources* (Tel Aviv, 1939), 60-61 [Hebrew].

3   See Numbers 18:7; see also BT Yoma 24a.

4   Rabbi Kook used the wording "extra soul" (*neshamah yeterah*) for the special inspiration provided by the Sabbath. See BT Betzah 16a; Taanit 27b. The genius constantly possesses such inspiration.

5   That is, in its inherent nature. The term *toledet* frequently appears in the writings of Rabbi Abraham Ibn Ezra with the meaning of "nature" (see, e.g., his commentary to Genesis 2:3). Genius is depicted as "power," that is, mental aptitude. Rabbi Kook presented this power as potential; it should be noted that he used this term to denote history, as well.

6   Rabbi Kook assumed that genius is a congenital trait ("property"—*segullah*).

eye will find a difference between natural genius and that which is acquired, like the same difference that usually exists between nature and labor.[7] Moreover, the excellent inclination for diligence and love of labor, in order to reach the peak of the lofty and the sublime—this, too, is one of the attributes of genius when present in great degree.[8] Accordingly, in the final analysis, the cause of genius is the quality of creativity, which man is capable of increasing or decreasing, as he chooses.[9]

First, we must note the definition of genius: Rabbi Kook maintains that genius is not limited to faculty and natural ability. The genius knows struggles. He fights "obstacles that [stand] in the path of the development of genius." The heart of genius, however, is God-given ("quality"—*segullah*). Rabbi Kook found no expression that more faithfully portrays the congenital trait than the aesthetic, and only poetry and song accurately reflect the spirit of genius. In *Shemonah Kevatzim*, the image of the righteous individual is characterized by poetry.[10] The righteous one is engaged in poetry,[11] and his knowledge of God is characterized by "the delight of every melody and song."[12] In *Eder ha-Yakar*, he stressed the poetic nature of the genius, as he writes in the continuation of this eulogy:

> But the poetical nature may elevate the soul, without excessive reasoning. This is the nature of genius in the might of its magnificence. If we are successful in removing the shroud that is drawn[13] over the innerness of the wondrous soul, that by the lot of Shaddai in the heights[14] He placed within the genius, that is especially present in the true genius, who is created for greatness.[15]

The aesthetic connection of genius is worthy of a discussion of its own.

---

7   The distinction between nature and craft was common in medieval Jewish thought.

8   That is, the greater the degree of genius, the greater the readiness for exertion and effort, even though genius is essentially congenital.

9   *Eder ha-Yakar*, 23.

10 For instance: "The divine poetry is astir within the soul of the greatest righteous ones" (*Shemonah Kevatzim* 1:206 [vol. 1, 82]). In another place he terms the congenital trait "natural disposition" (*Kevatzim*, vol. 2, 85).

11 "It is a great obligation incumbent upon the righteous to always engage in studies and poetry" (*Shemonah Kevatzim* 1:309 [vol. 1, 110]).

12 Ibid., 1:895 (vol. 1, 287).

13 Following Isaiah 25:7.

14 Following Job 31:2.

15 *Eder ha-Yakar*, 23-24.

Poetical Nature

What is the meaning of Rabbi Kook's defining genius as poetry? In order to answer this question, we will briefly examine his conception of poetry. Rabbi Kook channeled the aesthetic discussion to the clearly epistemological realm: poetry and music first and foremost express (and are presented in his writings as) an epistemological and experiential access to the profound, inner, broad, and infinite realm beyond rationality and the scientific thought that reflects it. This sphere is dynamic and fluid, and as such cannot be expressed by language and reason. The realm beyond the consciousness manifests the divine presence and the heavenly vitality that ripples throughout the natural and human reality.[16] In this respect, Rabbi Kook gave theoretical and philosophical expression to Hasidism's characteristic emphasis of divine immanence. Obviously, Hasidic thought was not the first to formulate the inner divine presence. However, it transformed this divine presence into a central conceptional link, and the meeting point for other ideas. For Rabbi Kook, rational knowledge is incapable of absorbing this lively, flowing inner divine presence. The realm that transcends the consciousness (and is immanent in the natural reality) is what he calls "holy" (*kodesh*) in his writings.[17] The following are contentual, literary, and formal features of the holy in these writings:

(1) The holy expresses a realm that is beyond rationality, although not necessarily contradicting it.

(2) The holy refers to the theosophical plane that is depicted in the Kabbalistic literature (the *Sefirot* and divine emanation).

(3) The holy is parallel to "the thing in itself," in Kantian terminology.[18]

---

[16]   The conception that scientific perception is limited, and that there is a realm that extends beyond its capabilities, was discussed at length by Ish-Shalom, *Between Rationalism and Mysticism*, chap. 1.

[17]   I will not address the question of the precise definition of the "*kodesh*," which is an object of dispute among the scholars who explore Rabbi Kook's writings, from Samuel Hugo Bergmann and Nathan Rotenstreich to current scholars. In this study I will present a number of characteristic features, without presuming to have the final word on this question. Moreover, the transcendental term relates solely to reason and rational thought. At times, it is specifically the content beyond reason that is the immanent content, that is, the divine presence and the like.

[18]   Like many other religious Zionist thinkers, Rabbi Kook, too, related to "the thing in itself" as

(4) The holy relates to an inner, dynamic, and vital examination of the reality ("life").

(5) The holy reflects the divine presence in the reality.

(6) The holy cannot be particularized, and is universal.

(7) The holy is perceived as concealed content.

Poetry and song are seen in Rabbi Kook's writings as representing the manner in which the holy is conceived and perceived; this, however, refers to intuitive, spontaneous, and mystical contemplation, and not to rational conception. Additionally, this refers primarily to the perception of symbols and their representation. Symbolic perception, portrayed in poetical and musical terms, is capable of penetrating the hidden layer of reality. We know from the mystical literature that the esoteric is generally expressible only in symbols.[19] On occasion, poetry and music characterize the realm beyond reason, as well, and not only the approach to this sphere, and at times they represent the combination of rationalism and mysticism.[20] For Rabbi Kook, poetry is, first of all, an epistemological and contemplative representation and instrument. In this aspect, we hear the echo of the distinction between Rabbi Kook and the Hasidic sources with which he was familiar. The Hasidic thinkers sought the experiential in the hidden realm. The dominant value for them was communion with the divine presence. Rabbi Kook, in contrast, strove primarily to *know* the holy. Accordingly, music and poetry for Hasidism are, first of all, a means for uniting with the concealed, the hidden Presence, while for Rabbi Kook they are clearly epistemological values.

In Rabbi Kook's writings, poetry and music represent the activity of the pure sentiment, the "poetical sentiment,"[21] while at the same time

a concrete being, and not as a term that merely expresses the limits of cognition. See, e.g., D. Schwartz, *Faith at the Crossroads: A Theological Profile of Religious Zionism*, trans. B. Stein (Leiden, 2002), chaps. 2-3.

[19] In Rabbi Kook's thought, "poetry" is parallel to the "secrets of wisdom" (*Kevatzim*, vol. 1, 143; this passage does not appear in the parallel edition: *Writings of Rabbi Abraham Isaac ha-Kohen Kook*, notebook 13 [Jerusalem, 2004]). Likewise, the "concealed" requires attentiveness and the ability to listen (*Kevatzim*, vol. 2, 158).

[20] See, e.g., *Shemonah Kevatzim* 1:602 (vol. 1, 192).

[21] Ibid., 6:116 (vol. 3, 41).

they express an aesthetic dimension of epistemological perception and experiential consciousness. Following Kant's *Critique of Judgment,* and similar to the philosophers who advocated idealism of various sorts (such as Penny, Schelling, and Hermann Cohen), Rabbi Kook, too, believed that the aesthetic sense can be subject to philosophical discussion, with its definitions and schematism.[22] Aesthetics characterize both the entity and the conception, and therefore can be subject to positive discussion. He most likely was also influenced by thinkers who set forth cognitive theories of art, such as Schopenhauer and Schelling.[23] Aesthetics was an important component of the philosophical conceptions of these thinkers. Traces of the conception of music of Nietzsche,[24] who sharply attacked the cognitive idea of art, are to be found in Rabbi Kook's discussions, as well. Thus, Rabbi Kook used aesthetic criteria to a dual purpose:

(1) the definition of ontological and moral values;
(2) delineating the way to know or experience these values.

The main functionality of poetry and music lies in their use as a metaphor of consciousness: the realm that Rabbi Kook called the holy is characterized by the very fact of its being sung. At times he also used the term "harmony" to mean balance in the realm beyond thought. This terminological usage, along with "poetry," attests to the musical dimension of the lyric. Sound, poetry, and melody reflect what transcends human logic and the approach to it. In a number of instances, Rabbi Kook set forth a scheme of gradual emanation or crystalization: the nucleus that is inexpressible in thought—the holy—is symbolized in song, and when it develops or descends and materializes, it can be expressed in thought and speech. Conversely, when the mental perception ascends, it is transformed into poetry and melody. Rabbi Kook connected the realm of the holy

[22] See, e.g., A. Kolender, *Transcendental Beauty* (Jerusalem, 2001) [Hebrew].

[23] See, e.g., S. Rosenberg, "R. Abraham Isaac Hakohen Kook and the Blind Crocodile (*Orot ha-Kodesh* and the Philosophy of Schopenhauer)," in *Beoro: Studies in the Teachings of R. Abraham Isaac Hakohen Kook and the Ways of Teaching It*, ed. H. Hamiel (Jerusalem, 1986), 317-52 [Hebrew]; A. Rozenak, *Prophetic Halakhah: Rabbi A. I. H. Kook's Philosophy of Halakhah* (Jerusalem, 2007) [Hebrew].

[24] Rabbi Kook compared Nietzsche with Sabbatai Zevi. For him, the latter's apostasy was comparable to the former's madness. See *Kevatzim*, vol. 3, 56.

(expressed by means of music) with the image of the perfect man. For him, this sublime individual naturally and primally expresses himself in poetry.[25] He writes:

> The righteous individual always stands between God and the world. He connects the silent and dark world to the divine speech and light. All of the true righteous one's senses are dedicated to the divine connecting of all the worlds. All his desires, wishes, inclinations, thoughts, actions, conversations, practices, movements, sadnesses, joys, distresses, and delights, leaving nothing, are chords of the holy music, which are used by the divine life—which flows through all the worlds—to give it its fierce voice. Endless souls, the limitless treasures of life, fill all that exists; only they, by their exertion to ascend from the bottom of the depths of the desolate baseness to the sublimity of the divine joy of freedom—the source of pleasure and delight[26]—motivate all the deeds of the righteous one, who is always employed in the service of the holy, for his entire life is sacred to the Lord.[27]

The righteous individual's existence is an expression of the holy. His mental and physical activities are depicted in musical terminology ("chords"). Consequently, the righteous one occupies the middle ground: on the one hand, he is a corporeal and worldly creature, while on the other, he is an expression of the divine realm, which is poetical, lyrical, and musical. Rabbi Kook concluded from this that the functional stance of the righteous individual is one of mediation: he connects the world to God. The motive force of the righteous one is the elevation of reality, in which he succeeds because he is planted in the transcendental world.

Rabbi Kook argued that righteousness also entails paradox: the aesthetic faculty of the righteous "is multiplied mightily."[28] That is, it is specifically the righteous one, who does not ascribe much worth to material life, and is not limited to the corporeal reality, who is capable of appreciating the sublime and the beautiful in both the visual and musical spheres

---

[25]   "The soul of the natural pietists is full of divine murmuring, their heart and their flesh will shout for joy to the living God [following Psalms 84:3]" (*Shemonah Kevatzim* 7:88 [vol. 3, 171]).

[26]   On pleasure and delight, see, e.g., *Zohar, Bereshit*, 1:26a.

[27]   *Shemonah Kevatzim* 3:30 (vol. 2, 22).

[28]   Ibid., 1:804 (vol. 1, 257).

("that is in sights, that is in song"). The righteous individual's conduct, as a personality that contemplates and acts in the depths of psychological and natural phenomena and life itself, is constantly characterized by the terminology of poetry and harmony. Rabbi Kook writes:

> Divine poetry constantly plays in the harmonic laws in the inner chambers of his [the righteous one's] soul.[29]
>
> Divine perfection, the tremendous and pure morality, the wonderful divine harmony with all its beauty and pleasantness, is always the happiness of the lives and pillar of their [the great souls'] spirits.[30]

The soul of the righteous "is always present within the [heavenly] sphere of the singing of the music of the melody of the pleasant holy."[31] The righteous ones' experience of the divine presence, too, is characterized by musical strains. The righteous individual walks with the *Shekhinah* (the Divine Presence) "freely, in an excursion [...] replete with delicate pleasures, the fragrances of spices, a multitude of harps and lutes, the secret utterance, the song of *shinanim* [a class of angels], and the exalted gentle voices of the holy angels."[32] Music reflects the righteous one's value of freedom ("freely, in an excursion"), and not only his communion. His pure aesthetic sense encompasses music.

Regarding "those of noble soul," Rabbi Kook states that "their poetry is constant,"[33] and attests of himself: "I must necessarily be a poet."[34] He describes the aesthetic foundation of the righteous one as follows:

> Intellectual and emotional righteousness is a special art, that must be constantly improved and developed by the one fit for it, and it itself will bring about the practical righteousness which has the standing

---

29   Ibid., 2:98 (vol. 1, 323).

30   *Kevatzim* 2, 83; for stylistic purposes, *nafsham* is rendered here as "their spirits."

31   *Shemonah Kevatzim* 4:8 (vol. 2, 134).

32   Ibid., 4:96 (vol. 2, 167).

33   Ibid., 2:85 (vol. 1, 320). See also 2:96 (vol. 1, 323). On the Temple poetry, Rabbi Kook maintained that "the majesty of this supernal poetry is revealed to them [the priests of the Lord] continually day after day" (ibid., 4:63 [vol. 2, 152]).

34   *Hadarav*, 61.

of craft, and is not on as high a level of art as that of emotion and intellect. The happiness of the world is dependent upon the self, the facility of righteousness, which is the good heart, and the inner clarity of perception of the righteous who are the foundation of the world. The nation, and the whole world, are firmly grounded on the proliferation of the quality of righteousness.[35]

The quality of the righteous individual is an inner dimension. It corresponds to art, and in the continuation of this passage, Rabbi Kook called it "the poem of the righteous." He writes of this poetry: "when it is magnified and is blessed from its godly source, it brings the joy of the worlds to humans."[36] He draws the following distinction: intellectual righteousness and emotional righteousness are "art," while practical righteousness is "craft." This is expressed in the following schema:

intellectual righteousness emotional righteousness	art
practical righteousness	craft

This teaches that the divine emanation that infuses his inner self impacts the righteous one, and this emanation has an aesthetic dimension, that is, such an inner effect upon the individual is expressed in art and poetry. This divine emanation also inspires the environment of the righteous one. His inner emanation enables other people, as well, to receive this ("song [emanation] to those who sing [i.e., receive the emanation]").[37] The practical righteousness, which is technical, comes into play here; this is the outer and "superficial" expression of the inner content. The song does not only reflect the processes of emanation within the Godhead, it also extends to such processes on the part of man. In other words, the various sorts of

---

[35] *Shemonah Kevatzim* 1:510 (vol. 1, 164). In another passage, Rabbi Kook states that the righteous are the few who maintain the many (ibid., 7:138 [vol. 3, 202]).

[36] Ibid., 1:510 (vol. 1, 164).

[37] Ibid., 1:588 (vol. 1, 186). This wording recurs, in another context, in 2:20 (vol. 1, 301).

emanation have a distinctly aesthetic dimension. The righteous individual, who is also the leader in the messianic time, is sensitive to the singing, in which he participates.

Song and Genius

I will now return to the description of the piety, righteousness, and genius of the Aderet, a portrayal that is replete with musical motifs. Rabbi Kook writes:

> He [the Aderet] viewed the Torah and all its commandments, with all their sections and clauses, in life, in study, and in action, as a great and mighty divine song, a love song.[38] Each commandment and each law has a special musical trait, to which *Knesset Yisrael* [the personification of the nation of Israel] is attentive and in which it delights, "It shall blossom abundantly, it shall also exult and shout" [Isaiah 35:2]. We must merely remove the seal from the ears of our children, "the thorns and thistles that encircle the supernal rose."[39] Song will strike waves in their heart, and raise their souls with the same natural elevation experienced by all those who saw fit to develop the nature of their Jewishness. The natural Jew, in the full sense, was the genius, the righteous one, the Aderet, of blessed memory. The natural harmony, that comes forth from the entire practical Torah in all its branches, would sing inward within his soul. Accordingly, he was bound by love to every commandment, whether minor or major. "Happy is the man who fears the Lord, who delights greatly in His commandments" [Psalms 112:1].[40]

The inner, vital world, of which each commandment is its outer and practical expression, is exposed in the genius's divine service. For the genius, the Torah is a song, and the observance of the commandments is its melody. Rabbi Kook presented this song as playing from itself, connecting it with nature (the "natural Jew"). The genius can listen to the song, that is, to the divine presence that is revealed through worship. And thus, too,

---

38 Following Psalms 45:1.

39 This sentence appears in some Hasidic works. See, e.g., Rabbi Israel, the Maggid of Koznitz, *Avodat Yisrael* (Munkacs, 1929), commentary to M Avot 5:4, fol. 92; Rabbi Joshua Heschel of Apta, *Ohev Yisrael* (Zhitomer, 1863), *Nitzavim*, fol. 87b.

40 *Eder ha-Yakar*, 47.

the influence of the genius upon the generation: in the end, the inner, vital dimension of divine life will radiate on the surroundings (the "children"), as well. This teaches of the patently aesthetic dimension of righteousness and genius, a dimension that is expressed in musical terms. The more tangible Rabbi Kook's description of the image of the genius (the Aderet), the more it was dominated by its musical characteristics (musicality, melody, attentiveness, harmony).

We learn from this that genius, as "poetical" nature, is a congenital trait that enables the genius to know the transcendental realm intuitively. The genius immediately perceives the holy, while other people must toil toward this end their entire lives. The genius knows the divine presence in reality directly, as he is gifted with a contemplative spirit. He has penetrating sight that sees the divine structure of reality. This congenital trait can be described only in aesthetic terms. Rabbi Kook emphasized that the poetic aptitude is natural, and is opposed to any purposeful interests. Rabbi Kook wrote in a letter from 1907 to his son Rabbi Zevi Yehudah that "no poetical works were written to any [concrete] end [...] the pure poetical spirit is not present in songs that are written for some aim."[41] We find an allusion in Rabbi Kook's writings to the distinction between genius and inspiration, which are concerned with the autonomous ability to uncover the concealed, and righteousness, to which the hidden is revealed by heteronomous divine manifestation.[42]

The "poetical nature" therefore finely elucidates that character of genius and righteousness. The aesthetic dimension of genius leads us to come to know it, within the context of its effect on the environment.

Types of Genius

In the following analysis of the eulogy delivered by Rabbi Kook, we will examine the two types of genius he describes ("the genius and aptitude of the intellect"; "the genius of morality and righteousness"). Rabbi Kook first spoke of intellectual genius. This concept has diverse sources. For some Enlightenment thinkers and Romantics, scientific innovation was no less

---

41   *Igrot ha-Re'ayah*, vol. 1, 37-38.
42   See, e.g., *Shemonah Kevatzim* 7:89 (vol. 3, 172).

creative than a work of art. Newtonian physics, for example, was included in the integrated and comprehensive philosophy of Friedrich von Schlegel, who sought to remove the partitions between the different disciplines and integrate them. According to Schlegel, founders of modern physics should indeed be viewed as artists rather than as philosophers.[43] In his doctrine of aesthetics, Kant compared nature to a work of art, and the firm foundation of the creative imagination to the basis of both mathematics and geometry.[44] Rabbi Kook, however, added another sort of genius, who is characterized by "morality and justice." That is, there is genius in morality and altruism, as well. In this sense, the characters of the saint and the genius merge. Rabbi Kook used the wording "the faculty of the genius of righteousness" to refer to the righteous individual.[45]

In the eulogy, Rabbi Kook first distinguished between the genius inherent in man's nature ("natural") and the genius acquired by toil and labor ("artificial"). If we apply this division to moral genius, we find that there is a natural moral genius—a person who is naturally inclined to justice and altruism to a creative and exceptional degree—and an artificial genius—a person who reached the zenith of his morality through his toil and exertion. The natural moral genius is a paragon of moral perfection.

Rabbi Kook did not specify what he meant by the "genius of morality and justice," but he let the reader assume the existence of a special form of inspiration, a sort of spontaneous creativity and brilliant intuition, in morality as well. Was his intent "pure" altruism,[46] in the sense of activity without the intervention of any egoistic consideration? And if

---

43 See F. von Schlegel, *Philosophical Fragments*, trans. F. Firchow (Minneapolis, 1991), para. 381. In that period, Newton's achievements were accredited to the creative imagination, and not only to reason. See J. Engell, *The Creative Imagination: Enlightenment to Romanticism* (Cambridge, MA, 1981), 127-28.

44 See D. Summers, "Why Did Kant Call Taste a 'Common Sense'?," in *Eighteenth-Century Aesthetics and the Reconstruction of Art*, ed. P. Mattick, Jr. (Cambridge, 1993), 133.

45 *Shemonah Kevatzim* 1:767 (vol. 1, 216). The hagiographical literature on Rabbi Kook writes that only exceptional individuals were called "the true genius" by him, such as: Rabbi Jacob David Willowski, Rabbi Hayyim Ozer Grodzinski, Rabbi Shalom Mordecai Shvadron (H. Lifshitz, *Shivhei ha-Re'ayah: What Was Related about Rabbi Abraham Isaac ha-Kohen Kook* [Jerusalem, 1979], 204 [Hebrew]).

46 We saw above that the new man has no independent will, and he devotes himself to the service of society and his fellow man (no. 14 in the above list).

so, is "moral creativity" needed to attain such a state,[47] and what type of creativity?

In his writings Rabbi Kook coined the terms "compassionate genius" and "the genius's generosity." He writes:

> In all genius, the eye of clarity, that penetrates to the spiritual content that is the cause of action, sees the grandeur of the spirit of genius in its self, in the might of its valor, in the splendor of its magnificence. In the compassionate genius of the greatly charitable individual, for whom lovingkindness and benefiting [others] are his ideal and the crowning glory of his life, his inner contemplation is cognizant of the inherent brilliance [*ziv*][48] of lovingkindness, which is something very precious and uplifting, more sublime and lofty than all the acts of lovingkindness and benefits that are realized *in actu*. We all will rejoice if the light of lovingkindness is spread among us. The world will rejoice, humanity will rejoice, and the nation will rejoice, when the sight of the genius's generosity is manifest in one of its sons. The divine spirit of generosity is the treasure of life, that gives tremendous worth to all, the breath of life[49] for every individual soul in the nation, which it embellishes in its entirety with the crown of everlasting beauty. At times this genius of lovingkindness is manifest

47 Rabbi Kook indirectly referred to a realm that has been intensively researched in recent years, that of moral creativity. One view defines moral creativity as a characteristic of brilliant moral responses to the dizzying technological and scientific development of the past century; while others present it as the transferal of moral values to artistic and aesthetic products. Following Aristotle, the scholars examining moral creativity discuss poetics as a teleological act, whose aim is the good outside it. According to this, art meets moral needs that were not satisfied before its creation, and it is bound up with revolutionary motives. See, e.g., M. Schwebel, "Moral Creativity as Artistic Transformation," *Creativity Research Journal* 6 (1993): 65-81; J. Wall, "Phronesis as Poetic: Moral Creativity in Contemporary Aristotelianism," *The Review of Metaphysics* 59 (2005): 313-31; D. Ambrose and T. Cross, eds., *Morality, Ethics, and Gifted Minds* (New York, 2009). Rabbi Kook was inclined to the aesthetic side. He defined in aesthetic terminology both the moral genius and the intellectual genius. On the connection between the saint and morality, see J. Horne, "Saintliness and Moral Perfection," *Religious Studies* 27 (1991): 463-71.

48 The literature of Habad Hasidism discusses the question of the *ziv* and its relation to the light. See D. Schwartz, *Habad's Thought from Beginning to End* (Ramat Gan, 2011), 32 [Hebrew]. In this literature, the *ziv* is an expression of the essence, such as the ray of the sun is an expression of the sun. Rabbi Kook apparently used this meaning, such that lovingkindness is the *ziv* of *Binah*; see below. In *Shemonah Kevatzim* 6:245 (vol. 3, 94), Rabbi Kook distinguished between the "renewal of the *ziv* of the world" and the soul of the righteous individual.

49 Following Genesis 2:7. The soul generally expresses the level of *Binah*.

among the poor of the land;[50] only, at times the holy glory of a life of lovingkindness dwells constantly within their hearts, while at other times it is actualized in practical generosity. When the aptitude of generosity meets the ability for this, when embodied in action, this spirit is even more wondrous. Those, however, who appraise life in its true worth, the philosophers and thinkers of pure thoughts, are conscious of the majesty of lovingkindness, even when it is wrapped in many veils[51] that prevent its manifestation.[52]

In this passage, Rabbi Kook presents the approach to reveal the foundation of genius. At least two interpretive strata present themselves in this passage:

(1) On the literal level, an analysis of moral genius (a term that appears in his work *Eder ha-Yakar*) uncovers an inner faculty of lovingkindness. The moral genius is blessed with the capability, and substrate, of lovingkindness, which is infinitely more sublime than actual acts of lovingkindness. The existence of this lovingkindness faculty is the cause of happiness and elevation for the whole world.

(2) On the symbolic level, contemplation of genius reveals the divine nobility that emanates lovingkindness. In other words, an examination of the righteous individual reveals the theosophical source of his inspiration and sweep of vision. The Jewish people, specifically, and the world as a whole are made fruitful by the righteous ones bringing down divine emanation.

We will now discuss the symbolic stratum of the "genius of lovingkindness." A careful analysis of the Kabbalistic symbols in Rabbi Kook's writings reveals a process within the Godhead of emanation. This process begins with *Binah* and concludes with *Malkhut*:

Binah ("Intelligence")
↓
Hesed ("Lovingkindness")
↓
Din ("Valor")
↓
Tiferet ("Beauty")
↓
Netzah ("Lasting Endurance")
↓
Hod ("Majesty")
↓
Malkhut ("Kingdom")

---

50 See Amos 8:4; Job 24:4.
51 See the commentary of Nahmanides to Genesis 38:15.
52 *Shemonah Kevatzim* 3:40 (vol. 2, 27).

This implies that the moral genius is built of two dimensions, the inner and the outer.

(1) The meaning of the inner dimension is that the genius is capable of absorbing the divine emanation of lovingkindness-without-bounds in his soul. That is, the genius is gifted with the pneumatic ability to be a receptacle,[53] to be a substrate for divine inspiration. At times this faculty is hidden, and requires an act of explication. Rabbi Kook states at the end of the eulogy that philosophers, theologians, and Kabbalists succeed in perceiving this ability and properly defining it.

(2) The outer dimension means that the divine emanation is channeled in such a way that it influences the genius's surroundings.[54]

According to Rabbi Kook, some geniuses were gifted only with the inner dimension, while others succeeded in influencing others, as well. In either case, genius is patently expressed in the ability to absorb and transmit lovingkindness to the surroundings. He stressed the national environment (the "single soul in the nation") of the genius of lovingkindness, as we shall see in the following discussion..

Moral Genius and Redemption

Since Rabbi Kook includes morality within genius, we should examine the image of the genius as a moral teaching for the public at large. In other words, the very discussion of genius is of educational value. The portrait of the genius goes beyond the realm of intellectual curiosity, and becomes an object for emulation. In the continuation of his eulogy for the Aderet, Rabbi Kook writes:

> As regards the benefit to be derived from knowledge of the *toladah*[55] of some genius, there is practical benefit, and theoretical benefit. The practical benefit is a sort of "the jealousy of scribes increases

---

53   Rabbi Kook called Moses "the most sublime vessel of the divine light that the human soul embraced" (*Olat Re'ayah*, vol. 2, 159).

54   Rabbi Kook used the Kabbalistic and Hasidic term of "pipe" (*tzinor*) for the righteous individual's receiving of the divine emanation, which he transfers to the world. See *Shemonah Kevatzim* 1:859 (vol. 1, 274).

55   Rabbi Kook used medieval terminology to refer to the nature of the genius, that is, his formative traits.

wisdom,"[56] such that the reader, who sees the inner splendor and majesty, sanctity, and grandeur[57] attained by the great man, will have the inner desire aroused within him for him, too, to try his strength, to follow in his ways. And if he is incapable of fully emulating him, at any rate, it is impossible that he will not at all be moved by this from the place of his lowliness to ascend to upper [realms]; that, he, too, will choose some such good ways and precious acquired virtues; when he exceedingly labors in them, this nature increases. The theoretical benefit is the greatness of the soul that increases at the foot of every sublime vision, majestic in holiness, that presents itself before him. The great vision itself elevates the soul and refines the heart, even if he [the possessor of the soul] will not think to adopt the practical ways to resemble what is much higher and loftier than him.[58]

Rabbi Kook described the double influence of the genius: active influence, the emulation of the genius by the public around him; and passive influence, the spiritual elevation of the public surrounding the genius.[59]

---

56 BT Bava Batra 21a; *Tanna de-Vei Eliyahu Rabbah*, chap. 21.

57 The terms used by Rabbi Kook (*hod* and *hadar*, *kedushah* and *tiferet*) might echo the emanation from *Tiferet* to *Malkhut*, through *Hod* and *Yesod*. Thus, he alluded to an additional stratum of meaning, namely, that the mental awakening of the genius has its roots in the supernal emanation.

58 *Eder ha-Yakar*, 23.

59 In the speech he delivered upon assuming the post of rabbi in Bausk in 1996, Rabbi Kook spoke of two types of parallel leaders, who engage in active and passive leadership. The passive leader "is of a very wondrous level, and is greatly elevated over all the people. Consequently, he dwells by himself and is engaged in perfecting himself, according to his worth, and as he is engaged in this, he leads the entire public, who follow him, even though his leadership is not in accordance with their own value. Rather, by the aspect of the great power of the leader he elevates and raises them, to deport themselves above their worth" (printed in *Otzrot ha-Re'ayah*, vol. 4, 64). The active leader is not gifted with such charisma, and he does not lead the public by force of his personality, he rather chooses "to act with them in accordance with their attributes."
     Rabbi Kook would later explain that the passive influence is anchored in two realms: (1) theurgic and magical notions. The saint brings down divine emanation, in an event that occurs totally between the saint and the Sefirotic world. He wrote, for instance: "The more the righteous one satisfies himself with the pleasantness of the divine delight, desire, the intellect, emotion, and its beauty, the more the entire world is filled with contentment and a feeling of expansiveness, delight, and tranquility" (*Shemonah Kevatzim* 1:697 [vol. 1, 222]). All this is grounded in the terminology of the bringing down of the divine emanation; (2) personal example: Rabbi Kook wrote of the "paramount righteous, God's mighty ones,"

We should address the question of the context and the motifs that Rabbi Kook incorporates in this passage. To denote the passive influence of the genius, Rabbi Kook uses the expressions "high and lofty" (Isaiah 6:1; 57:15); "majestic in holiness" (Exodus 15:11), and "lowliness." These three expressions appear in the blessing of redemption that immediately precedes the morning *Amidah* prayer.[60] Rabbi Kook understood the events of his time as stages in the last Redemption. He might have sought to imply that the approaching Redemption, to which the blessing of redemption alludes, is also dependent upon the influence of the genius, that is, Rabbi Kook himself, or at least those who share his paradigm. Moreover, the Redemption is being realized by the secular public, who threw off the yoke of religious observance. Rabbi Kook was convinced that the latter were tools in the hands of Divine Providence. However, the motive force that caused them to realize the divine plan was the passive influence of the genius. Rabbi Kook accordingly stated in the above passage that the genius passively influences those whose soul is in a "lowly place," which he raises to "upper [realms]."[61]

The motif of incorporation of liturgical wording from the blessing of redemption links genius and redemption.[62] Rabbi Kook summarized that "[to draw] the inner *tziyur* of the portrait of the great soul is undoubtedly a heavy labor."[63] "*Tziyur*" usually means "concept," although at times Rabbi Kook used it in its visual sense (i.e., picture); here, it is the act of depicting.[64]

---

whose "natural familial love soars until it spreads over all Israel" (ibid., 2:37 [vol. 1, 306]). Personal example, too, is not divorced from magical influence. In any event, the two planes are personal and passive, in that the saint does not directly address the public.

[60] The source of these inclusions reads as follows:
   "High and exalted/ great and awesome, He humbles the haughty down to the dust, and raises the lowly to the heights"/ "Who is like You, Lord, among the mighty? Who is like You, majestic in holiness?"

[61] The verse in Daniel (7:25) refers to the response of the wicked to Israel.

[62] This approach also found expression among Rabbi Kook's students, who saw his personality as a source of passive influence on the Land of Israel and on the entire world. See Cherlow, *The Tzaddiq*, 52.

[63] *Eder ha-Yakar*, 24.

[64] The source is the medieval rationalist literature, where it means "apprehension" (I. Efros, *Philosophical Terms in the Moreh Nebukim* [New York, 1924], 104). See, e.g., D. Schwartz, "Epigrams ('Siyyurin') of R. David Ibn Bilia," *Kiryat Sefer* 63 (1990-1991): 637-54 [Hebrew]. See also *Shemonah Kevatzim* 7:176 (vol. 3, 223). Cf. Cherlow, *The Tzaddiq*, 264 n. 10.

Thus, genius and its characteristic mental and theosophic processes are not easily depicted. This is especially true regarding moral genius. If we listen to what Rabbi Kook incorporated in Eder ha-Yakar, we learn that he alluded to a new conception of genius in the messianic era.

Moral Genius and Heresy

As we saw above, the genius's passive influence is significant for both his immediate environment and the national and messianic plane. In the eulogy, Rabbi Kook spoke explicitly of the former, while he merely alludes to the latter. Rabbi Kook continued to set forth the ways in which the genius passively influences the national plane, focusing on the question of belief and heresy.

The distinction that Rabbi Kook drew in Eder ha-Yakar between scientific and moral heresy was discussed once or twice in the scholarly literature,[65] and requires further clarification. In short, scientific heresy is atheism, while moral heresy is the perception of religion as immoral.

Rabbi Kook asserted that two factors determine the progress of the human race: ability (intellectual and scientific achievements) and moral will (the good). If these factors develop in tandem and with mutual adaptation, the result will be the "general and perfect good,"[66] and "the natural divine love"[67] will be revealed. If, however, ability develops without the corresponding development of the moral will, this will result in materialism and heresy, which have their roots in self-love and narcissism. Rabbi Kook then turned to explaining the ways of heresy.

Rabbi Kook identified scientific heresy with the denial of God's existence, and moral heresy with the claim that religion[68] harms the moral development of the human race. He advanced two arguments regarding these two types of heresy:

---

[65]   See Yaron, *Philosophy*, 26-27; S. Rosenberg, "Introduction to the Thought of Rabbi Kook," in *Yovel Orot: The Thought of Rabbi Abraham Isaac ha-Kohen Kook, of Blessed Memory*, ed. B. Ish-Shalom and S. Rosenberg (Jerusalem, 1985), 84-88 [Hebrew].

[66]   *Eder ha-Yakar*, 36.

[67]   *Eder ha-Yakar*, 35. The idea of cosmic divine love reflects the divine emanation, that by its nature radiates to all. The nature of narcissism, however, is the opposite.

[68]   Theology; as Rabbi Kook puts it, "the studies of God" (*Eder ha-Yakar*, 37).

(1) Scientific heresy is a child of the modern age. Greek philosophy believed in the existence of gods, and it discussed the question of providence, that is, whether the gods are involved in what occurs in earthly existence.[69] Moral heresy, in contrast, is both an ancient phenomenon (the Epicureans) and a new one (socialist and Marxist ideologies).

(2) Scientific heresy is based on moral heresy; the former has "no independent basis."[70]

The second argument implies that the effective effort to rout heresy must be directed primarily toward moral heresy. Rabbi Kook maintains that the response to moral heresy's infiltration of the Jewish people must be twofold:

(1) The active response: dissemination of the argument that the Torah does not harm man's morality; if it seems otherwise, the flaw lies in man's understanding of the Torah, and not in the Torah itself.

(2) The passive response: striving for religious perfection in the personal realm influences one's surroundings. "Consequently, whatever improves the deeds and attributes of those upholding the Torah and the

---

69 Once again, Rabbi Kook adopted the medieval rationalist conception that attributed universal and impersonal providence (that is, the preservation of the genus and species) to philosophy. He took pains to harmonize it with individual providence. See, e.g., *Shemonah Kevatzim* 8:154 (vol. 3, 292).

70 *Eder ha-Yakar*, 37. Although scientific heresy was deemed to be a branch of moral heresy, the former was of great concern to Rabbi Kook, usually more than moral heresy. First, regarding his eulogy of the Aderet: Rabbi Kook raised a number of arguments from the polemical literature in order to wrestle with scientific heresy. For example, the argument from the *Kuzari* concerning the factuality of the belief of Judaism ("historical truth"), and the argument that the discoveries of modern science did not shock Judaism, as they had unsettled Christianity ("there is no discrepancy, for example, between the opinion of Ptolemy and Copernicus and Galileo"; *Eder ha-Yakar*, 37). Second, in an essay published that same year (*Ikvei ha-Tzon*), Rabbi Kook maintained that the problem of the generation is mental. He wrote that "the terrible sickness of the generation does not lie mainly in the heart, not in emotion, not in desire and licentiousness, not in hands that do evil, and not in feet that run to evil, although all these are sick and in pain, rather, the illness has its basis in the mind [literally, the brain]—the power of thought. At the very summit of thought, that encompasses all, hides a fierce illness, which is deeper than any habitual language. Because of it, a person will not understand the language of his fellow, and all the additional instances further increase the spread of the

faithful will lessen natural moral heresy, and its decline will be matched by a similar decline in its scientific derivative."[71]

The passive response is the dominant one, led by those individuals who have attained religious perfection, that is, the exceptional individuals. This conception provides the framework for a discussion of heresy in *Eder ha-Yakar*, which it opens and ends. Rabbi Kook writes at the beginning and end of this discussion:

> [1] The natural divine love, which is confirmed in the ways of life, was always manifest in Israel among the exceptional individuals, even in the most wretched times. For individual examples that indicate the general picture, we may use the acts of the righteous[72] and their state of mind.[73]
>
> [2] For only moral good deportment, with good deeds and good attributes, that comes from righteous and God-fearing observers of the Torah, is the most correct guarantee for removing the erroneous element of moral heresy. When it is removed, the weakness of scientific heresy is revealed, and the imaginary iron yoke[74] of negation, that weakens the strength of Israel, is broken on its own, and obviously,

human sickness, and our eyes see and pine" (*Eder ha-Yakar*, 110). The metaphor of the Tower of Babel, that is, the lack of communication in language, teaches of the intellectual and cognitive root of heresy. Third, additional arguments that focus on the intellectual aspect are to be found in Rabbi Kook's *"Moreh Nevukhim Hadash"* (A New Guide for the Perplexed), on which Rabbi Shahar Rahmani wrote his PhD dissertation.

71   *Eder ha-Yakar*, 37.

72   The reference to the genre of stories of the righteous is typical of the eulogy's style. The stories, however, about the Aderet that Rabbi Kook relates are not the main content of the eulogy, which is concerned with the ideas of the perfect man and his place in the national awakening.

73   *Eder ha-Yakar*, 35.

74   Rabbi Kook argues that the heretical literature is "moral literature of spoiled fantasy" (*Eder ha-Yakar*, 37). He thereby once again followed the medieval rationalist style, which blamed the error of heresy on the dominance of the imaginative faculty. See, e.g., Z. Harvey, "Maimonides and Spinoza on the Knowledge of Good and Evil," *Binah* 2 (1989): 131-46.

the divine light returns[75] to illuminate the souls, the national forces[76] unite, and the blessing of life and peace[77] nears Israel.[78]

This teaches that the main passive influence is wielded by perfect individuals. Although all those who "uphold the Torah" and the "faithful" influence their surroundings, it is the righteous individual who removes the influence of heresy. Thus, the discussion of heresy is joined to that of genius. In the final analysis, it is the moral genius who routs moral heresy by the force of his personality and its passive influence.

These passages reveal a bit more of the moral genius's influence on the public at large. We have already mentioned the distinction between the cosmic divine love and narcissistic love, which is the cause of heresy. Rabbi Kook says here that as soon as moral heresy and scientific heresy have vanished, the divine light "obviously" emanates onto the souls and fills them. This echoes the fundamental Kabbalistic model that evil has no inherent existence, and is only secondary to the good. As soon as the divine spark is exposed and evil is differentiated, it is put away and disappears.

Here an additional aspect is portrayed. The divine emanation, expressed in the metaphors of "love" (passage [1]) and "light" (passage [2]), is beneficent to all equally. Heresy, which emphasizes the individual and his self-love, conceals and clouds over the divine emanation. Rabbi Kook might possibly allude to the model of the moral genius: since the moral genius acts on behalf of all, and also influences all by his very personality (passive influence), then he drives out self-love from his soul until it vanishes;[79] and the moment that self-love disappears, the cosmic love—which is the divine (or Sefirotic) emanation—shines forth. Rabbi Kook ended by writing that the righteous individual's action and passive influence also have an effect on

---

75 Rabbi Kook observed in his letters that "the great ones of the nation, who illuminate its path, are capable of casting a special light before it" (Igrot ha-Re'ayah, vol. 1, 321).

76 Rabbi Kook linked strength, righteousness, morality, love, and genius when he related to the Aderet: "Such tremendous strength, along with his righteousness and his good and fine morality, was our proud glory [or might; gaon uzeinu], of blessed memory" (Eder ha-Yakar, 43).

77 In the Kabbalistic literature, the righteous individual is symbolized by the Sefirah of Yesod, which is also called "Shalom" (literally, "Peace").

78 Eder ha-Yakar, 43.

79 On the negation of the self in Rabbi Kook's writings, see Cherlow, The Tzaddiq, 82-86.

the national level. Here, too, love of all pushes aside love of the individual.[80] The righteous individual unites the "national forces" by overcoming self-love in favor of influence over the society as a whole. This, then, is another instance of Rabbi Kook directing our attention to the period of the national renaissance.

Summation

Rabbi Kook's discussion of the genius and his traits in his eulogy for the Aderet is based on four assumptions:

(1) Genius is divided into rational genius and moral genius;
(2) Genius is described in aesthetic terms;
(3) Genius exerts both active and passive influence;
(4) Genius is indirectly connected to redemption.

The inclusion of the idea of the moral genius within the aesthetic realm ("song"), and the allusions to the passive influence of such genius in the redemptive time, make a substantial contribution to the conception of the saint. Rabbi Kook concluded his eulogy of the Aderet with a discussion on the attribute of piety, reiterating the existence of "clean, exalted, and pure" piety,[81] within a clearly national context. Lovingkindness toward one's fellow is also lovingkindness toward God.[82] The eulogy opens with the image of the genius, and ends with that of the pietist; the eulogy offers a journey from moral genius to the praxis of lovingkindness. The feature common to both the pietist and the genius is their influence on others, from the individual level to the national. The eulogy is an important document, because Rabbi Kook collected in it his thoughts on the person who is morally exceptional. Although much remains hidden, and Rabbi Kook left

---

[80] This, indeed, is how Rabbi Kook presented the Aderet: "The love of Israel was fixed within him in a twofold bond, from the aspect of the simple love of the direct natural inclination of love of his people, and from the aspect of the divine influence, because it is the people of the Lord, a holy people which the Lord chose for His portion from all the peoples on the face of the earth" (*Eder ha-Yakar*, 44).

[81] *Eder ha-Yakar*, 63.

[82] Ibid., 64.

the range of meanings of moral genius to the imagination and speculation of the reader, his formulation remains clear and focused.

We should take into account *Sitz im Leben*, that is, the historical and social background of the eulogy. The allusions to the genius that Rabbi Kook embedded in the text suggest the manner in which he viewed his own contribution to the national revival ca. 1906, the year in which *Eder ha-Yakar* was published. Rabbi Kook had immigrated to the Land of Israel less than two years earlier, and he was still under the influence of his first exposure to the national awakening there. He referred to the Aderet, but he sketched an outline that enables us to understand the personality of a genius, in general, and specifically, his own personality. The question of whether he did so consciously or not is not relevant to the self-image of the saint. His contribution to this issue is his presentation of moral genius, which refers to the altruism that results from inspiration and creative brilliance, in light of the stormy messianic reality. This inspiration can be described in aesthetic terminology.

As noted above, passive influence is extremely important for understanding Rabbi Kook's character. He quickly learned that he did not substantively and actively influence the nonreligious public. The dialectics of the elevation of the soul in the presence of Zionist activity, on the one hand, and the abandoning of religious observance by the *halutzim* (pioneers), on the other, characterized him since his arrival in the Land of Israel. Avinoam Rozenak already noted the revival of Torah effected by the unification of opposites at the time.[83] Accordingly, all that remained for Rabbi Kook was to pin his hopes on the genius's passive influence and intimate service of the Lord.

---

83   Rozenak, *Rabbi A. I. Kook*, 54-57. See also *idem*, "Halakhah, Aggadah and Prophecy in Torat Erez Israel through the Prism of 'the Unification of Opposites' in the Writings of Rabbi A.I.H. Kook," in Sagi and Schwartz, *Hundred Years*, vol. 1, 261-85 [Hebrew].

Chapter Four

PROFILE

Up to now we have examined a certain personality type, the genius, and his contribution to fashioning the image of the saint. This discussion is important, because Rabbi Kook was intensively occupied with such a figure in an essay that he himself readied for publication. We will now turn to an exploration of the structural lines of the saint in Rabbi Kook's thought, this time with an analysis of conceptual thoughts, and not only typological ones as in the discussion regarding the genius type.

The Reflection of the Godhead

In Kabbalistic and Hasidic thought, processes within the Godhead were copied to the soul, as in the use of the *Sefirot* of *Hokhmah*, *Binah*, and *Da'at* in the depiction of the cognitive process. At times, the transferal moved in the opposite direction, as in the anthropomorphic portrayal in Lurianic Kabbalah of the primal divine structure ("*Adam Kadmon*"—primordial man) after *Tzimtzum* (the act of divine "withdrawal"). Rabbi Kook, too, transferred processes within the Godhead to the saint, and the perfect man became the reflection of the supernal world. It seems, however, that he did so in an unusual and extreme fashion, in both stylistic and contentual terms. In this he was guided by the figure of the saint. The following passage draws a parallel between the suffering of the righteous individual and that of the *Shekhinah*:

> The great anguish that each righteous one feels within himself over the diminution of the divine communion that he senses within himself, that does not satisfy his great thirst, from which all his limbs are shattered always, out of his longing, and he has no rest from any delight or pleasure in the world—this is the actual anguish of the

Shekhinah.[1] The content of the life of all the worlds longs for the supreme divine perfection that is revealed in them.[2]

Just as the worlds thirst for elevation and the revelation of the divinity within them, so too, the righteous one desires communion with God. And just as the fact that divinity is not fully manifest in the world distresses the *Shekhinah*, the fact that the righteous individual does not attain the highest levels of communion is the cause of his physical flaccidity and unease. Rabbi Kook, however, adds that this is "the actual anguish of the *Shekhinah*." That is, the personal and the cosmic processes are united. The righteous individual feels God's anguish, and in this respect he is a reflection of the *Shekhinah*.

Thus, the saint undergoes processes parallel to those of the divine *Sefirot*:

> For he [the true holy righteous one] always ascends in his thought and will to the spiritual supernal world, in which there are no limitations,[3] in which all can enter, and obviously, all that is good can gather together. He acts with his supernal power,[4] so that the good that is dispersed among all the individuals in Israel, and in the entire world, and in all the worlds, will assemble together. There are unfathomable degrees in this trait. The most righteous man encompasses the most comprehensive breadth, and he has no contraction of strict judgment.[5] For he, in his entirety, is replete with

---

[1]   See, e.g., Rabbi Joseph Albo, *Sefer ha-'Ikkarim* (*Book of Principles*), 4:45 (ed. I. Husik [Philadelphia, 1946], vol. 4, 2, 446), II. 12-13. Cf. Rabbi Kook's more moderate statement: "The anguish of the righteous [...] is in accordance with the anguish of the *Shekhinah*" (*Shemonah Kevatzim* 8:195 [vol. 3, 309]). The righteous are distressed at the withdrawal and concealment of the divine light.

[2]   *Shemonah Kevatzim* 4:47 (vol. 2, 146).

[3]   See BT Berakhot 51a; Shabbat 118a.

[4]   The term "supernal power" has a magical-astral context; see below.

[5]   The contraction mentioned in this verse clearly appears in a Kabbalistic-symbolic context. *Arikh Anpin* (literally, "the Long Face"; that is, "the Long-Suffering," referring to God [G. G. Scholem, *Major Trends in Jewish Mysticism* [New York, 1969], 270), parallel to the *Sefirah* of *Keter*, too, has no dimension of strict judgment; this might have been Rabbi Kook's intent here. In other places in his writings, he states that the righteous individual distances himself from this contraction, that means strict judgment and inflexibility. He writes: "The one with the rich soul, with its great song and splendor [*tiferet*], suffers especially from the contraction of the wisdoms that are concerned with external and random matters" (*Shemonah Kevatzim* 1:880

lovingkindness and many mercies, and truly desires the good of all. He loves to find merit for all people, and hates to find guilt in them and convict them. The world is incapable of recognizing this degree of righteousness, and every paramount righteous one must enclothe his supreme righteousness in many garbs, since after they restrict the light, people can derive benefit from him.[6]

We should take note of the Kabbalistic symbolism in this passage. This would seem to be a routine process of divine emanation, such as Rabbi Kook described in many places, and the likes of which we discussed above. The saint brings down the divine emanation from *Binah* ("his supreme righteousness") to *Malkhut* ("righteousness"). Wordplay is at work here in Rabbi Kook's choice of words: the righteous individual (the *tzaddik*) effects emanation from the supreme *Tzedek* to the lower *Tzedek* (*Binah* and *Malkhut*, respectively). In schematic form, this is the process:

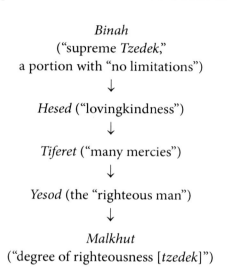

Binah
("supreme *Tzedek*,"
a portion with "no limitations")
↓

Hesed ("lovingkindness")
↓

Tiferet ("many mercies")
↓

Yesod (the "righteous man")
↓

Malkhut
("degree of righteousness [*tzedek*]")

[vol. 1, 281]); "The supreme righteous cannot contract themselves to a special view, since they see the Lord's lovingkindness and light spread over all, it is outstretched everywhere" (3:261 [vol. 2, 97]). Rabbi Kook maintains that if the "completely righteous one" had not been born with an Evil Inclination, he would completely negate all strict judgment (8:167 [vol. 3, 299]). In his letters (*Igrot ha-Re'ayah*, vol. 2, 186), he explains that he is among those capable of engaging in Kabbalah ("the inner secrets of the Torah"), and as such, "he is exceedingly replete with the light of lovingkindness of the Torah, and it is incumbent upon him to engage in the rectification of the fallen and the drawing close of those who are distant (in the language of the masters of the esoteric teachings [i.e., Kabbalists], this is also included in the category of the collection of the holy sparks from within the husks." Finally, Rabbi Kook writes in his commentary to the Passover *Haggadah* that "the fundamental line that distinguishes Israel from the [non-Jewish] peoples is the light of lovingkindness, which is the primal light of the Patriarch Abraham, may he rest in peace" (*Olat Re'ayah*, vol. 2, 264). On the extraction of the sparks, see below in this chapter.

6   *Shemonah Kevatzim* 1:575 (vol. 1, 182).

The saint succeeds in bringing down the divine emanation because of his adherence to the trait of lovingkindness; that is, he loves all people and contains them, despite their being many and diverse. Rabbi Kook wrote that the righteous individual does not experience any "contraction of strict judgment." His endless love and giving remove the *Sefirah* of *Din*-strict judgment from the process of emanation. Rabbi Kook mentioned elsewhere that even if the righteous one is angry, this anger is on the level of external expression and behavior, and not on the deep inner level.[7] Since the righteous individual has a comprehensive view of reality (which is all light and good), he finds no real reason to become angry.[8] Only a righteous individual who does not know himself in depth falls to "the anger of fools."[9] The personality of the righteous individual is all love. As Rabbi Kook noted about himself, "Great is my love for all creatures, for all the reality."[10] The righteous individual loves the entire reality, while being anguished at its lacks.[11] If, however, we return to the claim that the righteous one does not experience the contraction entailed in strict judgment, this might be an allusion to the level of such an individual, that reflects the state of *Ein-Sof* [a term relating to an aspect of God that is beyond definition] before *Tzimtzum*, which, for example, is frequently mentioned in the Habad literature. The righteous individual transforms the "divine *Ayin* [naught]" to "*Yesh* [being]."[12] In any event, the righteous one is a reflection of processes that occur within the Godhead. In many passages, Rabbi Kook presented the righteous one as a reflection of the universe, who "elevates the inner nature

---

7   "But this does not come from the heart" (ibid., 3:170 [vol. 2, 70]). See *Mussar Avikha*, 138.

8   Rabbi Kook wrote that "the supreme righteous, possessing clarity of cognition [...] are cognizant that the pure light is much greater than the world's ability to bear it, notwithstanding which, he must illuminate in the world, and there must be many masks to hide it; these masks are evil and its bearers. Consequently, all these, too, are part of the rectification of the world, then why should they be angry and rage?" (*Shemonah Kevatzim* 7:207 [vol. 3, 234]). Thus, evil is a sort of mask (*masakh*) that restricts the divine light, which the world could not withstand. This use of "*masakh*" originates in the Hebrew translation of Maimonides, *Shemonah Perakim*, chap. 7.

9   *Shemonah Kevatzim* 8:6 (vol. 3, 245).

10 Ibid., 8:116 (vol. 3, 279). See the collection of passages on love in *Middot ha-Re'ayah* (within *Mussar Avikha*, 92-97).

11 *Kevatzim*, vol. 2, 122.

12 *Shemonah Kevatzim* 2:319 (vol. 1, 393).

[of the reality] by his elevation of himself."[13] Here, however, the righteous individual is a reflection of the Godhead itself. With this approach, Rabbi Kook stretched the microcosm metaphor to its limits.[14]

An analysis of this passage reveals the symbolic dimension of Rabbi Kook's discussion. We should also, however, consider the two additional strata of the passage:

(1) The realistic meaning: the righteous individual is distinguished by his love of the nation, and his advocacy of it. He derives the good from all members of the nation, and channels it into national and messianic missions.

(2) The magical sense: the righteous one brings down the divine emanation, through his profound knowledge of its channels; he is gifted with "supernal power." In the first stage, he engages in activity resembling the gathering of the divine sparks, the significance of which will be discussed at length below. In the second stage, he brings down the divine emanation.[15]

Rabbi Kook then identified the divine emanation with the inspiration of the saint. Now, the godly illumination that expresses its presence in the worlds is the same illumination possessed by the righteous individual. Rabbi Kook writes:

> All the opinions, movements, wars, preparations [konaniyyot], foundations,[16] literatures, and social and personal aspirations prepare life, how to have the fresh light—in which the supreme holiness in its full glorious freedom lives—be absorbed within them and infuse them.[17] This is the light of the righteous, the supreme mighty ones, who are armed with the pure supernal might, the holy

---

13 Ibid., 2:113 (vol. 1, 327).

14 See A. Altmann, *Studies in Religious Philosophy and Mysticism* (London, 1969), 1-40. In *Shemonah Kevatzim* 1:692 (vol. 1, 220), Rabbi Kook writes of "the spiritual waves in the individual soul and in the world." An additional depiction of the reflection of the *Sefirot* in the righteous individual appears in *Shemonah Kevatzim* 8:115 (vol. 3, 279).

15 In another passage, Rabbi Kook states that "those great of soul [...] draw down [*mamshikhim*] the supernal light of life into mundane affairs" (*Shemonah Kevatzim* 2:7 [vol. 1, 295]).

16 Or: bases, following II Chronicles 4:14.

17 On freedom in the image of the saint, see below, Chapter Eight.

might of the brilliance and splendor of life, as they appear from their
source, full of splendor and burnished finery.[18]

According to this portrayal, the righteous are a sort of personification of the
divine emanation. The multifaceted reality in its entirety is a preparation
(disposition, in medieval terminology) for receiving the righteous
individual's emanation. Rabbi Kook must have taken into account the
perfect man bringing down emanation by means of his theurgic and
magical activity. In this passage he further alludes to the representation of
the light by the righteous individual, and concludes, in dialectic fashion,
with the might of the righteous, who at times must use the forceful attribute
of strict judgment. Indeed, Rabbi Kook uses the term "*gevurah*" three times
in the conclusion of the passage.

To draw this into closer focus: Rabbi Kook had fervently argued, as
we have just seen, that the saint does not experience strict judgment. Now
we see the dialectic nature of this argument. Rabbi Kook finds the saint
rooted in lovingkindness, but, notwithstanding this, he undoubtedly also
acts in the limited path of strict judgment. As one example of this, Rabbi
Kook compared the sinners of Israel to those drowning in the sea, whom
the righteous one saves:

> Additionally, all the souls that seem to be drowning in the depths of
> the tempestuous sea, all the souls of the basest sinners of Israel, all,
> without exception, strive, swim, and flow, cry out from the depths of
> the sea to those mighty in strength [see Psalms 103:20], the righteous
> of the world, to come to their aid, to throw them a life buoy, a rope
> to grasp. The righteous, the mighty ones of the world, the servants of
> the Lord, who fulfill His word with love, lovingkindness, and great
> courage, are filled with compassion, and in their great compassion
> throw them the means of rescue and protection, and food to sustain
> them alive, for as long as they struggle with the waves in the darkest
> places, in the depths [see Psalms 88:7].[19]

Rabbi Kook mentions the emanation of lovingkindness, strict
judgment ("great courage"; the term *gevurah* has both meanings, each of

---

[18] *Shemonah Kevatzim* 6:153 (vol. 3, 54).

[19] Ibid., 2:14 (vol. 1, 298).

which relates to power),[20] and beauty ("compassion"). The metaphor that he employs is reminiscent of that provided by Rabbi Saadia Gaon in the beginning of his philosophical work *Beliefs and Opinions*.[21] Rabbi Saadia compared himself, as the author of a book on matters of faith, to one who extricates those who are drowning in a sea of doubts. Both infinite love and fixed and unyielding strict judgment are bound up in the act of rescue. Occupation with strict judgment is a fall for the righteous one; the saint pays a price for saving the drowning. As Rabbi Kook writes elsewhere, the saint's "slightly leaving" lovingkindness suffices for him to experience "filth," "bitterness," "darkness," and a fall.[22]

The symbolic meaning finely expresses the position of the saint as reflective of the divine processes. The responsibility that he feels for the generation motivates him to use various theurgic and forceful means, at times even against his nature. On occasion, lovingkindness enjoys exclusivity in the work of the saint, while at other times he employs a combination of lovingkindness and strict judgment. In either case, the saint reflects processes within the Godhead, and his proximity to the latter sometimes leads to a blurring of the distinction between the two.

Inclusion and Toleration

The saint can be comprehended from his interaction with all the worlds, which is the heart of the idea of the microcosm: the saint is the reflection of all creation. Both the divine world and the material reality are reflected in him. The saint contains "many aspects of life."[23] Furthermore, he is the purposeful dimension of the world, imparting meaning and purpose to all the universe. Rabbi Kook wrote that "the world lacks aim, as long as the

---

20 This might be an allusion to *Binah*, that in the Zoharic *Sefirot* is perceived as the root of strict judgment. At any rate, in this and many other passages he compared the righteous to "those mighty in strength."

21 Saadia Gaon, *The Book of Beliefs and Opinions*, trans. S. Rosenblatt (New Haven, 1948), 7.

22 *Shemonah Kevatzim* 2:163 (vol. 1, 341).

23 *Shemonah Kevatzim* 2:331 (vol. 1, 397). On toleration and openness in Rabbi Kook's writings, see, e.g., B. Ish-Shalom, "Tolerance and Its Theoretical Basis in the Teaching of Rabbi Kook," *Daat* 20 (1988): 151-68 [Hebrew]; T. Ross, "Between Metaphysical and Liberal Pluralism: A Reappraisal of Rabbi A. I. Kook's Espousal of Toleration," *AJS Review* 21 (1996): 61-110.

supreme soul does not shine in it. When it comes and casts its precious light,[24] then the world advances, and Heaven and earth rejoice in the joy of their creation."[25] In Aristotelian terminology, the saint is the formal and final cause of all existence.

Consequently, the saint contains all. On the epistemological level, he absorbs different perceptions, even when they include contradictions or inconsistencies. Furthermore, his ability to embrace also extends to notions that do not suit the style and nature of his character. Such an approach indirectly assumes that the saint seemingly contracts his personality, in an act of withdrawal, in order to contain all. On the religious, social, and national level, this saint also receives those who have cast off the yoke of religion and its attendant observances. Rabbi Kook frequently wrote of the inclusiveness of the exceptional individuals. At times, he did not hesitate to speak in such a vein of himself, such as: "I must absorb all."[26] The following representative passages present the impression of all existence in the soul of the saint:

> The great souls are ready[27] for the all-encompassing vision to shine in their inner self.[28]
>
> The great souls feel in the depths of their being that they belong to all the reality, and certainly to all the people that they know, and certainly to every human being.[29] These ideas, that are powerful and very inclusive, give strength to rising and falling power[30] that

---

[24]   Following Zechariah 14:6.

[25]   Following the order of the Seven Blessings of the wedding ceremony and feast, as mentioned in BT Ketubot 8a; the beginning of Tractate *Kallah*; *Shemonah Kevatzim* 1:830 (vol. 1, 267). In 1:848 (vol. 1, 271), Rabbi Kook writes that "the righteous elevate the entire world," and their will "is implemented, following the supernal model."

[26]   *Shemonah Kevatzim* 3:233 (vol. 2, 89).

[27]   It is unclear from the style of writing whether "*mukhanot*" means that they are prepared (disposition) for the reflection of all, or whether this means the consent (of the perfect ones) to this reflection.

[28]   *Shemonah Kevatzim* 1:187 (vol. 1, 76).

[29]   That is, if the perfect individual feels affiliation with inanimate nature, or with the lower life forms within it, he must certainly feel affiliation with human beings.

[30]   The use of the phrase "rising and falling" refers to the different audiences addressed by the righteous one. The "rising and falling" sacrifice is determined in accordance with the financial ability of the one offering it; it "rises and falls" in value according to the individual's budget; see, e.g., M Shevuot 3:7.

examines the most individual lineage,[31] of them and their families, their people, and such lineages. The details of the genealogies join together and generate a new way of life.[32]

The great righteous ones include all in their soul.[33] They possess all the good of all and, also, all the evil of all; they suffer tribulations on account of all, and they derive pleasure from all; they transform all the evil of all to good. By force of their being elevated by means of the sufferings they endure, all is elevated by them, for in the root of their soul are all the very vast branches of all the souls,[34] of which the righteous are the foundation.[35]

The individual with a "great soul" undergoes a process of ascents and descents. He descends to the particulars, examines the general dimensions within them, and thereby succeeds in generalizing and universalizing them. The descent to particulars causes the righteous one to suffer, and their inclusion—that is, revealing their shared root—heals this suffering.[36] To a certain degree, we have here the Sabbatean and Hasidic notion of the righteous one who descends to the husks (the surrounding evil) to extract the sanctity within them, albeit in a general model.[37] In another

---

31 There might be a concealed messianic nuance here, since the Messiah is to designate the Israelites by their tribal lineage. See Maimonides, *Mishneh Torah, Hil. Melakhim* (Laws of Kings) 12:3.

32 *Shemonah Kevatzim* 1:203 (vol. 1, 81)

33 Rabbi Kook wrote elsewhere that the righteous individual "encompasses within him all [*kol*] opinions, thoughts, ideas, and influences" (ibid., 1:676 [vol. 1, 216]). The word "*kol*" has a rich history, beginning with its singular uses by Rabbi Abraham Ibn Ezra. Rabbi Kook, however, undoubtedly meant its Kabbalistic sense, namely, the *Sefirah* of *Yesod*, which reflects the righteous individual.

34 Avivi understood this wording as the bringing down of *mohin*. See Avivi, "History as a Divine Prescription," 761. The *mohin* descend from the soul's highest level, which is the *Yehidah* ("the source of the soul").

35 *Shemonah Kevatzim* 1:210 (vol. 1, 82).

36 "The anguishes felt by the one great in soul from the necessity of occupation with minor details, whether in study or in action, are healed only by the deep and expansive thought, that each minor detail is the product of an entire entity, and every manifestation reveals an entire world within itself, and agitates infinite worlds" (*Shemonah Kevatzim* 1:401 [vol. 1, 134]).

37 See ibid., 1:617 (vol. 1, 196); Cherlow, *The Tzaddiq*, 70-73. Rabbi Kook even said that the righteous engage in "strange things" (*Shemonah Kevatzim* 1:803 [vol. 1, 257]). On the aspect of the righteous one descending to the society, see *The Tzaddiq*, 153-63.

place, Rabbi Kook states that the service of some of the righteous lies in their occupation with particulars and their rectification, while others act in a more general realm.[38]

According to these passages, the saint's inclusive power is expressed in a number of interrelated matters:

(1) The soul of the exceptional individual is reflective of all.[39]

(2) This soul encompasses all.

(3) This soul is not private, it rather belongs to all.

(4) This soul acts, and has an effect, on all.

(5) This soul derives benefit from all, and suffers on behalf of all.

One of the noteworthy meanings of the connection between the saint and universality is its intellectual sense. The saint acquires all knowledge, from "the most profound depths of the profundity of halakhah" to "all the languages and their literatures" and "human science in all its aspects."[40] The intellectual side of this inclusiveness is especially expressed in Rabbi Kook's consciousness in his rationalist conception of Divine Providence. He writes:

> Maimonides rejoiced when, for him, the nature of Divine Providence acquired an intellectual level. This is worthy of rejoicing, since as long as this belief, that is the basis of the life of the world,[41] remains without an intellectual aspect [literally, attribute], it is not involved with all the living waves of the wise soul [nefesh],[42] that seeks intellectual cognition. Once, however, it has received its intellectual

---

38   See Avivi, "History as a Divine Prescription," 740-41.

39   Elsewhere Rabbi Kook speaks of the centrality of the righteous individual's soul (Shemonah Kevatzim 1:217 [vol. 1, 85]).

40   Shemonah Kevatzim 2:361 (vol. 1, 506).

41   That is, Divine Providence orders the world. Rabbi Kook might also be alluding here to the immortality of the soul (the "World to Come"), that Maimonides equates with the immortality of the intellect. See, e.g., D. Schwartz, Messianism in Medieval Jewish Thought, second extended edition (Ramat Gan, 2006), 71-74 [Hebrew].

42   The meaning is undoubtedly the intellect. The term "nefesh hakhamah" frequently appears in the writings of thirteenth-century Kabbalists (e.g., Rabbi Jonah ben Asher Gerondi and Rabbi Bahya ben Asher); especially noteworthy is its appearance as the title of the book by Rabbi Moses de Leon. It is in this light that we are to understand the unification with the "soul [neshamah]," that appears later in the passage.

form, then it takes root in the depths of the soul [*neshamah*], in all its chambers[43] and depths, and man finds himself happy, when his spiritual [*ruhanit*] form is joined into a single entity.[44]

According to Maimonides (*Guide of the Perplexed* 3:18), Divine Providence applies to a person in accordance with the scientific knowledge he has attained. Maimonides's rationalist students in the thirteenth century already disagreed regarding the degree of naturalism in this conception.[45] In my opinion, Rabbi Kook's starting point was Kabbalistic. He referred to the tripartite *nefesh* ("soul, life force")—*ruah* ("spirit")—*neshamah* ("breath, soul, soul-breath") structure, and mentioned "the depths of the soul," which is a mental level higher than the other two.[46] He felt, however, that the works by the Kabbalists lacked the rationalist dimension. They disregarded the longing to acquire scientific knowledge, while medieval rationalism viewed scientific law as the supreme intellectual content of cognition. Most of the Kabbalists rejected the ideal of intellection as man's goal in life. For Rabbi Kook, the Kabbalists' concept was one-dimensional. He therefore used the motifs of rejoicing and happiness. For him, completeness, even if based on discordant notions (mysticism and rationalism), expresses the emotion of joy and elevated spirits.

Much has been said about the metaphysical dimension of inclusion and universalism in Rabbi Kook's thought. However, he also applied inclusivity in the ideological-political realm. Relating to the Uganda controversy (as a possible location for Jewish resettlement), Rabbi Kook wrote that "it is a bad sign for the party if it thinks that it is the exclusive source of life, of all wisdom and all integrity, and that anything beside it, 'all is vanity and a striving after wind' [Ecclesiastes 1:14 and more]."[47]

---

[43] Following BT Berakhot 10a; *Yalkut Shimoni* on Psalms 103, para. 857.

[44] *Shemonah Kevatzim* 1:13 (vol. 1, 5).

[45] See D. Schwartz, "The Debate over the Maimonidean Theory of Providence in Thirteenth-Century Jewish Philosophy," *Jewish Studies Quarterly* 2 (1995): 185-96.

[46] The translation of these terms follows *The Zohar*, trans. and commentary D. C. Matt (Stanford, CA, 2004) 1:206a (vol. 3, 262 n. 26).

[47] *Igrot ha-Re'ayah*, vol. 1, 17.

Standing

We have seen thus far in our discussion of genius that at times this standing is acquired following tremendous efforts and labor. Such an acquired standing, however, is inferior to that of the one blessed with this gift from birth. In contrast, when Rabbi Kook discussed the righteous individual, he both directly and indirectly negated the acquisition of such a status through exertion. The righteous individual is substantively distinguished from his surroundings. He writes:

> The righteous weary themselves in spiritual toil when their belief in themselves is diminished, and then they think that they are like all the masses of people. Even if they imagine themselves to be the most rectified and learned among them,[48] then, too, they are not saved from inner humility. Only, they must know that the quality of their soul [*neshamah*] is a completely different supernal quality, for the holy light and divine communion are demanded of them every moment,[49] and they must constantly influence all souls, that are succored by drawing upon their great and encompassing soul.[50]
>
> The truly righteous, the holy ones of the Most High,[51] inherently soar above all labor and toil. Although they would be desirous of all labor and toil, all tribulations and distress, all self-sacrifice, and all exhausting labor in the world, just in order to do the will of the living God, the everlasting King,[52] the Creator of their soul, the King of Israel, its Redeemer,[53] the Master of all people,[54] the God of all souls;[55] despite their will, they are replete with repose and contentment, and a plethora of delights constantly flows through their holy soul.[56]

---

[48]   See BT Sanhedrin 39b.

[49]   The quest for communion typical of the religious consciousness finds expression in a few passages in *Shemonah Kevatzim*; see e.g.: 3:280 (vol. 2, 102); 4:15 (vol. 2, 136).

[50]   Ibid., 1:705 (vol. 1, 225).

[51]   Following Daniel 7:18, 22, 25, and more.

[52]   Following Jeremiah 10:10; the "*Yotzer Or* [who forms light]" blessing in the Morning Service.

[53]   Following Isaiah 44:6.

[54]   See PT Berakhot 1:5, 10b; *Tanhuma, Hukat* 6.

[55]   See *Deuteronomy Rabbah* 11:10.

[56]   *Shemonah Kevatzim* 4:71 (vol. 2, 156).

The saint is gifted with intuitive thought, speedy and immediate perception, and congenital faculty. In this respect, he differs from other humans. Even if he wanted to toil like other people, he cannot.

Furthermore, the saint must have self-confidence and self-confirmation.[57] He must relate to himself as being a cut above ordinary people, including the best among them. An egalitarian image of the saint and other people results in his humility.[58] Rabbi Kook further alludes, at the end of the first passage, that if the saint loses his self-confidence, this will likely harm his role and the mission that is imposed upon him. The saint's influence on the surrounding society is dependent upon confirmation of the mental distance between him and all others. Rabbi Kook used the term *yenikah* (translated above as "drawing upon") because he drew a parallel between the processes within the Godhead (*ibbur* ["impregnation"], *yenikah* ["suckling"], *mohin* ["intellect," "aspect of consciousness"]) and those that occur within the soul. Consequently, the influence on others is effected by *yenikah*. While the righteous one is not dominant in Lurianic Kabbalah, for Rabbi Kook the regularization of these processes is dependent upon such an individual. The next section examines the relationship between the saint and the masses.

Dialectic

In his metaphysical teachings, Rabbi Kook explained that perfection is the unity of opposites. In this respect, his perception of the soul reflects metaphysical doctrine. The great soul, the holy soul, is of a containing and uniting nature. He declares that "the true holy righteous one unites within himself all the opposites."[59] He attests of himself, in a famous passage:

> I am full of joy, full of greatness, full of abjectness, full of bitterness, full of pleasantness, full of delight, full of love, full of jealousy, full of anger, full of lovingkindness, full of good to all; "Happy is the man who listens to me" [Proverbs 8:34], happy is the one who gives

---

57   The righteous one must believe in himself. See ibid., 2:193 (vol. 1, 349).

58   Rabbi Kook declared that "one must fear humility more than self-exaltation, and 'they are exalted through Your righteousness' [Psalms 89:17]" (*Shemonah Kevatzim* 1:894 [vol. 1, 687]).

59   Ibid., 1:575 (vol. 1, 182).

me the inner worth that suits me, according to the loveliness of my
unique quality. He [the righteous one] will lift up, yea, bear, he will
be exalted above all poverty,[60] he will sanctify and purify, and the
Lord our God is with him.[61]

Polarization and oscillation are common traits of mystics. Rabbi Kook,
however, raised this to a theoretical discussion, as we see from the motif of
the uniting of opposites in his *Ikvei ha-Tzon* (1906). Rabbi Kook treated the
issue of fear at length in this essay. He wrote that the fear characteristic of
the Jewish people throughout the ages ensued from two causes:

(1) the external element: the antisemitism and persecutions during
the long years of Exile;

(2) the inner element: apprehension of the ascent to perceiving the
unified stratum of existence. Rabbi Kook attributed this apprehension to
the influences of the imaginative faculty, which distorts reason,[62] probably
referring to reservations about studying Kabbalah.[63]

Although the external cause of fear still threatened, Rabbi Kook
believed that it was about to disappear following the national awakening
of the Jewish people. In contrast, the inner element, which was the focus of
Rabbi Kook's thought on this point, is still at the peak of its strength in the
light of secularization. Furthermore, Rabbi Kook understood secularization
among the Jews as the beginning of the process of liberation from fear.
He anticipated and longed for the return of prophecy—and a trembling
prophet cannot prophesy. It is at precisely this juncture that we find the
activity, and duty, of the perfect person:

---

[60] See *Shir ha-Yihud* for Thursday, in *Shirei ha-Yihud ve-ha-Kavod*, ed. A. M. Habermann
(Jerusalem, 1948), 36 l. 51 [Hebrew].

[61] *Shemonah Kevatzim* 3:235 (vol. 2, 90). See the midrashic dictum cited by Nahmanides at the
end of his commentary to Exodus 12:12.

[62] "The most harmful fear is intellectual fear, that the false imaginative faculty imposes on
the most refined and magnificent part of the human race" (*Eder ha-Yakar*, 119). We already
noted the source of the medieval tradition for this conception. See Harvey, "Maimonides and
Spinoza."

[63] See, e.g., M. Idel, "On the History of the Interdiction against the Study of Kabbalah before the
Age of Forty," *AJS Review* 5 (1980): i-xx [Hebrew].

In the End of Days, in the footsteps of the Messiah, when the divine light stands behind our wall,[64] the beginning of all the preparations is the removal of thought's excessive fear from the universal soul,[65] especially from the souls of the outstanding individuals, who are blessed with good intellect, with the aptitude of sanctity and righteousness. They are more susceptible to fear and weakness, impelled to this by the opposite power—the power of impertinence that must increase at this time, with no fear where it manifests itself.[66] Even though it [impertinence] comes from the side of baseness [see Ezekiel 17:24], from the side of intoxication and tumult, as distant as the skies are distant from the earth,[67] from that courage that comes from Heaven's blessing of the soul's riches and the strength of its righteousness—nonetheless, it [the power of impertinence] acts with its fierce power to take from itself the good part, the sparks of holiness, the innermost contents—[this is] the prevention of the intellectual fear of the promised power that is concealed in the treasury of our life. Then the courage [*gevurah*] [of insolence] will be set in the holy frame, and thought will blossom.[68]

This passage teaches of the soul of the saint, who possesses "the aptitude of sanctity and righteousness": the higher the saint's level, the greater his inner fear. The tearing down of the walls by the secular *halutzim*, who are driven by pure ideology (socialism, etc.), shines on the saints as well. By merit of the *halutzim*, the saints are released from their fear. Rabbi Kook established a polar hierarchy, which is the framework for the essay he wrote on this fear:

---

64 Following Song of Songs 2:9.

65 Rabbi Kook uses here Neoplatonian terminology, which repeatedly appeared in medieval Hebrew translations. See D. Schwartz, *Philosophy of a Fourteenth-Century Jewish Neoplatonic Circle* (Jerusalem, 1996), 161-70 [Hebrew]. Mention has already been made of the impression that Rabbi Solomon Ibn Gabirol's ideas made on Rabbi Kook: see M. Z. Sole, "The Monotheistic Worldview in His Teachings," in *Ha-Re'ayah: Collected Articles from the Teachings of Our Master, Rabbi Abraham Isaac Hakohen Kook* ..., ed. Y Raphael (Jerusalem, 1966), 88 [Hebrew]. In the passage cited here, Rabbi Kook referred to the collective spiritual dimension of the Jewish people ("the universal soul of this people girded with might" [*Eder ha-Yakar*, 119]). See Ish-Shalom, *Between Rationalism and Mysticism*, 254.

66 The intent is to "the power of impertinence."

67 Following Isaiah 55:9.

68 *Eder ha-Yakar*, 120-21. On fear as a component of the personality of the "great soul," see also *Shemonah Kevatzim* 1:91 (vol. 1, 32-33).

(1) Man: fear increases in accordance with his thought's breadth of vision and scope. As Rabbi Kook writes elsewhere in this essay: "As man's aptitude to understand and acquire wisdom increases, so too, does his imagined fear of intellective acts grows."[69]

(2) The people of Israel: the Jewish people's intellectual advantage lies in its mission to contain and find unity in multiplicity: the Jewish people "gathers and connects all that is scattered and separate in the sublime and the holy into a single comprehensive unit."[70] The fear increases in light of the daunting dimensions of this task, thereby requiring special courage from the people when faced with a pagan world, in which evil is rampant.

(3) The saint: the soul of the saint, which is the zenith of the people of Israel, is more polarized and torn than the two previous levels. The saint oscillates between the way of absolute truth, which demands corresponding behavior, and fear and aversion.

In this passage, Rabbi Kook suggests a therapeutic method that alludes to the fourth of the eight chapters in Maimonides's *Shemonah Perakim*, written in accordance with the principles of Aristotelian ethics. For a limited period of time, the saint must act in the opposite manner (that of insolence). Fear is at one pole of the hierarchy of traits, and impertinence at the other. In the period of the beginning of Redemption, which is the transitional period from Exile, the saint must act extrovertedly, impertinently. But what causes this change in the behavior of the saint?

Between the lines, we can understand that it was the *halutzim* who imparted the faculty of impertinence to the exceptional individuals. That is, in their blunt behavior, with no sense of commitment to the traditional generation of their parents, they paradoxically serve as an example for the saints, whom they might also spur to act in an extroverted manner. Their casting off of the yoke of religion is a model of the "opposite power": extroversion ("impertinence") as the routing of fear. The saint, too, must adopt this extroversion. In practice, he is to situate this impertinence and extroversion within holiness ("in the holy frame"). He must transfer this daring and "courage" from secularization to religion. Rabbi Kook is

69   *Eder ha-Yakar*, 119.
70   *Eder ha-Yakar*, 119. By "intellectual," I mean a body of knowledge that requires study, but not necessarily rational knowledge. At times mystical activity, too, requires intellectual effort.

apparently speaking to himself. The saint must manifest his personality, and reach the entire community.

Rabbi Kook further explained that the saint's activity is directly addressed to the collection of the "sparks of holiness"—the sparks of light that, in Lurianic Kabbalah, fell during the breaking of the vessels, and were captured within impurity.[71] The Redemption will come to pass when these sparks return to their source. This restoration of the sparks results in the collapse and disappearance of impurity, because the spark paradoxically revives impurity. Rabbi Kook understood the extraction of the sparks as an act that elevates the world. The extraction of holiness (i.e., spark) from impurity is perceived as the work of the perfect individuals. "They [the righteous] are capable of extracting from every speech and from every movement, from every report and from every occurrence, the words of the living God."[72] Rabbi Kook felt that he was acting during the messianic era, which is the time of the collection of the sparks.[73]

This teaches us a few points about the saint as a character who oscillates between the poles:

(1) Personality: the saint is characterized by the dialectic between self-confirmation and fear.

(2) Interaction between the saint and his community: at times the saint requires the extroverted behavior of his surroundings, in order to draw strength and learn modes of action. Here, as well, the holiness-secularization dialectic is the source of the saint's activity.

(3) Purposefulness: the saint engages in the extraction of the sparks, which is a dialectic occupation that encompasses impurity and purity at one and the same time. The righteous individual descends to impurity in order to reveal purity.

The saint is a dialectic personality, and his way of life is dialectic, as is obvious from every detail of his conduct. One example is Rabbi Kook's

---

71   See, e.g., I. Tishby, *The Doctrine of Evil and the "Kelippah" in Lurianic Kabbalism* (Jerusalem, 1984) [Hebrew].

72   BT Eruvin 13b; Gittin 6b; *Shemonah Kevatzim* 1:903 (vol. 1, 290). The collection and extraction of the sparks also refers to philosophical approaches ("foreign opinions"); see, e.g., *Shemonah Kevatzim* 8:147 (vol. 3, 290).

73   See Cherlow, *The Tzaddiq*, 68-70.

paradoxical statement: "When the true righteous one speaks in his own praise, he is filled with very great humility."[74] When Rabbi Kook depicted the unity characteristic of the "great soul," he listed these poles: "All the wars are incorporated in the ladder of peace; all the impurities, in the level of the holy; and all evils, in the summit of good."[75] Thus, there is a purpose to all these movements. In the end, all the dialectic is resolved, but the perfect resolution will be attained only in the messianic future. We see, therefore, that the dialectic figuration (some of whose elements were defined in *Ikvei ha-Tzon*) is typical of the way of the saint. Tension and fluctuation characterize both the relationship between the saint and society as a whole, and the intimate sphere. Indeed, Rabbi Kook did not erect any partition between the saint as individual and his relationship with the community.

Revealed and Concealed

Although Rabbi Kook did not formulate a hierarchy of saints, here and there in his writings we can find the foundation for such a gradation, especially in references to prevalent Jewish traditions. He distinguished between a revealed righteous individual and a hidden one.[76] According to this division, the revealed righteous one contends with the given reality, in which contraction and illumination, limitation and expansion, and evil and good are all intermingled. The hidden righteous one, in contrast, strives for illumination without limitation, which is called in Habad Hasidism, for instance, "the light of *Ein-Sof* before the *Tzimtzum*." Rabbi Kook called the primal state of illumination, before its contraction, the "good that is above any measure and extent," "the foundation of all the expanses," "the light of all lights," and a "portion with no limitations." According to this, the descriptive "hidden" does not refer exclusively to this individual's actions and relationship to society, but also, and perhaps mainly, to his aim of attaining the deepest dimension of existence (the light of *Ein-Sof*, *Binah*, and the like) and restoring all existence to it. Rabbi Kook states in a series

74   *Kevatzim*, vol. 2, 173.
75   *Shemonah Kevatzim* 3:98 (vol. 2, 49).
76   Our discussion is based on ibid., 7:162 (vol. 3, 214). See the interpretations that Cherlow offers for this distinction: *The Tzaddiq*, 180-84.

of passages that there is a hierarchy of the righteous that begins with the "pure" hidden one and continues to the revealed righteous individual.[77] The distinction drawn by Rabbi Kook reveals his view that the righteous individual who acts in an intimate manner and conducts the work of rectification far from the sight of others constitutes the highest level in this hierarchy. His influence on the surroundings is substantive. Furthermore, Rabbi Kook left an important place also for the revealed righteous, who have their roots in the concealed. In this manner, he did not limit his description of the righteous to any one type.

The Saint and Inspiration

The profile of the saint cannot be properly understood without taking into account the aspiration to prophecy in an era perceived as messianic. In the following passage, Rabbi Kook delineated the boundaries between saint and prophet, or alternately, between the saint who is within nature and the one who is above it.

> The arm of the Lord is outstretched to us in this manner:[78] we see that, in the depths of the soul [nefesh], Knesset Yisrael [the personification of the nation of Israel] has almost been healed in the part affected by its moral illnesses,[79] [that is,] its former iniquities.[80] The lengthy, terrible, and awful Exile had an iron crucible[81] that refines and purifies, with all its frightful tribulations, "like a smelter's fire and like fuller's lye" [Malachi 3:2] [...] [the nation] was burnished and purified. The heart is a new and pure heart,[82] the inner consciousness [kelayot, literally, kidneys] is ready for all that is lofty, sublime, and holy. Nothing, however, is actualized, coming from the potential to the actual, that which is concealed in the heart of the people and its hidden powers—this is the work of the sages of the generation, the

---

77 Shemonah Kevatzim 7:163-165 (vol. 3, 214-17).

78 Following Isaiah 9:11; Jeremiah 21:5; I Chronicles 21:16, and more.

79 Following Psalms 103:3.

80 Following Psalms 79:8.

81 An appellation for the Egyptian exile. See Deuteronomy 4:20; I Kings 8:51; Jeremiah 11:4.

82 Following Psalms 51:12. In the classical medical literature, the heart and the kidneys (and the liver) were deemed to be central organs, as opposed to the peripheral ones, and this notion entered Jewish thought.

righteous ones, preachers, sages and scribes, to whom will be added through the ages,[83] more sublimely, poets, with the Lord's spirit on His people, visionaries, prophets, the mighty, in accordance with the future elevation, degree by degree, "Arise, shake off the dust, sit [on your throne], Jerusalem" [Isaiah 52:2].[84]

At the end of this passage, Rabbi Kook distinguishes between two types of perfect individuals. The first category includes those superior individuals blessed with special, unique faculties, while the second refers to those who, in addition to natural ability, also possess charisma, the quality that comes from heavenly inspiration. Rabbi Kook writes of "the Lord's spirit," which is frequently used in reference to Samson,[85] whose strength was divinely inspired. He also uses the wording "through the ages," and afterwards, "degree by degree," signifying continuity.

Consequently, the appearance of these charismatic individuals will not be sudden, just as the Redemption itself emerges from within the conclusion of the Exile. The visionary and the prophet are the direct continuation of the genius and the righteous one. For Rabbi Kook, the present-day saint leads directly to the saint who is blessed with the divine gift of prophecy. The saint of the present time is of a degree that approaches the saint who receives "feedback," that is, actual inspiration from Heaven.

---

83   Following Isaiah 51:8; Palms 72:5; 102:25.

84   *Eder ha-Yakar*, 115.

85   See, e.g., Judges 14:6, 19; 15:14.

Chapter Five

FACULTIES

One of the topics that most interested Rabbi Kook was the mental structure of the saint. Each saint has defined mental faculties that drive his behavior and influence. Rabbi Kook was especially interested in the physical, intellectual, and creative abilities of the perfect man. He was not, however, satisfied by these traits, and demanded universality and generalization. He therefore discussed a personality faculty that is not limited to the definitions of other faculties.

Physicality

Rabbi Kook draws our attention to the material and physical dimension of the perfect man. Scholarly research has already noted Rabbi Kook's calls for a renaissance of physicality as part of the national awakening, and the importance he placed on physical fitness (exercise) as an act of repentance after the long years of Exile, in which the Jew was seen to be weak.[1] In a few passages, Rabbi Kook discussed the value of the righteous individual's eating, which he maintained was a "noble" and "ideal" activity.[2] We further learn that the perfect man is included in physical repentance. Rabbi Kook writes: "There are righteous ones whose entire repentance must be maintaining the fitness of their body."[3] Such statements are not

---

[1] See Yaron, *Philosophy*, 107-8; J. Garb, "Rabbi Kook: Working out as Divine Work," in *Sport and Physical Education in Jewish History*, ed. G. Eisen et al. (Netanyah, 2003), 7-14 [Hebrew]. On the Second and Third Aliyot's emphasis on physicality, see, e.g., B. Neumann, *Land and Desire in Early Zionism*, trans. H. Watzman (Waltham, MA, 2011).

[2] See, e.g., *Shemonah Kevatzim* 4:54 (vol. 2, 148-49).

[3] *Kevatzim*, vol. 2, 165. Rabbi Kook further wrote that "the righteous must make efforts to be healthy and mighty in spirit and body, and then the desire for justice [*tzedek*] will intensify

straightforward. The saint contains, inter alia, an ascetic dimension, since his consciousness is heavenly-directed. Rabbi Kook adopted a Neoplatonian style and ascetic tone when he asserted that the soul of the righteous is unwillingly connected to the body; only the divine mandate makes possible the material life of the "congregation of the righteous."[4] Thus, the tension in the righteous individual's physicality arises. Rabbi Kook wrote:

> Strength, the body's power, must be present in the righteous, the upright,[5] so that the appearance of the desire for the good will be decisive in the world. The weakness of the strength of the righteous, who must be girded with might,[6] attenuates the light of the world.[7]

The return to physicality is one of Rabbi Kook's tidings, and is anchored in his messianic conception of the national renaissance. In addition to his highlighting the quality of the saint's physical existence, for Rabbi Kook the very mention of this individual's physicality and worldliness is important. He writes:

> The righteous must truly be natural people, with all the natural features of the body and the soul present in them, as a trait of life and health. Then, in their self-elevation, they will be capable of elevating the world and all existence together with them.[8]

in the world" (167). He wrote elsewhere, in a somewhat different vein, "At times a spiritual lack cannot be filled by any labor or repentance, but only by increasing physical strength" (*Shemonah Kevatzim* 1:45 [vol. 1, 14]). The development of physical fitness is viewed in these passages as preparation for repentance, and not as repentance itself.

4   *Shemonah Kevatzim* 5:192 (vol. 2, 290). Rabbi Kook argued (apparently following the traditions that connected Plato with the prophets) that Plato's approach was possible as a result of the parallel period of the prophets. He alluded that the return to Plato is a milestone in the return to the prophets (ibid., 5:229 [vol. 2, 310]). The influence of Hermann Cohen's *Judische Schriften* is evident here. Rabbi Kook's connection to Plato and Neoplatonism is deserving of a study of its own. In this work, a single example of the Platonian conception of ideas will suffice: Rabbi Kook stated that societal arrangements must parallel the divine order ("the supernal model"), and correspondence to the supernal order is the aspiration and mission of "the holy exceptional ones" (ibid., 7:68 [vol. 3, 159]).

5   See Psalms 32:11; 64:11.

6   Following Psalms 65:7. On *gevurah* (rendered here as "might") as strict judgment in worship by the righteous, see above, Chapter Four.

7   *Shemonah Kevatzim* 1:44 (vol. 1, 14).

8   See Psalms 94:16; *Shemonah Kevatzim* 2:33 (vol. 1:305).

If the righteous individual were divorced from the world, it is questionable that he could elevate it. The need for physicality and physical and mental health follows from the task that is imposed on the righteous one, and the responsibility for the world that he is to feel. The elevation of the world includes the material, worldly dimension, and the righteous individual reflects and advances this process. His physical weakness is a consequence of both his still not having attained spiritual perfection and the fact that the spiritual world, by its very definition, is more sublime than the material one.[9]

Thus, Rabbi Kook presented a moderate psychosomatic approach,[10] in which body and soul correspond to one another. The degree of the body's health and strength is matched by the power of the soul's emanation.[11] Rabbi Kook formulated the body's closeness to the soul as follows:

> The body listens to the sounds of the soul [*tziltzelei ha-neshamah*][12] above, it senses the mysterious plethora, how it flows, how it emits rays full of great brilliance, how it penetrates and descends until it comes to the verbal sense, how speech knocks,[13] and it absorbs within itself the supernal essence, how life is poured within every speech of lips.[14] It listens and trembles, hears and overflows; it knows

---

9   *Kevatzim*, 27, 72.

10 I use the wording "moderate approach," because Rabbi Kook was not completely convinced of the full correspondence of body and soul, as he states outright in the following passage: "And if I am weak in my body, will my soul, too, suffer from this? And if my flesh will oppress me a thousand times, will my spirit be oppressed by this?" (*Shemonah Kevatzim* 7:196 [vol. 3, 230]). The dilemma regarding physicality is evident in other passages as well. On the one hand, the righteous who suffer from physical weakness were intentionally meant to engage in physicality and materiality, in order to elevate them; on the other hand, weakness results from flawed faith. According to Rabbi Kook, such righteous ones "have not perfected the supernal power of faith, to believe in the holiness of the light of the Lord that emanates on their lives and on the content of all their values, and also on their material system. Because of this lack of faith, they must suffer weakness, so that they will be compelled to care for the affairs of their body" (ibid., 8:72 [vol. 3, 264-65]); see above, n. 1.

11 Ibid., 3:302 (vol. 2, 108).

12 A wordplay based on Psalms 150, that speaks of "resounding cymbals [*tziltzelei shema*]."

13 Following Song of Songs 5:2 ("Hark, my beloved knocks"). Rabbi Kook alluded that speech is conducted in rhythmic units, like the beating of the heart.

14 Following Isaiah 57:19.

that it yet has much to do, it must exert itself and toil, it must expand the bounds of the light and the holy, it must be filled with greatness, faith, humility, courage, and life, and the word of the Lord will be known to him.[15]

This passage portrays the descent of divine emanation from the uppermost levels of the soul to the body, and the opposite process of elevating the body. Those party to the descent of this emanation are *Binah* ("life"), *Hesed* ("greatness"), *Din* ("courage"), and the like. The body itself seeks to overcome its physical state, to "overflow" and unite with the level of the soul. Elevation, symbolically meaning that the vessel draws near the light, and the material near the divine emanation, is a recurring motif in Rabbi Kook's thought. The process of elevating the body is depicted as the path from the idea to the word. Mental elevation ("the supernal essence") is the source of the idea, and the material linguistic action of speech connects the idea with physicality.

Besides its psychophysical depiction and its Kabbalistic meaning, the passage also contains a messianic layer of meaning. It is the second in a pair of passages that are concerned with physicality; in the preceding passage (3:302), Rabbi Kook wrote of "the sound of the *shofar* [ram's horn] of Redemption" following "the sign that already intrinsically refines the flesh." Rabbi Kook adopted the apocalyptic messianic conception that nature would change in the future world. This thought also gave rise to the notion of the "refined body," according to which in the messianic era the body will be purified, and will have no need for eating or for secretions. The Habad sources went so far as to claim that the future body would have both conception and cognition.[16] Rabbi Kook claimed in a similar spirit that "the flesh of the Israelite body is actually holy, as the holiness of the soul."[17] This statement apparently also bears messianic significance: in the future, the body would verge upon the the soul. Three strata of meaning of the elevation of physicality parallel one another: the psychophysical, the Kabbalistic, and the messianic. It is noteworthy that the above passage

---

15   *Shemonah Kevatzim* 3:303 (vol. 2, 109); see Jeremiah 28:9. Rabbi Kook further stated that the purity of the soul also means the purity of the body (ibid., 8:209 [vol. 3, 317]).

16   See Schwartz, *Habad's Thought*, 278-79.

17   *Shemonah Kevatzim* 3:364 (vol. 2, 127).

concludes with the return of prophecy, following the intensification of the divine emanation.

It should similarly be noted that Rabbi's Kook's discussions of the worldly nature of the saint are usually written in simple and direct prose, thus reflecting the importance he assigned to his emphasis of the saint's involvement in the material and the physical.

Rationalism

Rabbi Kook never freed himself of the influence of medieval Jewish rationalism, and especially not from the decisive influence of Maimonides. The *Guide of the Perplexed* directed him to the same extent as Kabbalah influenced him. Obviously, he could not adopt the Maimonidean principles as they had originally appeared, in their historical environment, even though the rational quest characterized Rabbi Kook's oeuvre. Thus, he saw the saint as an intellectual who valued the acquisition of knowledge. In Rabbi Kook's thought, as in the medieval rationalist environment, this conception is given a clearly elitist coloration. He wrote:

> For a great man, the refined contemplation of the act of Creation and *Maaseh Merkabah*,[18] psychology, ethics, and all the supreme spiritual views can serve as Talmud, and when this is joined by recitation[19] and the diligent study of the Bible and the Mishnah, he only infrequently is in such great need of the casuistry of the Talmud. This was the opinion of Maimonides in the study regime for the singular exceptional individuals, in accordance with his book.[20] This path, however, is possible only after the one of this standing [literally, virtue] has already acquired deep and considerable knowledge of the casuistry of the Talmud, and has acquired expertise in the order of [Talmudical] argumentation and the ways of its *sugyot* [discursive units]. Then he need not be so frequently absorbed in them that they will keep him from his elevated contemplations. [Rather,] he will set special times for them [i.e., Talmud study] when he will find

18 In the Maimonidean approach, these two terms denote physics and metaphysics, respectively; see the introduction to the *Guide of the Perplexed*.

19 Hebrew: *higayon*, also with the meaning of "logic."

20 See Maimonides, *Guide of the Perplexed* 1:34; Schwartz, *Contradiction and Concealment*, 220-24.

his spirit suited for expansive occupation with matters of Talmudic argumentation. His soul, however, will be mainly bonded to the place where it naturally aspires to gaze upon the beauty of the Lord and to frequent His temple [Psalms 27:4], the pleasantness of worship and esoteric intellection.[21]

Rabbi Kook gave a singular interpretation to two main concepts in the life of the perfect man:

(1) Torah study;
(2) setting fixed times for Torah study.[22]

Rabbi Kook stressed in the beginning of this passage that, for the perfect man, the study of theoretical disciplines (physics, metaphysics, psychology, and ethics) is like Torah study, with the consequent redefinition of "setting fixed times for Torah study." The original and intuitive interpretation of this concept is leaving aside one's mundane affairs in order to engage in Torah study on a regular basis. According to Rabbi Kook, this means forgoing these other realms of knowledge in favor of Torah. Thus, the perfect man, who has already acquired broad knowledge of Talmudic methodology and its application, spends most of his time engaged in the theoretical disciplines. His consciousness is directed to the acquisition of abstract knowledge in physics, metaphysics, psychology, and ethics. "Setting fixed times" now means that this individual returns to classical Talmud study. Rabbi Kook's adaption of the Maimonidean conception to his own ideas is especially striking in the end of this passage, in which he incorporates "esoteric intellection," that is, Kabbalah, within the context of rationalism.

In numerous aspects, the perception of the perfect individual as an intellectual connects many of Rabbi Kook's ideas. In the essay "Worship" (that appears in *Ikvei ha-Tzon*), he discusses rite, the applied dimension of which seems to be a collection of practical directives. Rabbi Kook drew an analogy to corporeality. Judaism rejected corporeality, but frequently used it in its sources, especially in the Bible and in Kabbalah; by the same coin,

---

21 *Kevatzim*, 168.
22 See, e.g., BT Shabbat 31a; *Shulhan Arukh, Orah Hayyim* 155:1.

worship is "worldly" and base, but expresses the most sublime experiences.[23] Here is the analogy, in graphic form:[24]

earthly stratum	corporeality	worship
noble stratum	sublime "inner apprehension"	"religion" and universality[24]

The following passage details how Rabbi Kook situated the exceptional individuals according to this analogy, while maintaining his complex style:

> And just as the low corporeality is the antithesis of Judaism, the Torah nevertheless spoke in such free language,[25] with no curb or limitation, with all its [divine] attributes. It is specifically these which have led us, together with the intellect and wisdom—the two of which together are forever "the lamp of the Lord in the earth"[26]— to the heights of the purist perceptions, by which the exceptional ones among us in each generation are living and enduring testimony. Similarly, the universal perception, usually called "religion," which is the concept of "the service of God." This is like "a stairway was set on the ground and its top reached to the sky, and angels of God were going up and down on it" [Genesis 28:12].[27]

---

23 Reading between the lines, we find the interpretation that Habad Hasidism gave to "Their beginning is inherent in their end" (*Sefer Yetzirah* 1:7), namely, in circular fashion, the lowest level touches the highest. Rabbi Kook wrote that "specifically the simplest and lowest language, together with the soaring logic that is stored in it, generally and in detail, together built the entire supernal and worldly palaces, to store within them the divine intelligence at the highest summit of the intertwining of its branches and the lowest depth of the ramification of its roots, to be a place for inquiry after both the absolute truth and righteousness in the life of the individual, the nation, humankind, and the reality" (*Eder ha-Yakar*, 142). On personification in Kabbalah, see also *Shemonah Kevatzim* 1:856 (vol. 1, 273).

24 See below, towards the end of this chapter.

25 In accordance with the principle: "The Torah speaks in human language" (i.e., it expresses itself in ordinary language; BT Berakhot 31b; Yevamot 71a; Ketubot 67b, and more). Rabbi Saadia Gaon understood this as referring to anthropomorphism.

26 In quotation marks in the first edition, this is a citation from *Behinat Olam* by Rabbi Jedaiah ha-Penini Bedersi, chapter 19 (Premishla, 1872, fol. 53a); also cited in additional works, such as *Pahad Yitzhak* by Rabbi Isaac Arama, *Shaar* 44.

27 *Eder ha-Yakar*, 152.

This passage portrays a process in which the base and worldly existence undergoes a process of purification, and manifests itself, with a different countenance, in a sublime and refined existence. The standing of the exceptional individual in this process is presented in two thoughts, one implicit in Rabbi Kook's writings, and the other stated outright:

(1) The exceptional individual reveals the lofty and refined meaning of the mundane. Rabbi Kook uncovers the profound symbolic significance of corporeality (usually by means of Kabbalah), thereby explaining its frequent appearance in the Bible and Midrash. At the same time, he extracts the deep meaning of religious action, namely, the observance of the commandments (ethical, magical, and theurgic ramifications). The one of great spirit connects the halakhah (Jewish law) with aggadah and the other components of the Jewish corpus, and thereby reveals its universality.[28] This intellectual task entails abstract symbolic thought, and it is the saint who engages in this.

(2) The exceptional individual is exemplary ("you are My witnesses"—see Isaiah 43:12) in that he lives an elevated life within the world. This individual lives an experiential life both by force of the symbolism in corporeality and by force of the observance of the commandments.

We now can present the righteous individual in the analogy as follows:[29]

earthly stratum	corporeality	worship	"flesh and blood" *tzaddik*
noble stratum	sublime "inner apprehension"	"religion" and uni-versality[29]	divine emanation

28 Rabbi Kook was aware of the rarity of exceptional individuals who are proficient in all disciplines, and he therefore spoke of such individuals in different fields (*Eder ha-Yakar*, 143).
29 See below.

The inclusion of Jacob's ladder in the end of the passage shows the saint's sense of mission. He connects the bottom and the top of this stairway, that is, the diametrically polar strata of reality, and casts them in a unifying light.[30] The saint fulfills this mission by means of his intellectual activity.

In "Worship," Rabbi Kook discussed at length the concept of "*dilug*" (literally, "skipping"). This concept, which originates in Hasidic thought, refers to the gap that exists between one divine world and the next and which is bridged by the divine influence.[31] In the well-known Kabbalistic conception, there are four worlds (*Atzilut*, *Beriah*, *Yetzirah*, and *Asiyah*), each of which is built of ten *Sefirot*, with gaps between the worlds. Continuous emanation cannot pass such a gap; it can be passed only by skipping. Rabbi Kook connected this concept with the belief of Islamic theology (*Kalam*) that reality also includes phenomena that are not subject to scientific rules ("for there is everything in reality").[32] Rabbi Kook also referred to the steps of the Redemption, while in *Shemonah Kevatzim*, he directed this principle to the rational. He wrote:

> The great ones must skip, in order to reflect on great thoughts. A man must be cognizant of his inner faculty, and know by himself if he was created for great things. Let him not be alarmed by the iniquity of pride, as he is cognizant of the level of his intellect, and the value of the inclination of his will. To the contrary, one must take greater care regarding invalid modesty, which represses the soul,[33] and blurs the divine light in the soul. When the great ones experience intellectual elevation, all the world is elevated together with them, by sensing [the influence of the great ones], in accordance with the common nature of all human souls. To a greater degree, however, this shared

---

30 This passage contains a fundamental magical stratum, according to which the saint uses supernal powers. See, e.g., *Shemonah Kevatzim* 1:309 (vol. 1, 110), which depicts the righteous individual's activity arousing the "supernal delight" and "the drawing down of the emanation of delight," and numerous other examples. See Cherlow, *The Tzaddiq*, 112-13.

31 See Schwartz, *Habad's Thought*, Index, s.v. "*Dilug*." Rabbi Kook mentioned the Hasidic source of this notion in *Shemonah Kevatzim* 5:62 (vol. 2, 218).

32 *Eder ha-Yakar*, 154.

33 Rabbi Kook stressed that the cognition of the righteous is a source of joy (*Shemonah Kevatzim* 1:513 [vol. 1, 164]), and, conversely, sadness and depression preclude this cognition. It is also noteworthy that he states in the same passage that "the joy of cognition," too, is connected with *dilug* ("the constant skipping").

nature is active among Israel, who enjoy absolute unity from the aspect of their soul.[34]

This passage discusses the influence of the intellectual achievements of the perfect ones. It categorizes the influence of the latter as passive: when the perfect ones have intellectual accomplishments, they advance the entire human race, and especially Israel. Rabbi Kook further asserts that the saint must possess self-confirmation and self-confidence. This is a process of intellection. He additionally wrote in his collections that "whoever is capable of studying the sciences of the world but does not do so, because of some weakness in his soul, diminishes the image [of God], for it is said, 'For in His image did God make man' [Genesis 9:7]."[35] Rabbi Kook accordingly distinguished between two types of the righteous:

(1) Those "whose worship is by means of the intellect and inquiry, and who are filled with wisdom and reason [higayon]."
(2) Those righteous "whose entire character consists of the worship that consists of simple feeling."

Rabbi Kook asserted that the former are preferable, since they are aware of worship based on the emotions and even experience it, but think that intellectual activity is superior. The latter, in contrast, are not cognizant of intellectual activity, and therefore attack rationalism, which they deem to be dangerous.[36]

In his writings, Rabbi Kook frequently mentioned the centrality of the intellectual dimension of the saint's worship. One expression of this is the mainly contemplative nature of the perfect man's prayer ("the

---

34   Ibid., 1:318 (vol. 1, 113).

35   *Kevatzim*, vol. 2, 119. This passage is indirectly based on Maimonides, *Guide of the Perplexed* 1:1, in which Maimonides understood the image of God as intellectual cognition. Medieval rationalism is evident in Rabbi Kook's style and ideas; this is deserving of serious research. Rabbi Kook already wrote in *Mussar Avikha* (29), in a wordplay, that "the nature of the intellect [ha-sekhel] is to engage in cognition [le-haskil], specifically." From a certain aspect, this composition was intended to defend the need to devote intellectual efforts to ethical teachings, even though it was deemed inferior to the sciences in the medieval literature. It should be recalled that Rabbi Kook challenged Zeev Jawitz's critique of Maimonides's rationalism. See below, Chapter Twelve.

36   *Kevatzim*, vol. 2, 173.

depth of clear knowledge"), in which the imagination does not play an essential role.[37] Additionally, the saint literature sometimes describes states of mystical communion in terms of prayer. For example, Teresa of Avila (1515-1582) called the first stage of such union the "prayer of quiet." Unlike verbal prayer, this is meditation on a sacred ceremony or event from the life of the saints, which results in an experience of proximity to God. She termed the second stage the "prayer of full union," which is marked by the manifestation of the divine presence within the soul. This results in the union of God and the soul in a mutual embrace. The third stage is the ecstatic.[38] According to this depiction, prayer is merely a reflection of the different levels of the mystical experience. Rabbi Kook viewed prayer as an expression of the saint's mystical influence on his surroundings, in a clearly intellectual context. He wrote:

> The great righteous ones must pray so that the light of the favor of the Lord[39] will be drawn [*yitmashekh*] into all sciences and all languages, so that the glory of the Lord will appear everywhere, the beams of the Torah's light will shine everywhere, and the prayer of the righteous and the illumination of their will shall make an impression so vivid that it will have no limit or conclusion. They must especially direct their prayer to this when they see the great attraction to languages and sciences, and it would be impossible to struggle with all those who turn to [these fields], the current need [for the sciences and languages] is obvious—then the inner righteous arise to effect salvation, with secret worship, and greatness of spirit [to the levels of] *Hayah* [and] *Yehidah*; they come to open the blocked channels,[40] to reveal the presence of the Lord within all His sciences—and the Lord's sciences are everything in the world, especially whatever effects the rectification of the world.[41]

Prayer is a response to the intensification of the intellectual disciplines and sciences that attract people's minds. The response of the saint is to infuse

---

37   *Shemonah Kevatzim* 1:665 (vol. 1, 212).
38   See N. Pike, *Mystic Union: An Essay in the Phenomenology of Mysticism* (Ithaca, NY, 1992), 1-11.
39   See Psalms 90:17.
40   On the righteous individual as a pipe, that is, a receptacle through which the divine emanation flows, see below, n. 47.
41   *Shemonah Kevatzim* 1:887 (vol. 1, 285).

these wisdoms and sciences with the divine emanation, and to turn them into a tool for the mending of the world. Such activity is to be done by means of prayer. Rabbi Kook depicted the spiritual ascent of the soul to the levels of "*hayah*" and "*yehidah*," which in the Kabbalistic literature denote the levels of the soul closest to the Godhead. Spiritual ascent succeeds in drawing down the divine emanation, and enables the channeling of the disciplines to the aim of the mending of the world. This elevation and drawing down are effected by means of prayer. Yet again, Rabbi Kook formulated the saint's passive influence. The saint does not come into conflict with scientific accomplishments, nor does he struggle with the cultural and social influences of science. He draws within himself and engages in mystical activity, in this case, mystical prayer. Prayer is discussed in the context of the acquisition of knowledge. Consequently, the image and influence of the saint hardly appear in Rabbi Kook's commentary to the prayerbook, *Olat Re'ayah*. A comparison of *Olat Re'ayah* with other works, such as *Ikvei ha-Tzon* or *Shemonah Kevatzim*, reveals the relative absence of the saint from this composition. This is because prayer, in its institutionalized form, is conducted with the masses (in a quorum of ten, *minyan*), and because of the central place of supplications in prayer. The righteous individual is mentioned by Rabbi Kook only in the context of contemplative prayer.

We see from many of Rabbi Kook's discussions that at times the intellectual ideal is not the pure ideal of the acquisition of knowledge, but a mix of science, ethics, aesthetics, and especially Kabbalistic perception. Saints "should make great efforts to increase the desire to explore the greatness of the Lord, in all the great, intellectual, moral ways."[42] Such a mix is at the basis of the intellectual activity of the righteous. Rabbi Kook, however, viewed the acquisition of knowledge to be of great intrinsic value. He maintained that intellection requires restraint and tranquility. The stormy overflowing emotions that are typical of many righteous individuals do not enable proper intellectual perception.[43] Rabbi Kook frequently drew upon medieval rationalist literature, from which he adopted the distinction between the perfect man and the mass (see Chapter Six, below).

---

42 *Shemonah Kevatzim* 1:88 (vol. 1, 28).
43 Ibid., 7:164 (vol. 3, 215). *Mussar Avikha* speaks in praise of restraint.

He frequently used the appellation of medieval rationalists for perfect individuals: "the remnants who invoke the name of the Lord."[44] For Rabbi Kook, the saint is subject to the tension between belief and reason. On the one hand, he does not experience any conflict between the two,[45] while on the other, the lack of correspondence between human thought and ideas and the perception of God and communion with Him causes the saint inner shame.[46]

Thus, Rabbi Kook ascribed great importance to the saint's rational dimension. We will see below that the saint acts upon the entire universe, and succeeds in mediating between the upper and lower spheres. Rabbi Kook naively believed that scientific development would eventually provide a full explanation for the action of souls on other souls,[47] which would make possible the comprehension and mapping of the regularity of the influence wielded by saints. He deeply believed in the capabilities of human thought and its development. In his heart of hearts, he awaited the time when the esoteric teachings would become scientific truth. We can easily understand that the intellectual dimension of the saint is an important building block in the edifice of his personality.

Aesthetics

The saint does not only address existing creative forces, but also turns to those that are dormant. For religious and social reasons, aesthetic creativity

---

44 Following Joel 3:5. See, e.g., *Igrot ha-Re'ayah*, vol. 2, 147. This expression appears a few times in *Shemonah Kevatzim*, as well. An example of this is the righteous addressing the root of the soul: "At that very time [the footsteps of the Messiah], the remnants, who have the courage of the Lord in their heart, must illuminate with the supernal light of the soul" (8:83 [vol. 3, 269]). See J. Garb, "'Alien' Culture in the Circle of Rabbi Kook," in *Study and Knowledge in Jewish Thought*, ed. H. Kreisel (Beersheva, 2006), 253-64.

45 "The practical intellect of the great ones of the world might be very exalted and developed, while at the same time possessing sublime belief and greatness of spiritual insight, with tremendous and illuminating imagination, who sense the supernal emanation with clarifying and lucid intellect" (*Shemonah Kevatzim* 3:204 [vol. 2, 80-81]).

46 Ibid., 6:90 (vol. 3, 32-33).

47 "The souls acts on each other in sublime actions; the future awaits the appearance of the science that will clearly reveal the value and essence of these sublime actions, and will show the channels [*tzinorot*; also translated as "pipes"] that go from one soul to another in the manner of their emanation" (*Shemonah Kevatzim* 3:34 [vol. 2, 24]).

did not occupy a central position in Jewish history.[48] In a certain sense, it could be said that aesthetics was repressed, and to the extent that it arose, it was concentrated in quite specific visual and musical fields (synagogue art, cantorial music, *klezmer* music, and the like).[49] In our discussion of genius, we spoke of Rabbi Kook's return to aesthetics, and we cannot distinguish between the interpretation of present events and the aesthetic renaissance. Rabbi Kook wrote:

> At the time of the nation's failure,[50] which is, concurrently, the time of [national] revival and renaissance, we must engage in great spiritual labor, that of the extraction and purification of sentiments and opinions, and especially, the labor of the extraction of the aesthetic sense, [that is,] the limitation of the imaginative faculty, [followed by] its strengthening on faithful foundations, to the extent that it is beneficial and strengthening, but to remove it where it breaches its fence[51] and walks on a road not built up.[52]

Once again, Rabbi Kook used terminology typical of Lurianic Kabbalah, which was given much broader meaning in Hasidic teachings: namely, the "labor of extraction." We spoke above of the collection of the sparks that were captured by the shells and their uncovering. The labor of extraction is particular. It requires the righteous one to relate to distinct events and defined publics and to derive the good.[53] The labor of extraction relates to all fields of activity and creativity, with emphasis on the aesthetic faculty. For Rabbi Kook, the extraction of the divine spark, in the aesthetic sense, means enclosing creativity and setting bounds for its freedom and passion.

---

[48] See, e.g., K. P. Bland, *The Artless Jew: Medieval and Modern Affirmations and Denials of the Visual* (Princeton, 2001).

[49] See D. Schwartz, *Music in Jewish Thought* (Ramat Gan, 2013) [Hebrew].

[50] We may reasonably assume that Rabbi Kook related generally to the phenomenon of secularization as a "religious failure." He might also, however, have alluded to a specific event that occurred at the time he wrote this passage, such as the murder of two members of *Ha-Shomer* (the association of Jewish watchmen in the Land of Israel in the early twentieth century) in 1911, whom he eulogized.

[51] Following Ecclesiastes 10:8. See *Midrash Temurah ha-Shalem*, chap. 5, *Temurah* 7 (in S. A. Wertheimer, *Batei Midrashot*, vol. 2 [Jerusalem, 1953], 197).

[52] Following Jeremiah 18:15. The citation is from *Shemonah Kevatzim* 1:25 (vol. 1, 9).

[53] Rabbi Kook distinguished between the labor of extraction and the elevation of the worlds, which is a general action that relates to all existence. See *Shemonah Kevatzim* 2:49 (vol. 1, 309).

Rabbi Kook frequently wrote about the place of aesthetics in the existence of the perfect human being. As we saw above, he systematically discussed the image of the genius. He also argued that freedom is a condition for creativity.[54] According to him, the righteous individual confirms the material world, because its beauty is a reflection ("pure brilliance") of the supernal beauty, and the way to attain the latter. The righteous are gifted with "the sentiment of loveliness and beauty" of the material world,[55] and their worldview, to a great degree, is aesthetic. He wrote:

> Even a secular artist sees the entire world in a completely different way, more magnificently, than it is seen by all other viewers; and this is certainly so for the righteous, who see with the spirit of divine inspiration—the entire world appears before them with the attribute of supernal beauty and magnificence [*tiferet*], such as the splendor [*hod*] that no eye has seen, O God, but You, who act for those who trust in You [Isaiah 64:3].[56]

Now aesthetic creativity has become a worldview for the perfect ones. The end of this passage also anchors such creativity in the divine emanation: from *Tiferet* to *Hod* and *Yesod*, the *Sefirah* that, in Kabbalistic symbolism, expresses the righteous individual himself. By focusing on aesthetics, Rabbi Kook expressed the creativity that had been dormant among the Orthodox public, certainly until his time.

In his occupation with innovation ("the flow of innovation"), Rabbi Kook was especially concerned with the "great souls," who are "creative masters." He depicted innovation as a continual process of illumination and emanation ("riches"). The highest level of the soul illuminates and emanates to its lower dimensions. He writes:

> Richness so increases until it comes to the geniuses of thought, the masters of abstract thought [*tziyur*],[57] to such a marvelous degree that many are amazed by the insights that are manifest from the fruit

---

54   "It is specifically the free soul that is creative" (ibid., 4:85 [vol. 2, 162]).

55   Ibid., 1:804 (vol. 1, 257).

56   Ibid., 8:176 (vol. 3, 301).

57   In another place, Rabbi Kook indirectly referred to artistic innovation, and noted its destructive potential: "It would blur the form of every element, before any building had been erected on it. This is the fear of art" (ibid., 6:70 [vol. 3, 25]).

of their thoughts, even though the revealed part must necessarily be the inferior soil in the core of creation.[58] But the concealed Creation, the wonders of its acts, the speed with which the streams of the intellect flow, do not enable us to perceive the inner nature, essence, and details of these flowing streams. The greater aptitude consists of penetrating the depth of our self.[59] This penetration—all that one must know is the ease with which it is conducted,[60] the degree to which the labor and toil of the soil harms the noble heights,[61] the degree to which the [creative] one must be attentive to the need for the joy of inner tranquility.[62] To this degree the brilliance of the content of the creative work will increase, and the holy sparks will begin to shine on all life and its spiritual ramifications. At every moment we create, either knowingly or unwittingly, a measureless multitude of creations; if we were only to learn to sense them, to bring them to the realm of our heightened awareness, to become accustomed to bring them into the context of the expressions suitable for them, then their splendor and majesty would be revealed, and their effect would be seen over all of life. The eternal truths will become a flowing spring [that emanates] from [the highest degree of] the soul [neshamah] that knows not vanity and falsehood; it is derived from the torches of truth,[63] and all that shall stream from its light is truth and justice, forever.[64]

According to this quite complicated discussion, the saint is capable, primarily, of contemplating, and being attentive to, his own self. The

---

[58] In other words, creativity takes shape in the upper levels of the soul, and when it devolves to the lowest level, its base and mundane aspect is revealed.

[59] That is, the ability to be cognizant of the supernal source of creativity, namely, the soul.

[60] Rabbi Kook sought to explain that introspection, that is, the knowledge of the soul, must be passive on the part of the one engaging in it; he must look and listen, but without any active intervention. Conversely, the more he attempts to impose his scientific and epistemological criteria on the object of his cognition, the soul, the less he will know it.

[61] This is because the source of the influence is attained intuitively, and not discursively ("labor").

[62] This refers to the supernal root of *Malkhut*, namely, *Binah*. See, e.g., Rabbi Moses Cordovero, *Or Ne'erav, Shaar ha-Kinnuim* (Vilna, 1899), fol. 36b; *Midrash Ne'elam, Lamentations*, ed. Margaliot, fol. 91d.

[63] See Rabbi Isaiah Horowitz, *Shnei Luhot ha-Berit* (Warsaw, 1930), vol. 2, fol. 18a.

[64] *Shemonah Kevatzim* 4:82 (vol. 2, 161).

faculty of introspection is perceived as genius. The introspective process of contemplation is dialectic to a certain degree; it is a receptacle or conduit, and at the same time, it is self-confirming. The following are the inner elements of innovation, all of which Rabbi Kook alluded to in this passage:

(1) Withdrawal: the genius withdraws within himself, in a seeming act of humility. He contemplates the source of emanation, namely, the soul, without the use of any preexisting mental patterns. This is a purely introspective contemplative action.

(2) Self-assurance: the action described in (1) paradoxically ends in self-enhancement, since this contemplation uncovers the creativity of the genius, who possesses a "great soul." In other words, this is a process of self-confirmation. The genius is cognizant of the fount of innovations, and is aware of their nature.

(3) Reflection: nonetheless, the "innovation" is not an expression of personal originality, but rather of the emanation that comes from the divine *Sefirot*. The soul's emanation is actually a reflection of theosophic and cosmic processes.

Rabbi Kook sought to formulate the saint's process of innovation and the ways to understand it, and resolve his tremendous self-confirmation with his humility.[65] Innovation itself is an action of the highest level of the soul. It can be perceived intuitively, while the other ways diminish it and pose difficulties for its comprehension.

Universality

One special faculty with which the saint is blessed—universality, or generalization—can hardly be defined by the criteria we have already used. For Rabbi Kook, the higher the level of a person's cognition, the more general his perspective. The perfect man has an inherent propensity for all existence, and he encompasses all. This inclusion is based on a special faculty, which has two aspects:

---

[65] See *Igrot ha-Re'ayah*, vol. 3, 4. Cf. Y. Cherlow, "On Modesty and Regeneration: An Exchange of Letters between R. Kook and R. David Cohen," *Iyyun* 46 (1998): 441-50 [Hebrew].

(1) The cognitive aspect: the ability to acquire all the sciences, wisdom, and knowledge; the ability to absorb cognitive, ethical, and aesthetic knowledge.

(2) The emotional aspect: the ability to love all. The soul of the saint is, in effect, the reflection of all. The faculty of love applies, first and foremost, to humans, but it expands to include all existence.

The emotional faculty is largely altruistic. Since the life of the saint is channeled to his fellow and to all that is outside him, he must be prepared to waive his independent personality on behalf of the other ("self-voiding").[66] The saint's altruism is his formative and defining trait. He is uplifted above being an individual person with wills and desires. "Whoever has a moral-poetical soul always thirsts to be engaged with the general";[67] "the saint's love and thirst is not for himself alone, but for the entire world."[68] Rabbi Kook pointedly emphasized the saint's inability to limit himself to a certain orientation; he rather includes all. In one passage, he labeled the individual characterized by self-voiding as follows: "Who is from the attribute of *Malkhut* [...] this individual is capable of absorbing all within himself."[69] Such a saint is a "receptacle." As was noted above, the saint loves all people.[70] This aspect of the saint has a special national aspect: "The soul of the righteous one is comprised of the totality of the souls of *Knesset Yisrael.*"[71]

This teaches that such inclusiveness is possible due to a special faculty. Rabbi Kook wrote that "those of great soul cannot be separate from the more comprehensive totality, their entire desire and aspiration is always

66   See Wyschogrod, *Saints and Postmodernism*, 33.

67   *Kevatzim*, 69.

68   *Shemonah Kevatzim* 7:208 (vol. 3, 234).

69   *Shemonah Kevatzim* 6:212 (vol. 3, 82). The *Sefirah* of *Malkhut* is perceived as reflecting the other *Sefirot* and as a conduit for transmitting their emanation, without an independent nature of its own. This passage, too, is clearly dialectical, and Rabbi Kook speaks of "the depth of the righteous one's self." On the righteous individual's voiding himself of his particularism, see, e.g., ibid., 1:692 (vol. 1, 220); 3:47 (vol. 2, 30).

70   Ibid., 7:165 (vol. 3, 215); see above, Chapter Two, at n. 15.

71   *Kevatzim*, 175.

for the good of all, the all in its full breadth, height, and depth."[72] In this same passage, he defined inclusivity and generalization as a special faculty. When the saint is faced with disagreements, quarrels, and struggles, he embraces all. That is, he understands that the opposites ensue from focusing on details. He therefore engages in the action of embracing, "to include all, to stitch together, to unite."[73]

We should now ask: what is the mechanism of inclusion? How does the righteous individual elevate the reality to the level of the general and absorb it in his soul? Three keys were given to the exceptional individual:

The cognitive key for the act of inclusion reveals the uniting factor within a multitude of details. The perfect man examines historical, social, and national processes, and uncovers the general dimension that is the root of all the individual events, and that is nothing other than the good. The exceptional individuals are capable of "always receiving the best, the healthiest, and the gentlest in every collective, and planting it in the soil of the all."[74]

The emotional key for the act of inclusion is love. Rabbi Kook definitely ascribed great importance to love of the nation. He mentions in many passages that love of Israel is the motive force for the activity of the perfect man. By the same coin, however, the saint's absolute dedication to humanity cannot be understood without his love of every human being. Rabbi Kook set forth a hierarchy of love: in his writings he emphasized love of humans and nature,[75] but focused the love within the perfect individual on the nation, that is, Israel.[76] We may reasonably assume that the passive influence that the righteous individual radiates to his surroundings is

---

[72] *Shemonah Kevatzim* 1:101 (vol. 1, 33). A series of passages on the topic of inclusion were printed in *Hadarav*, 121-40.

[73] *Shemonah Kevatzim* 1:101 (vol. 1, 34).

[74] Ibid., 1:119 (vol. 1, 42). See Avivi, "History as a Divine Prescription," 726-27.

[75] See the well-known passage, which was first published in *Arpilei Tohar*: "I love all. I cannot but love people, all the peoples. I desire from the depths of my heart the splendor [*tiferet*] of all, the mending of all. My love of Israel is more fervent, deeper, but the spreading inner desire consists of the might of its love, actually for all" (*Shemonah Kevatzim* 2:76 [vol. 1, 318]). On the standing of the Jewish people in Rabbi Kook's thought, see Schwartz, *Challenge and Crisis*, 233-46.

[76] See, e.g., the discussion by Cherlow, *The Tzaddiq*, 223-53.

probably anchored in his love of the nation, even though Rabbi Kook expanded its meaning to include active love.

The psychological key for the act of inclusion is the interaction between the strata of the soul. The perfect man is blessed with psychological harmony. Rabbi Kook writes that

> whoever is greater in thought [*mahashavah*], the more closely interconnected are the parts of his soul and all the values of his life; and his power of speech [*dibbur*], and all his movements [*tenuotav*], are connected in a larger fabric, which is perceived with an inner sense in his entire inner being, and the greater this is, [the more intimately he is connected] to all existence.[77] It is impossible for one of original thought to permit himself to engage in worthless talk, or to participate in a conversation on mundane affairs,[78] and whatever he says must be filled with Torah and knowledge.[79]

The "noble souls" are a paragon of the unity of thought and action.[80] The mundane use of mental powers leads to two consequences: (1) the undermining of the mental harmony, and (2) the undermining of the cosmic harmony. The missions incumbent upon the saint in the personal and national spheres are rooted in his unified mental structure.

Finally, the inclusion mechanism is anchored in the metaphysical notion of the saint's responsibility for all, and especially in his willingness to suffer on behalf of all. Rabbi Kook situated this inclusion mechanism in the emotional key: "The saint's suffering the iniquity of the generation, and his atoning for them by his tribulations, is an emotional matter."[81] The

---

[77] Once again, Rabbi Kook made use of the idea of the microcosm. The psychological harmony of the one "greater in thought" reflects the cosmic harmony. Rabbi Kook additionally spoke of the "inner sense," which might possibly echo the approach of the *Kuzari* (4:3), concerning the inner eye (imagination), which is the basis of prophecy. Regardless of whether this alludes to heavenly inspiration, psychological unity is revealed by an inner sense. It is also noteworthy that Rabbi Kook's terminology alludes to the Kabbalistic threefold concept of thought (*mahashavah*), speech (*dibbur*), and act (*maaseh*).

[78] See BT Yoma 19b; Sukkah 28a; Avodah Zarah 19b.

[79] *Shemonah Kevatzim* 1:736 (vol. 1, 235).

[80] Ibid., 8:192 (vol. 3, 308).

[81] Ibid., 1:149 (vol. 1, 58). Rabbi Kook continues: "for each individual from Israel, according to his measure, is anguished by the iniquity of the generation." Rabbi Kook thereby moved away from the Christian sense of the individual who endures the suffering of the world. Since the

saint is responsible for the entire generation, and this responsibility entails sacrifice and suffering.

Quietism

Rabbi Kook did not forgo the dimension of the saint's negation of his self and will. Due both to his unique personality and the weighty responsibility and tasks imposed on him, the saint retreats from any expression of egoism. At times, the faculty of inclusion is anchored in this withdrawal from personality. Rabbi Kook expressed this self-abnegation and total reliance on God (quietism) when he spoke of the perfect man's prayer:

> For the great righteous ones, prayer is very difficult, for they have no will of their own, and their greatest cognition is connected to their pristine faith in the light of divine lovingkindness, which ameliorates everything for them. How will they pray to be saved from any distress, since they have no distress in reality? After the profound contemplation[82] that follows [self-]elevation—for, in the final analysis, man and his needs, the world, life, and all their connections, all the emotions, all the inclinations, and all the natural demands, life and the love thereof, their possessions and their value, all these are the stratagems of the [divine] light of the great lovingkindness of which He said the world will be built,[83] and prayer itself, its utterance, its directions, and the very nature of the desire to order everything in the world according to their nature and character, life, honor, wealth,[84] children, peace, joy, satiety and repose,[85] and above them, wisdom and the sanctity of will and delight, all these are manifestations of the supreme lovingkindness, whose full worth is accentuated by prayer at any time, and especially in time of distress; and the outer will [hefetz] that is revealed by the light of the inner will [ratzon] of the righteous, who are the foundation of the world, whose soul is continuously revived by the

righteous individual is an exalted personage, and he draws down the divine emanation for the benefit of all, he bears the iniquities of the generation to a much greater degree than would an ordinary person.

[82] I.e., highly significant cognition.

[83] Following Psalms 89:3.

[84] Following Proverbs 22:4.

[85] See Judah Loew ben Bezalel (*Maharal*), *Gur Aryeh* to Leviticus 26:6.

supernal divine manifestation,[86] is in itself one of the foundations
of life and the construction of the reality, as breathing air, as eating
and drinking, as building and sowing, as healing and bathing—by
this the spirit of prayer will once again stir the righteous, the upright
of heart, and they will abandon the supernal [strict] judgment
that infuses all the treasures of life, facing which [human] will is
negated,[87] and they will remain servants of their Maker, who pour
out their hearts like water,[88] seeking will, life, physical health, and
the supernal light.[89]

The perfect man's divorce from his will and any personal interests voids
prayer of its meaning. Rabbi Kook undoubtedly meant the institutionalized
structure of prayer, including the supplicatory blessings in the *Amidah*
prayer, which relate to a person's or society's physical and mental needs.
Additionally, not only does the righteous one ignore material needs that
are meaningless to him, he also disregards troubles. The latter make no
impression on him, even though, physically, he might experience suffering
and pain; on the contrary: the saint reaches a state of equanimity.

In the first stage, prayer is of no concern for the righteous individual,
while in the second he once again takes an interest in it. This individual's
"return" to prayer results from the revelation that, in the final analysis,
physical and mental needs, and tribulations, are an expression of God's
lovingkindness. The righteous one realizes that, just as his special soul and
the emanation that he receives are a "natural" law, ensuing from divine
lovingkindness, needs and troubles are also natural law.

---

[86] I.e., the emanation that comes from the inner will to the outer one. The inner will apparently
is parallel to the "innerness of the soul," which the Habad literature identifies with the level of
Yehidah. The emanation descends until the "outer" mental will.

[87] Rabbi Kook argues here that the righteous individual manifests the superiority of prayer as an
expression of the divine presence ("the great lovingkindness"), and therefore returns to ask for
material needs that express human will. This means that the righteous individual leaves the
God of strict judgment (i.e., the divine attribute of *Gevurah* associated with strict judgment,
which does not allow for human will, but only that of God), before which all desires and needs
are negated, and returns to the hidden presence that allows for desires and needs.

[88] From the prayer recited by the Reader during the repetition of the *Amidah* prayer for Yom
Kippur; and also from Hoshana Rabbah, in the "*Ta'aneh Emunim*" liturgical hymn.

[89] From the *Yekum Purkan* (May Deliverance Arise) prayer recited on the Sabbath before the
Mussaf Amidah; the citation is from *Shemonah Kevatzim* 3:67 (vol. 2, 38-39).

All that the saint requires in the earthly realm is that which is an expression of divine lovingkindness. He lacks self-will, and all his activity is guided by the needs of society and the universe. For his part, he would conduct himself in accordance with strict judgment, which would mean the total negation of his existence in the face of the Godhead. He prays only when he discovers that his personal supplicatory prayer elevates the entire world. And even when he returns to pray, the very act of prayer is difficult for him. This understanding of prayer is consistent with Rabbi Kook's antinomian conception.[90]

From Faculties to Ideology

A discussion of the faculties of the exceptional individual would not be complete without any reference to ideology. Rabbi Kook asserted that the perfect man's faculties are made fruitful and ascend when they are anchored in the national condition. In other words, adherence to nationalism is an integral component of the nature of the perfect person's faculties. He writes:

> When the light increases in the soul of the heads of the nation, the choicest of the sons, those of great faculty, emanation flows, the great lives begin to flow, to be revealed in spiritual and material circles, in literature, in society, in nature and temperament, in the pleasantness of souls [nefashot] and generosity. Supernal splendor will begin to spread the beauty of its cloud and the grandeur of its glory, and the Lord's great name will be seen once again over His people.[91] The hidden [national] quality will emerge and rise against all its detractors and refuters. All the peoples of the earth will see that the Lord's name is proclaimed over you [Deuteronomy 28:10], and all who see them shall recognize that they are a stock the Lord has blessed [Isaiah 61:9].[92]

90 See below, Chapter Eight.

91 See I Samuel 12:22.

92 *Shemonah Kevatzim* 4:20 (vol. 2, 138). The following passage (4:21), that had been previously discussed in a number of studies, presents the longing for prophecy ("we are called to the wellspring of prophecy"), and the messianic enhancement of the awakening of the faculties described in this passage.

Thus, the national awakening amplifies the various faculties possessed by the saint. This awakening pertains to his physical dimension, that is, his physical nature ("nature and temperament"), as it does to intellectual and aesthetic creativity ("literature"). Now the spiritual leaders, "those of great faculty," will also be "the heads of the nation." The impetus of the exceptional individuals and the intensification of their faculties reveal the nation's special quality, which had been dormant ("hidden") for so many years.

This discussion leads us to one of the most paradoxical aspects of Rabbi Kook's philosophy of the perfect individual—the national dimensions of the saint.

Chapter Six

NATIONAL TASKS

Rabbi Kook undoubtedly thought that religious genius was not limited to a specific religion. The exceptional individual is, first and foremost, human and universal. This said, he proposed a cosmic and human hierarchical structure. He maintained the existence of a hierarchy among saints, and a number of times referred to non-Jewish perfect ones whose very being lacked the component that defines the Jew. The Jewish saint is the archetype of maximal perfection. As we shall see below, in *Eder ha-Yakar*, Rabbi Kook plainly accepted the existence of a universal saint. For him, universality was, in a way, an extension of Judaism. His starting point, however, was the general human hierarchy of saints.

The saint has, primarily, connection to a community, and Rabbi Kook emphasized his reliance on the Hasidic conception of the *tzaddik*.[1] At the present time, however, the Jewish saint has a substantive connection to a much broader circle: the nation. He ascribed a completely new dimension to the saint, the national dimension. He forcefully advocated the special quality of the Jewish people. Accordingly, his definition of the saint is rooted in the Jewish national renaissance and his theological support of the Zionist enterprise. He therefore devoted much attention to the national tasks of the exceptional individuals.

Redefinition

Since the image of the saint occupied Rabbi Kook, it was only natural that he would fundamentally link the saint with the national awakening. Furthermore, this tie is so enrooted that it requires a redefinition of the

---

[1] See *Shemonah Kevatzim* 1:227 (vol. 1, 87); see also above, Chapter One.

saint and his role. This direction is given striking and forceful expression in several passages. For example:

> In the [time of] the footsteps of the Messiah, whoever's heart is inclined to be connected to the salvation of Israel has the soul of a supernal righteous one, who cannot be deemed of intermediate standing.[2]

> When the true righteous one is enrooted in the Land of Israel, the love of the Land of Israel that he had in the Diaspora is negated, and in its place a new love sprouts, that is born solely in the Land of Israel, that begins with sentiment and ends in knowledge.[3]

> But it is those who await salvation, "and the knowledgeable will be radiant like the bright expanse of sky,"[4] who bring the Redemption; it is they who report a saying in the name of its originator, and the word of God is truly in your mouth;[5] and it is they who are the mighty ones, who desire, specifically, the complete Redemption, and the entire center of their divine service is solely that perfect expectation, which is flawless, for whom only the supernal dimension of redemption is fitting.[6] The entire nature of those who are engaged in the inner essence [literally, soul] of the Torah is devoted, bound to, and needs the soul and appearance of Torah, they await the light of the Lord,

---

2 Ibid., 2:66 (vol. 1, 315). In the preceding passage, Rabbi Kook defined the end of the middle way: "that I eat in order to study, pray, perform the commandments, and the like" (ibid., 2:65 [vol. 1, 314]). Thus, eating and other activities of survival are only a means. That degree of the righteous, in contrast, is that eating itself is holiness, and then becomes an end in itself. It also should be noted that Rabbi Kook sought to expand the potential for being a righteous one (even though he speaks of congenital faculty in his discussion of genius). E.g., "Everyone has a point of good and righteousness" (ibid., 6:223 [vol. 3:86]).

3 *Kevatzim*, 174; "*ha-regesh*" could also be rendered "sensibility."

4 Daniel 12:3; see also 12:10. This might be an allusion to the introduction to the *Kuzari*, which states that "the knowledgeable will understand" (following Daniel 12:3). Rabbi Kook, too, maintains that the Redemption will be concealed, and anticipation is needed ("those who await salvation") in order to follow its progress. Elsewhere he mentions that these knowledgeable ones are sensitive to the sparks that are located in places known only to them. "The brilliant knowledgeable reveal treasures [that were] in darkness, and hidden caches in places where no person would think to search" (*Shemonah Kevatzim* 6:267 [vol. 3, 100]).

5 Following I Kings 17:24.

6 Following Jeremiah 10:7. This means that only the supernal dimension of Redemption is suitable for such anticipation.

and the fullness of the supernal glory [*ha-kavod ha-elyon*].[7] They guard the footsteps of our Messiah, they know that the entire world and the fullness thereof, all the complexities of nature and all its creations, are merely steps in which the light of the Messiah treads.[8]

Mental involvement in the process of redemption by itself turns a person into a saint. Rabbi Kook's style in these passages leads us to presume that Redemption is perceived as a national, altruistic act, and the partner to this seemingly loses his individual personality and his diasporic history. All his actions are intended for the benefit of all Israel. It is noteworthy that, according to what Rabbi Kook says about those "who await salvation," the transformation of a person into a saint is not dependent on tangible action; it suffices for the individual's consciousness to be directed to the nation as a whole and the processes that it undergoes. Two principles characterize the connection between the saint and the historical and national process:

(1) Identification: Rabbi Kook emphasized that this refers to the "inclination of the heart" and "awaiting salvation," and not necessarily activism. This statement by Rabbi Kook is anchored in the theological sphere: Divine Providence acts covertly, and moves the entire universe to its redemption. The elevation of the world is effected without tangible dependence on human beings. The saint senses the cosmic flow and is cognizant of it. The very cognition and mental partnership in the given processes makes a person a saint.

(2) The way to the goal includes the goal itself: Rabbi Kook obliquely explained that the expectation for salvation is itself a sort of salvation, and possibly even more than this. He writes elsewhere: "'But those who turn to the Lord shall not lack any good' [Psalms 34:11]—all good is already present in the very turning to the Lord."[9] Just as prayer itself is no less important

---

7   The wording "the supernal fullness" appears with the meaning of the world of souls. See, e.g., Nahmanides, *Ramban (Nahmanides): Writings and Discourses*, trans. C. B. Chavel, vol. 2, *The Gate of Reward* (New York, 1978), 542: the "higher reward [*ha-gemul ha-elyon*]." See the commentary of Abrabanel to Deuteronomy 34:5:7. "*Kavod*" (glory) expresses the emanation from the highest *Sefirah* (*Binah* or *Tiferet*, sometimes called "supreme glory") to the lowest (*Malkhut*). The fullness of the *kavod* is the fructification of *Malkhut* by the supernal emanation.

8   *Igrot ha-Re'ayah*, vol. 3, 19-20.

9   *Shemonah Kevatzim* 6:233 (vol. 3, 89). In the following passage (234), Rabbi Kook mentions the dictum: "the reward of a commandment is another commandment" (M Avot 4:2), and alludes to the Maimonidean interpretation that the reward for a commandment is the fulfillment of the

than the fulfillment of the requests it contains, so too, the anticipation of Redemption is no less important, and possibly more, than its realization.

Rabbi Kook directly applied these two principles to a messianic interpretation of contemporary events, which led him to redefine the saint. Now, the saint is whoever senses the hidden and latent messianic processes of reality and identifies with them. Moreover, the saint's connection to and dwelling in the Land of Israel cause him to undergo a sort of metamorphosis. The second passage highlights the change in his conduct in regard to love of the Land of Israel, both emotionally and intellectually ("that begins with sentiment and ends in knowledge"). This love is seemingly a metaphor for the general change experienced by the exceptional individual upon his moving to the Land of Israel.

The Saints of Ideas

One of the essays in *Ikvei ha-Tzon*, "The Thoughts," grades metaphysical and moral ideas in relation to nationalism. An analysis of the essay clarifies the standing of the saint in Israel and among the nations of the world. In this essay, Rabbi Kook proposed a threefold division of ideas:

(1) Universal, noble ideas that have neither contentual nor stylistic connection to nationalism. The example given by Rabbi Kook is the existence of God, which is independent of any nation or style.

(2) Noble ideas that are universal in terms of their content, but which acquire a special style in the Jewish people.

(3) Particular, noble ideas that are unique to the Jewish people, in both content and style.

"The Thoughts" aims to exemplify the second category of ideas. Rabbi Kook made no effort to illustrate the third category, but he probably meant Kabbalistic knowledge that is not transitive. He called to foster these particular ideas in the era in which "nationalism intensifies, Israel is on the path fit for sanctity and blessing."[10] He illustrated the second category

---

commandment itself (Maimonides, *Commentary to the Mishnah*, Introduction to Chapter Eleven of Tractate Sanhedrin).

10   *Eder ha-Yakar*, 123.

with the aspiration for justice, integrity, and truth—which are universal ideas and values—that is present in the heart of every Jew. He set forth the following argument:

(1) Justice, integrity, and truth constitute the divine light that shines into the Jewish soul.

(2) The divine light needs a receptacle to contain it.

(3) The religious ethos of Judaism (commandments, customs) is the receptacle that contains the light.

(4) The urge of every Jew to remain attached to his people, despite its lowly condition, ensues from the preceding arguments. Accordingly:

(5) Universal noble ideas are imprinted in the Jewish people.

Rabbi Kook embedded a number of Kabbalistic and Hasidic terms, both revealed and concealed, in this argument.[11] It highlights the special imprint of the Jewish people in its internalization and dissemination of these universal ideas. The saint is mentioned a few times in connection with the second type of ideas: once, as a universal saint, and another time, as a Jewish one. We will begin with the universal saint. Rabbi Kook wrote, when he presented the second type of idea:

> At times there will be mighty ones, skillful ones,[12] who are capable of straining and refining the inner content, that is equal in essence,[13] to finely bring it in the singular and pure Israelite style. Then it will be beneficial, as that blessing that comes generally to Israel from the outstanding converts: "When Israel does the will of the Omnipresent,

---

[11] The following terms are taken from the discussion in *Eder ha-Yakar*, 124. Truth and justice, which are the emanation to the Jewish soul, reflect *Tiferet* and *Malkhut*, respectively ("the sublime desire for the divine justice [...] to the divine, pure and uplifting light of truth and integrity"). These values ensue from the love of God ("the root of the love of God, that is hidden within our heart and soul"). Love is an expression of lovingkindness. The Kabbalistic literature frequently portrays the emanation from *Hesed* to *Tiferet* and *Malkhut*. Rabbi Kook added to this the inner point ("the hidden power," "the wonderful point of life to adhere specifically to this nation"), a notion which is prevalent in Hasidic thought. He thereby reveals characteristics appropriate for religious Zionist thought. See, e.g., Schwartz, *Faith at the Crossroads*, 176: the "point of Judaism."

[12] Following Exodus 28:3.

[13] That is, from the sociological aspect, it is equivalent to all, and possesses no national singularity.

the Holy One, blessed be He [both appellations for God] sees some righteous one in the non-Jewish nations such as Jethro and Rahab, and brings him to adhere to Israel."[14]

To read between the lines, Rabbi Kook apparently adopted the approach of Rabbi Judah Halevi, that the convert can adhere to Israel from the universal aspect, but not from the unique, individual aspect (for Rabbi Judah Halevi, this means that the convert is not able to become a prophet) expressed in the third type of idea. At any rate, the universal superior (and exceptional) individual is capable of adhering to such values, as if they were imprinted within him from birth, just like a Jew. Rabbi Kook consequently wrote that "among all the peoples, in accordance with the situation of the reality of the human race, only individuals are capable of rising up to the level of [absolute] righteousness."[15]

And now we turn to the Jewish saint. Rabbi Kook was of the opinion that the quality literature of Jewish thought finely distinguishes between the three (actually, four) types of ideas. He wrote:

Thought requires great routine, special erudition, and accustomed acuteness until it is capable of distinguishing between those parts, of not confusing a thing with something different. Consequently, there are those among the great ones of past[16] generations who use everything available to them from the greatest sages of the [non-Jewish] nations, even as regards the most sublime matters, while others completely flee from this, while yet others are in the middle, being inclined to here or there, drawing near with the right hand and thrusting away with the left;[17] and there are those who do the opposite. All depends on the part to which these matters come [i.e., the specific situation]. The inner holy sentiment guides the saints of ideas to the best goal; "the eye of the Lord is on those who fear Him" [Psalms 33:18], and "the integrity of the upright guides them" [Proverbs 11:3].[18]

14 PT Berakhot 2:8, 20a; *Song of Songs Rabbah* 6:10; *Yalkut Shimoni, Song of Songs* 6:991; *Eder ha-Yakar*, 122-23.

15 *Eder ha-Yakar*, 124.

16 "*Aherim*"; thus also in the 1906 edition; perhaps it should read "*ahadim*" (a few).

17 Following BT 47a; Sanhedrin 107b. The right hand is seen as dominant.

18 *Eder ha-Yakar*, 123.

Rabbi Kook referred here to Jewish thinkers who engage in the formulation of ideas: that is, philosophers. Only one who is occupied with the three types of ideas, including the third type (a characteristic of the Jewish people), need be concerned with the blurring of the distinctions between these types, as follows:

(1) The one who does not fear using all the philosophical and theological literature that was composed by non-Jewish thinkers (general literature).

(2a) The one who is more inclined to use Jewish literature, and less apt to use the general literature.

(2b) The one who is more inclined to use general literature, and less inclined toward Jewish literature.

(3) The one who uses Jewish literature exclusively.

Rabbi Kook suggested at the end of the passage that there is no guiding principle for the formulation of ideas. In order to create the ideal religious thought, one must be guided by the "inner holy sentiment." He called the thinkers who reach the level of perfection the "saints of ideas [kedoshei ha-ra'ayon]." This teaches us, once again, that the tradition of rationalist thought continued to nest in Rabbi Kook's thought, despite the dominance of the esoteric. The image of the saint includes rational activity, such as the stylizing of universal ideas in Jewish garb. The saint is a thinker, and he succeeds in correctly blending universal and Jewish values. Rabbi Kook drew a sharp distinction between the non-Jewish saint and the one who is "from the aspect of our pure stock."[19] Furthermore, the exceptional non-Jewish individual owes his lofty status to his adherence to the Jewish people. It is the Jewish coloration of the ideas that gives the saint his sublime nature.

In his article "The Thoughts," Rabbi Kook spoke of the non-Jewish saint and the Jewish saint who is Jewishly-oriented in particular. This leaves the Jewish saint who is humanistic by nature, and addresses himself to all humankind. This saint also appears in *Shemonah Kevatzim*:

> There are some righteous ones, who are very great and tremendous, who cannot contract themselves within *Knesset Yisrael* alone, and

---

[19]   *Eder ha-Yakar*, 123.

they always are concerned about and earnestly seek what is good[20]
for the whole world. Nevertheless, they are also connected in
their inner point specifically with *Knesset Yisrael*, because *Knesset
Yisrael* is the essence of what is good and outstanding in the entire
world, and the love and good that will come to *Knesset Yisrael* will
return and encompass every being. These righteous ones cannot be
nationalistic in the outer content of the word, since they cannot bear
any hatred or injustice, any restriction or contraction of good and
lovingkindness, They are good to all, as the attributes of the Holy
One, blessed be He, who is good to all and His mercy is upon all
His works.[21] They nevertheless are mighty envisioners of salvation,
since they know for a certainty and believe with their entire pure
soul that the salvation of Israel is the Lord's salvation, the salvation
of the world and the fullness thereof, and all in it, from the loftiest
heights to the deepest depths.[22]

The passage discusses Jewish saints, for whom, on a superficial level, all
humans are equal, since these saints are motivated by the "inner point,"
which, according to the Hasidic literature that influenced Rabbi Kook, is
unique to the Jew. He therefore acknowledged the humanistic orientation
of the saint, and at times the panhuman responsibility of the saint
becomes dominant. In the same breath, however, Rabbi Kook took pains
to state that humanism enhances this uniqueness. There are two reasons
for this:

(1) The psychological reason: the humanistic feeling itself ensues
from the "inner point" and from *Knesset Yisrael*.

(2) The ethical reason: what is good for Israel is also good for the
entire world. The redemption of Israel, too, is the redemption of the entire
human race.

Rabbi Kook explained that since these saints love the entire human
race, then, paradoxically, their love of Israel "is limited to a concentrated
place."[23] Consequently, this love is of a higher quality. We may presume

---

20   Following Proverbs 11:27.

21   Following Psalms 145:9.

22   Following *Sefer Yetzirah* 1:5; the passage is from *Shemonah Kevatzim* 3:4 (vol. 2, 6).

23   The continuation of the passage in *Shemonah Kevatzim* 3:4.

that these saints' love of Israel is focused because the Jewish people has intrinsically singular standing, and therefore has a special place in this universal love.

Thus, we learn that for Rabbi Kook there can be no humanism without national singularity. Even if the saint does not distinguish between Jew and non-Jew, he is driven by the same representative divine entity of the Jewish people (*Knesset Yisrael*).

The Saint and the Masses

The above discussions show that, for Rabbi Kook, the saint is bound together with the national dimension. Although the Redemption will be realized by the "inferior souls" (that is, the *halutzim* and others engaged in building the land), it owes its existence to the altruism of the "supreme saints."[24]

Continuing in this vein, it is noteworthy that a prominent message in Rabbi Kook's thought hinged on a change in the standing of the saint over the course of time. While in the past the religious genius was an exceptional personality, elevated above other people and impossible to emulate, at present this individual is close to the collective and is enrooted in it. In the past, the perfect individuals were on the highest level, while the masses were extremely base. Today, however, the masses have been elevated and have become increasingly moral and intelligent;[25] at the same time, the perfect ones have increasingly descended from their high level. This well-known notion of Rabbi Kook was formulated in 1906 in the article "The Generation," which spoke of the generation of the Second Aliyah. He wrote:

> In most historical periods, we find exalted sages, the great of spirit in the early generations whose greatness and fierceness of spirit leave us amazed, while the collective was in a lowly state, both in knowledge and in discipline.[26] The truth be told, the masses of our people are more exalted than any other masses in terms of the divine holiness

---

24   Ibid., 1:723 (vol. 1, 231).

25   Zvi Yaron already noted Rabbi Kook's deep appreciation for the members of the *moshavot* (agricultural settlements) from the Second Aliyah. See Yaron, *Philosophy*, 39.

26   Following Proverbs 12:1.

that envelops them,[27] and they became an example [nes].[28] In recent generations, the giants began to diminish, while the collective ascends. The ignorant among our people have decreased, and, on the other hand, the geniuses and the righteous have diminished and decreased.[29]

The source for Rabbi Kook's distinction between the exceptional individuals and the masses is to be found, once again, in medieval rationalism.[30] The gap between them is mainly intellectual, since in the beginning of the passage the masses are characterized by both intellectual and moral inferiority, while in the continuation of this text, the masses are compared only to "the ignorant [burim]." Additionally, we saw in the discussion of heresy (above) that morality is the foundation for scientific thought. Rabbi Kook consequently ended this passage with "the geniuses and the righteous [geonim ve-tzaddikim]": genius has two meanings, intellectual and moral, while the righteous individual usually is of outstanding moral stature.

Rabbi Kook maintains that the disparity between the perfect individuals and the masses of the people of Israel was not so great, because of their "divine holiness." Nonetheless, the distance between the people and the exceptional individuals has decreased, which explains, for example, the greatness of the Second Aliyah generation, especially the pioneers. Rabbi Kook further argued that the distance between the exceptional individual and the generation has lessened because of the former's intensive activity: such an individual elevates the generation by his occupation with the inner nature of the Torah.[31]

---

27   Following Deuteronomy 33:12.

28   That is, a significant event, one worthy of mention (following Numbers 26:10; see also Ezekiel 27:7).

29   Eder ha-Yakar, 111. This conception is formulated in different wording in Kevatzim, vol. 1, 121-22.

30   See T. Ross, "The Elite and the Masses in the Prism of Metaphysics and History: Harav Kook on the Nature of Religious Belief," Journal of Jewish Thought and Philosophy 8 (1999): 355-67.

31   Rabbi Kook explained that there is no development among the great ones of the generation, just as the object of their knowledge, the esoteric teachings ("the inner aspect of the Torah"), remains fixed: "Even though they [the "intellective structures"] are already revealed to those great of spirit in generations eternal, for the general spirit of the intellection of the early individuals stands as a banner forever, despite all the new individual discoveries [...] at any rate, the necessity to elucidate and bring down the sublime matters, to that degree of ordinary

Two statements emerge from this passage regarding the image of the saint, who is symbolized in the genius and righteous types:

(1) The fundamental traits of the saint themselves have not changed. The definition of the saint in our time remains as it was in previous generations.

(2) The number and quality of the saints has decreased in our generation. In this respect, Rabbi Kook adopted the notion of the decline of the generations.[32]

Taking into account the passages cited above on Rabbi Kook's self-consciousness as saint, we can see that his meaning here is dialectical: on the one hand, he is aware that his standing as saint is lower than that of his predecessors, who had a mythic aura; while on the other hand, there are few saints, and he therefore is a rare personality in his generation. Such a dialectic finely suits the character of Rabbi Kook. The gap between the exceptional individual and the masses is one of the reasons why "the person whose soul shines forth within him must frequently seclude himself."[33] He also differentiated between the exceptional individuals who are capable of emulating the behavior of the masses and mingling with them, at least temporarily, and those incapable of joining with the masses at all.[34] Even those who mingle with the masses repent for the "diminution of the communion [with God] of that time."[35]

In the collections of his thoughts (kevatzim), Rabbi Kook amplified the saint-masses distinction with a series of ontological insights. Now the saint's drawing closer to the masses, even as a dialectic pole, is brought into

matters, that same necessity makes them the possession of the entire collective. By this the people in its entirety is elevated to the supreme and lofty level" (Eder ha-Yakar, 143). The spiritual giants adopt the stable and sublime messages to the various generations.

32 See, e.g., M. M. Kellner, Maimonides on the "Decline of the Generations" and the Nature of Rabbinic Authority (Albany, NY, 1996); A. Melamed, On the Shoulders of Giants (Ramat Gan, 2003) [Hebrew].

33 Shemonah Kevatzim 3:319 (vol. 2, 114). On the merit of seclusion to attain self-awareness, see ibid., 8:149 (vol. 2, 290).

34 Ibid., 8:150 (vol. 3, 290-91).

35 Ibid., 8:185 (vol. 3, 304).

question. Rabbi Kook established a hierarchy of the strata of the people, in accordance with the components of the soul:[36]

> *neshamah* ("breath, soul, soul-breath"): "the righteous of the generation, intellectuals and knowledgeable, the pure and the mighty."
> *ruah* ("spirit"): "Torah scholars, [God-]fearing and perfect, possessing a refined soul, who desire the existence of the nation and of its holy light, together."[37]
> *nefesh* ("animative soul, life force"): "the masses are connected by their nature to the entirety of the nation and the simple faith."[38]

According to this hierarchy, the saint is next to the Torah scholar, and is not one who borders on the masses. The parallel Kabbalistic model of the soul also included emanation from the *neshamah* to the baser parts of the soul. The direct interaction, however, is between the saint and the Torah scholar. In general, "the men of action cannot fathom the thought of the men of spirit. The latter are completely alien to the former. They cannot sense any of their sentiments, they cannot understand their troubles or their delights."[39] The distinction between the exceptional individuals and the masses is, as we noted, ontological.

Rabbi Kook limited the altruism of which he had spoken, asserting that

> The natural material and spiritual health present in the masses, despite their coarseness and lack of knowledge, is superior in several degrees to all of this that is possessed by the great ones, whose ideas

---

[36] Ibid., 2:305 (vol. 1, 386). Rabbi Kook called the first level "the Israelite soul." This structure somewhat echoes the metaphor of the palace in the *Guide of the Perplexed* 3:51.

[37] We may assume from Rabbi Kook's gathering around himself circles of Torah scholars that they constitute the circle of the righteous individual.

[38] Rabbi Kook apparently assumed the existence of religious consciousness within every person. He wrote: "There is no man in the world without a bit of righteousness" (*Shemonah Kevatzim* 5:227 [vol. 2, 309]). The definitions of *neshamah*, *ruah*, and *nefesh* (all generally rendered as "soul") are based on *The Zohar*, trans. and commentary Matt, 1:206a (vol. 3, 262 n. 26).

[39] *Kevatzim*, vol. 2, 81. Rabbi Kook similarly distinguished there between educated and intelligent "plain men of spirit" and "divine men of spirit."

and spiritual ferment harmed their innocence, the tranquility of their spirit, and the purity of their soul.[40]

Since the masses are gifted with a direct and straightforward approach, the saint can learn from them, as well. However, he also explained that the masses are "coarse and lack knowledge," and the saint's approach to them is clearly paternalistic ("to benefit them and influence them").[41] At times, the perfect man is not built for the conceptions of the masses. He is incapable of acquiring "many studies that most people so delight in."[42] And this is not all: the masses create an economic and social system that eventually serves the perfect man. Additionally, the purpose of the wicked in the world is to give the righteous individual a reason to live a material life. If there were no wicked, the righteous individual would be drawn into the spiritual world, and would be completely divorced from the material. Thanks to the wicked, "the flame of [the righteous one's] love for the supernal world is cooled."[43]

Prayer has a central place in the saint-masses relationship. Rabbi Kook praised the proclivity of Hasidism to draw the simple folk to its ranks. He attributed its success, inter alia, to the "strengthening of prayer in comparison with Torah [study]."[44] He further explained that prayer is meant to connect the righteous one, not of his volition, to the masses. In other words, this individual has no real reason or incentive to mingle with the masses. Rabbi Kook writes:

> If it were not for the labor of prayer, there would be nothing connecting the learned with the masses, nor Israel with the entire great world in the End of Days, nor man with all that is animate.[45]

This passage describes the level of the saint in a very extreme formulation, while at the same time anchoring him in the ontological hierarchy of all

---

40 *Shemonah Kevatzim* 3:79 (vol. 2, 43).

41 See also *Kevatzim*, vol. 1, 103-4.

42 *Shemonah Kevatzim* 7:209 (vol. 3, 235).

43 Ibid., 3:110 (vol. 2, 53). On the other hand, the spiritual and material dimensions of the perfect individual are united (ibid., 3:161 [vol. 2, 67]).

44 Ibid., 7:138 (vol. 3, 202).

45 Ibid., 3:80 (vol. 2, 43).

existence, in the present and in the messianic future. Rabbi Kook implicitly drew the following analogy:

saint	Israel	man
masses	non-Jews	animate world

This analogy is reminiscent of Rabbi Kook's well-known statement before his arrival in the Land of Israel: "The internal difference between those who observe the Torah and those who have left the religion is greater than the difference between Israel and the nations."[46] It transpires that Rabbi Kook did not wish to retreat from the hierarchy to which he alludes: the relationship between the saint and the masses parallels that of man and the animate world, and the Jew and the non-Jew.[47] The unbridgeable, categoric chasm is formulated quite clearly in the following passage:

> No one can comprehend the profundity of the soul of the great noble ones, the people of Heaven, for whom the life of the spirit is the entire content of their lives. The world thinks that they are aristocratic, loving themselves, or ne'er-do-wells and lazy, while the entire world derives benefit only from their light, and none love work and man and participate in the lives of all those of baser standing as they do. Because they know their worth and the value of their lives for the world, they are aware of the great responsibility resting on them in maintaining their essential nature, faculty, and honor, to the extent that the entire world was created only to command this.[48] It is they who are the spiritual foundations of the world, to the extent that if their ideal will, that soars to the supernal holy height, were to cease for a moment, the entire world would sink into the mud that is sullied with the filth of life and its foul wickedness.[49]

In the beginning of this passage, Rabbi Kook used the wording "the profundity of the soul" to refer to the highest levels of the soul (*Hayah*,

---

46   *"Eitzot me-Rahok* [Counsels from Afar]," *Ha-Peles* 2 (1902): 530.

47   The substantial distinction between Jew and non-Jew was formulated in many passages in his work *Orot*. See Schwartz, *Challenge and Crisis*, 234-36.

48   BT Berakhot 6b; Shabbat 30b; *Yalkut Shimoni*, Ecclesiastes, 989.

49   *Shemonah Kevatzim* 4:75 (vol. 2, 157).

Yehidah), those that are in communion with the Godhead. It is specifically the context of communion, which Rabbi Kook called ascending to "the supernal holy height,"[50] that causes the divine emanation to be brought down to the material world. In the final analysis, this emanation causes the masses to blossom. The saints bear the burden of the masses ("love work and man"). Additionally, since the masses are not cognizant of the exalted status of the saint, he seems haughty to them.

This paragraph continues the elitist motif that Rabbi Kook expressed in the preceding passage, which maintains the ontic distinction between the saint and the masses. "Those with the faculty for piety, sanctity, the attainment of the secrets of the Torah, cannot compare themselves to the majority of people."[51] This distinction does not pass over the minutiae of everyday life; for example: when the saint speaks "as most of the people speak," he feels "the soul's protest."[52] Rabbi Kook further argued, in the previously-cited passage, that the saint is the purpose of the world. That is, in the first stage, the saint is responsible for the condition of the world, both in terms of his moral responsibility, and his activity (bringing down the divine emanation). In the second stage, the saint gives reason and purpose to the world, which was created solely for his sake.

It is noteworthy that Rabbi Kook's messianic vision included narrowing the gap between the masses and the exceptional individuals. This vision was fashioned before he came to the Land of Israel, as can be seen from the conclusion to the poem *"Mas'at Nafshi"* (My Soul's Desire):

> For the exceptional ones
> Shall be for flocks,[53]
> And in the darkest places, in the depths[54]
> They shall shine in every direction.[55]

---

50   The saint generally expresses the *Sefirah* of *Hokhmah*, but here, Rabbi Kook apparently referred to the three uppermost *Sefirot*: *Keter, Hokhmah,* and *Binah*.

51   *Shemonah Kevatzim* 6:26 (vol. 2, 12).

52   Ibid., 6:53 (vol. 2, 20).

53   Following Isaiah 17:2.

54   Following Psalms 88:7.

55   Rabbi Kook alludes here to Mount Nebo, which is at the gates of the Land of Israel (Numbers 27:12; Deuteronomy 32:49). The poem was printed in *Orot ha-Re'ayah* (Jerusalem, 1970), 30.

This vision is problematic, because the distinction between the exceptional individual and the masses is ontic. Moreover, paradoxically, the distinction between the perfect man and the masses is "a source of blessing for the many."[56] Rabbi Kook probably derived the vision of the narrowing of the gap from the apocalyptic messianic conception that sees a change in the laws of nature of the future world.

To sum up this point: the saint is an unusual phenomenon in the landscape of his generation. The difficulty of his mission is redoubled, since in the past, even though his authority was not official, it nevertheless went unquestioned. The great distance—the chasm—between the saint and the surrounding society afforded him his authority, although this did not necessarily lead to compliance. In the current time, in contrast, when the public is educated and is interested in ideologies and literatures, the saint's authority is no longer self-evident. We may assume that this fact is a source of frustration, since the saint-masses distinction is substantive. It is possible to ascend and approach the levels of the saint, but it is impossible to unite with him, because his is a congenital quality.

National Mission

What are the tasks of the saint, and what is expected of him in a situation in which he must establish his authority? The answer is to be found in the action of unification. In the past, this was mainly negative in nature: the removal of the divisive element, Christianity. In the present, however, unification is a positive action: the saint unites the tense and opposing strata. In ancient times, unification was performed by Rabbi Akiva, who is deemed to be a classical Jewish paradigm of the saint. Rabbi Kook writes:

> Laying hands on the holy, deriding the words of sages,[57] lashing out against the sanctification of the physical, despairing of the sanctification of world dominion, obscuring the awareness of the supernal chosenness of Israel, and the attenuation of the supernal

56 *Shemonah Kevatzim* 7:69 (vol. 3, 160).
57 In accusing Jesus of these, Rabbi Kook relied mainly on the polemical writings of the medieval period. See, e.g., the satirical book *Toledot Yeshu* (A Jewish Life of Jesus).

life-force by a terrible mental flaw[58]—all these came together in the war that *Knesset Yisrael* wages against the destructive force that came forth from within it, which, in the end, was directed outward, and was cast forth from the camp of Israel. This foreignness [to the unique quality of Israel] prevents the blessing of the inner spring, the root of life from the issuing forth of the spring of Israel. We therefore are called to constantly shelter with the God of Israel,[59] to encompass all the world, from the highest degree to the lowest,[60] connected in a single holy life, that flows and ebbs, ascends and rises, without stopping. Rabbi Akiva came to save the central leaf of unity[61] when it collapsed, and the entire world almost collapsed; and he was the head of the Ten Martyrs,[62] those who came to Mind first[63]—[rescue me] "from men, O Lord, from Your hand, from men whose share in life is fleeting" [Psalms 17:14]—who [the Ten Martyrs] gave their lives to exalt the glory of the Lord,[64] to aggrandize the holy of holies. The depths of evil, the depths of the sea,[65] completely left the place of the holy, as it took its part from those bodies garbed in the supernal souls, to which it thought to adhere. He expounded mounds of laws from every point [on the Torah],[66] but he did not expound [the word *et* in] "Revere only the Lord your God" [Deuteronomy 6:13; 10:20], he rather expounded that this includes Torah scholars,[67] and showed that the one who was insolent to the Sages had his roots in poison

---

58   Rabbi Kook alludes here to the Christian theological underpinning, whose force is evident beginning with the Gospel of John.

59   Following BT Berakhot 55a; *Exodus Rabbah* 34:1; *Tanhuma, Beha'alotekha* 10.

60   See, e.g., *Zohar, Bereshit*, fols. 1b, 20a. This wording was commonly used by the founders of Hasidism. See, e.g., Rabbi Schneur Zalman (Schneersohn) of Lyady, *Iggeret ha-Kodesh*, chapter 10.

61   The "central leaf" is the top of the spine of the *lulav* (the palm frond, one of the Four Species taken on the Sukkot holiday), consisting of leaves bound together. The Talmud (BT Sukkah 32a) discusses the case in which "the central leaf is split," that is, the two bound leaves separated, to which Rabbi Kook alludes.

62   The leading rabbis who were executed by the Romans; see BT Berakhot 61b; *Midrash Aseret Harugei Malkhut*.

63   See BT Menahot 29b.

64   Following Daniel 3:28.

65   Following Micah 7:19, in a reference to the shells that presumably received their wish in the corpses of the Torah scholars killed by the Romans.

66   Following BT Eruvin 21b; *Tanhuma, Bereshit* 1.

67   BT Pesahim 22b; Kiddushin 57a; Bava Kamma 41b; Bekhorot 6b.

weed and wormwood;[68] he was a son of a forbidden union and the
son of a menstruant woman [both extremely derogatory terms].
"Not like these is the Portion of Jacob" [Jeremiah 10:16], rather,
the inheritance of Esau is Mount Seir,[69] that will be desolate when
liberators shall march up on Mount Zion.[70] He [Rabbi Akiva] chose
to bring about his own death, rather than transgress the teachings
of his colleagues regarding the washing of the hands;[71] he was not
like one who is uprooted from the world, as if he had relations with
a harlot,[72] by eating their bread unclean among the nations;[73] "and
shall eat unclean food in Assyria" [Hosea 9:3]; "eating the flesh of
the swine, the reptile, and the mouse, shall one and all come to an
end—declares the Lord" [Isaiah 66:17]. "And the Lord shall be king
over all the earth" [Zechariah 14:9], "and everyone who breathes
shall declare, the Lord, the God of Israel, is King, and has dominion
over all."[74]

Clearly, at times the saint acts in forceful ways, if such action is needed, to
rescue the cosmic order. In ancient times he came to unite the nation and
the entire universe in two positive ways:

(1) Ascribing decisive importance to the Oral Law, that is, the halakhic
interpretation of the Rabbis, and the commandments and regulations that
they enacted.

(2) Strengthening the standing of the Rabbis by exegetical and
halakhic means.

In a negative aspect, the saint's activity was concentrated on the
rejection of Christianity, which threatened the authority of the Rabbis.

---

68 Following Deuteronomy 29:17.

69 Following Deuteronomy 2:5; see also Hosea 24:4.

70 Following Ezekiel 35:7; Obadiah 1:21.

71 Following BT Eruvin 21b. Rabbi Akiva preferred to use his rationed water for the ritual washing
of the hands instead of drinking it, thereby endangering his life, in order not to transgress
Rabbinic law.

72 Following BT Sotah 4b: "Whoever eats bread without washing his hands is as though he had
intercourse with a harlot, as it is said [Proverbs 6:26], 'For on account of a harlot, to a loaf of
bread.'"

73 Following Ezekiel 4:13.

74 From the *Mussaf Amidah* prayers for the Days of Awe. The passage is from *Shemonah Kevatzim*
6:3 (vol. 3, 76-77).

Thus, the saint devoted himself to buttressing the standing of the Rabbis, thereby maintaining the unity of the nation and the whole world.

In the present time, the saint's unification activity is conducted in the national sphere, in two planes:

(1) unifying the hidden and the manifest national motive forces;
(2) unifying the covert and the overt personal driving forces.

We will begin with the former. Rabbi Kook's national conception adopted a dual model. He spoke of the disparity and tension between the revealed national stratum and the concealed one. In the latter, the Jewish people stand on the threshold of Redemption, after the cathartic process of Exile. In his many references to the issue, at times Rabbi Kook preferred not to specify whether this was a divine reflection of *Knesset Yisrael* (the *Sefirah* of *Malkhut*), or the nineteenth-century Romantic concept of the "national spirit." In my estimation, he did so in order to leave the interpretive horizons for his writings open. In the manifest stratum, however, not only are there no signs of the religious metamorphosis from Exile to Redemption, it would seem that the opposite is the case. The contrast between the external and the inner is therefore double:

(1) On the one hand, the time of the Exile is difficult, and every day is harsher than its predecessor (manifest); on the other hand, the world develops and advances from day to day to its final Redemption (hidden).[75]

(2) On the one hand, the generation of Redemption lashes out at the values of religion (manifest); on the other, its inner driving force is the pure motive of seeking the Redemption (hidden).

The dual structure of history characterized Rabbi Kook's thought in different periods. In 1927, for instance, he wrote of "the great difference between the delusion that brings darkness to the world and the mysterious anticipation that always brings it the emanation of tremendous light, energy, and life."[76] The role of the intellectually, morally, and aesthetically perfect is to resolve the tension and bridge the gap. He therefore called the perfect the "masters of secrets."[77] This appellation refers mainly to Kabbalists and other

---

75 Ibid., 1:669 (vol. 1, 213).

76 Printed in M. Zuriel, *Otzrot ha-Re'ayah*, vol. 2 (Shaalvim, 2002), 1079.

77 *Shemonah Kevatzim* 1:669 (vol. 1, 213).

mystics, but also alludes to the ability to understand the concealed motive forces of the reality. Rabbi Kook had both of these meanings in mind, since it is the Kabbalists who uncover the inner meaning of existence. The role of the exceptional individual is the unification of the inner and the outer; he reveals the inner dimension of the reality, thus effecting harmony.

As for the second type of unification: in *Shemonah Kevatzim* Rabbi Kook fiercely opposes the argument that the national awakening was a result of secularization. For his part, he presented the paternalistic argument that those who argue for a secular source of this awakening are unaware of their profound and inner motives:[78] "They themselves do not know what they want." Rabbi Kook then provided a detailed description of the place of the saint:

> What must the righteous of the generation then do? To rebel against the spirit of the nation, even in speech, and to detest its treasures, is an impossible thing: the spirit of the Lord and the spirit of Israel are one and the same. Rather, they must toil exceedingly to reveal the light and the holy in the spirit of the nation, the light of God that is in within all these, until all those who possess those thoughts in the general spirit and all its assets will find that they actually stand embedded, enrooted, and living in the life of God, shining in the supernal holiness and might.[79]

The saint fights nothing. Rabbi Kook's starting point is not tragic; the righteous-hero does not wage war, out of pure valor, against all odds. Even before the saint is aware of his true self, he is naturally attracted to the light of *Ein-Sof*.[80] To the contrary, Rabbi Kook states that righteousness is consistent with the biological teaching of evolution and its cultural implications: the righteous individual is integrated in developmental processes, with the aim

---

[78] On the denial of substantial secularization in religious Zionist thought in general, see Schwartz, *Faith at the Crossroads*, 175-87.

[79] *Shemonah Kevatzim* 1:71 (vol. 1, 23).

[80] "There are many times in the life of the supreme holy princes in which they are not cognizant of themselves as a special personality, which has personal existence and content, and certainly desire, aspiration, and wishes. Then in that general trait there is no differentiation of individual, volitional, and free essence and will; rather, there is a general reality here, that is drawn by the streams of its brilliance after the light of *Ein-Sof*; the righteous one [brings] life to all life, light to all worlds" (*Olat Re'ayah*, vol. 1, 85).

of bringing the nation and the world to perfection.[81] The righteous one interacts with the world;[82] he is responsible for its mending;[83] his activity results in pardon for the iniquities of the generation's sinners.[84] Thus, the exceptional individual acts with the nation, and not against it.

What is the saint's activity in the national sphere? Faced with presumed substantial secularization, the saint engages in a process of revealing the inner essence. His basic assumption is that the inner motive of the *halutzim*, those building the Land of Israel, is a distinctly divine one. The saint does not confront the outer motive (secularization), he rather uncovers the inner motive force.

Rabbi Kook hardly detailed the social actions the saint must initiate in order to reveal the inner stratum of the members of the nation, and to unite their inner and outer strata. The saint's activity is intimate. Exposure and unification are components of the work of the world's mending and elevation, that is, the drawing down of the divine emanation into the worldly reality, which it fructifies. He refrained from openly depicting political and social activity; at the most, he spoke of the need for literary activity. Rabbi Kook frequently advanced the argument that passive influence is the central mode of influence of the perfect individuals. Additionally, "the sanctity of the Land of Israel" aids in the saint's mending of the world.[85]

Clearly, the saint is gifted with a penetrating and comprehensive view of the inner motives of psychological and historical processes. He therefore succeeds in uniting the inner essence with its outer expressions. Attention

---

81   "The calculation is simple: since everything develops beneficially, then everything ascends, and similarly, all is prepared for the banquet and for complete good. Satisfaction from the reality is manifest, and supernal lovingkindness is poured into the entire fullness of the soul. This is the orientation of the good attribute of the righteous, whose labor is the love of God and the love of the world and all people" (*Shemonah Kevatzim* 1:511 [vol. 1, 164]). The "banquet" is an allusion to the banquet that the Lord will prepare for the righteous in the future.

82   The biography of the exceptional individual is also the biography of the reality. Rabbi Kook writes: "All thoughts and ideas, the great desires, the tremendous tests that are experienced by each righteous one in his individual soul, they all are experienced by the nation in its entirety, generally by humankind in its entirety, and even more generally by the world in its entirety, and all the worlds" (ibid., 1:598 [vol. 1, 190]).

83   Ibid., 1:638 (vol. 1, 202).

84   Ibid., 2:338 (vol. 1, 399).

85   Ibid., 3:367 (vol. 2, 128).

should be paid to Rabbi Kook's understanding of the problematic nature of the dialogue and persuasive efforts with the Second Aliyah generation. His works accordingly mention the need for "preachers" and "scribes" who are capable of addressing the educated. Regarding the charismatic group that is driven by heavenly emanation, he mentioned the visionary and the prophet, who are entrusted with the nation's moral situation.

Praxis

The metaphysical and mystical tasks imposed on the saint are the unification of the manifold, the mending of the rift between inner and outer, and the extraction of the holy from within the impure. These duties are conducted mainly in the personal drama between the saint and his God. In the intimate realm, far from the public eye, the saint perseveres in his struggles and his special labor. Notwithstanding this, there are also communal and national aspects to the missions imposed on the saint. The task of presenting complex metaphysical content to the public in understandable language is an example of such a clearly personal aspect. "In our generation, whoever has an all-encompassing soul must engage in introductions, in the clarification of keys to every sublime manner."[86] The saint is to make two topics accessible to the public at large: belief and morality.

Rabbi Kook thought that, ultimately, the saint is to be the true leader. The "inner" task of uniting the internal and the external in the nation becomes an external mission; he is to lead the people. I mentioned earlier the Degel Yerushalayim movement. A few years earlier, Rabbi Kook had asserted that the secular leaders, who are motivated by principles and ideals and who have a divine inner core ("point of sanctity"), will eventually be replaced by the saints:

> Instead of strength being manifest in the beginning, in the form of *tohu* [the primeval unformed],[87] it will be taken from the wicked and given to the righteous, those who are mighty as lions, who will

---

86   Ibid., 1:683 (vol. 1, 217).

87   The soul of the wicked is "from the lights of *tohu*" (ibid., 1:683 [vol. 1, 217]). In another passage he states that these souls are "higher than the souls of *tikkun* [i.e., those in the world that has been mended; a notion from Lurianic Kabbalah]" (ibid., 1:297 [vol. 1, 107]).

reveal the veracity of the mending and building with the fierce spirit of clear and brave intellect, and with the inner bravery of sentiment and fixed and clear revelation.[88]

Rabbi Kook held the idealistic generation in great esteem, although, ultimately, it will be the activity of the saints that will lead to the final realization of the utopian world.

Significantly, Rabbi Kook frequently used such terms as "strength" and "courage." The righteous and the supreme individuals are "mighty creatures."[89] The saint has "the strength to rule," and "all the powers of Creation submit to his word."[90] Rabbi Kook emphasized that the terminology of strength and power refers to both spiritual and material strength.[91] The ideal that he set before himself is a model of the saint as spiritual, military, and political leader. There is tension between such an ideal and the passive influence of the saint, to which Rabbi Kook ascribed much importance. The following passage by Rabbi Kook places the saint's tension in proper perspective:

> There are some mendings of the world that cannot be performed by the righteous, but rather by the wicked and people who are flawed in opinions and deeds. By repentance out of love[92] and the exertion of great effort to increase holiness in the world, by the sincere prayer of the righteous, the righteous, too, will be able to participate in such mendings, that, in the usual course of affairs, can be effected only by the wicked and those who are distant from holiness. These mendings include social mendings, such as implements for working the land, wars, of which there are some that are greatly needed in the world, practical inventions. Others of them are spiritual mendings, of several practical and theoretical wisdoms into which the soul that is adorned with pietism and the elevation of the soul for holiness cannot penetrate. It is only by the great ascent of the spiritual process that this supreme blessing can be attained, that of the appropriation

---

[88] Ibid., 1:243 (vol. 1, 91).

[89] Ibid., 1:520 (vol. 1, 166); 1:540 (vol. 1, 173), and many more.

[90] *Ein Ayah*, Berakhot, vol. 1, 18.

[91] See *Shemonah Kevatzim* 1:251 (vol. 1, 95); see Garb, *Chosen Will Become Herds*, 41-43.

[92] That is, the repentance from love of the righteous. In another passage, Rabbi Kook wrote that by merit of repentance "all the sins become merits" (*Shemonah Kevatzim* 3:32 [vol. 2, 23]).

[literally, conquest] of all the improvements of the world by the righteous and the holy.[93]

Rabbi Kook specifies the fields in which the saint does not participate naturally: agriculture, army, and modern technology. He had no reservations about presenting these domains as dominated by the wicked and the ignorant (of Torah). Like other religious Zionist thinkers, he was aware that the effort of establishing a political entity included agriculture, an army, and technology.[94] Rabbi Kook was silent regarding the ways in which saints participate in these material realms, whether they were to actively participate, or to lay the spiritual foundation that facilitated material activity. It seems to me that the saints' participation in this activity was limited to prayer and theurgic and magical activity (i.e., drawing down the divine emanation). The saint seeks to appropriate these fields, too, as the end of the passage appears to teach, but, in most instances, his activity is to bring about the elevation of the world by means of his intimate activity. Such a saint looks upon "practical matters," as he puts it, "from above, [looking] down."[95] If he nevertheless is forced to be involved, in any fashion, in practical matters that are not under his control, then he experiences a descent from his lofty level.[96]

This teaches that the true drama of the saint is played out within his inner world, and his actual influence is by means of his intimate struggles. In this respect, Rabbi Kook maintained the fundamental paradox of the saint, namely, that his power ensues from his very relinquishing of power.[97] To be precise, we can now state that the saint is caught between his aspirations and his awareness of his tangible limitations. Rabbi Kook writes in numerous passages that the saint possesses self-awareness. He is cognizant of the special structure of his soul and his capabilities. A saint who does not believe in his abilities will ultimately fail.[98] Those passages,

---

93   Ibid., 2:191 (vol. 1, 349).

94   See Schwartz, *Faith at the Crossroads*, 140-51.

95   *Shemonah Kevatzim* 2:300 (vol. 1, 384).

96   Ibid., 2:335 (vol. 1, 398).

97   See Wyschogrod, *Saints and Postmodernism*, 57-58.

98   See, e.g., *Shemonah Kevatzim* 8:46 (vol. 3, 257); *Kevatzim*, vol. 2, 125. Rabbi Kook addresses his own soul with the call to "Know your worth" (*Shemonah Kevatzim* 8:69 [vol. 3, 264]).

however, almost invariably speak of self-assurance and the recognition of special faculties and his singularity. However, in his discussion of the praxis, Rabbi Kook focused on self-awareness in the sense of placing boundaries and being aware of limits.

Summation

Rabbi Kook's understanding of his time as the messianic era necessitated the refashioning of the image of the saint. Two dominant factors shape the discussion of the national saint:

(1) Adaptation: the altruistic and functional characteristics (the elevation of souls, the channeling of the divine emanation), on the one hand, and on the other, the ontological distinctions between the saint and all that lies beyond him were funneled into the new situation in which the Jewish people, and actually, the entire universe, found itself.

(2) Expansion: holiness spreads to many among the Jewish people (to some, in potential). Altruism almost becomes a national characteristic. "The faithful of the Chosen People [...] live and suffer for all the handiwork [of God]."[99]

Nor did Rabbi Kook refrain from drawing connections between the saint and the Messiah. He wrote: "Every righteous one [who is] an everlasting foundation [see Proverbs 10:25], wherever he is, whether revealed or hidden, constantly redeems the souls of all people; he is the Messiah of the God of Jacob."[100] Rabbi Kook's writings are marked by the tension between the public and leadership dimension of the saint and his intimate worship. Rabbi Kook tended to transfer the saint's political and messianic drama to the inner realm, that of mendings and the elevation of the souls of the generation. Whatever his place, the saint is not measured by the classical criteria of sainthood.

---

[99]   *Shemonah Kevatzim* 7:94 (vol. 3, 176).

[100] Following II Samuel 23:1; the passage is taken from ibid., 6:263 (vol. 3, 98). See also S. Cherlow, "Messianism and the Messiah in the Circle of Rav Kook," *Moreshet Israel* 2 (2006): 42-87 [Hebrew].

Chapter Seven

MORAL AND AESTHETIC TASKS

The saint in Rabbi Kook's thought is purposeful. He acts in accordance with his goals, and he fulfills what is incumbent on him by force of his responsibility and perfection. We saw in the preceding discussion that his national tasks are an important motive force for the perfect individual's religious, social, theurgic, and magical activity. While the influence of this activity is important, we should also take into account the influence of the saint's sweeping personality, which is a source of inspiration of lovingkindness and love for his environment. Thus far we have been occupied with the central task imposed on the saint, namely, the mending of the world in the ontological plane (the elevation of the sparks, and the advancement of the nation and the world to their final redemption). Along with this mission, however, the saint is engaged in the attainment of additional aims, as we will see below.

Contending with Evil

The saint contends with evil on the level of cognition and action. Rabbi Kook was aware of two classical metaphysical models as he wrestled with the question of evil: one, the Neoplatonian concept of evil as negation, and the other, the substantial concept of evil. In the first understanding, evil has no independent existence, and in effect, the world is fundamentally good. Evil appears as the good (that is, the spiritual reality) disappears. Thus, evil is a negation. The second notion has the source of evil in the divine world, in the domain of the shells. According to this, evil is a self-standing reality that is identified with a certain aspect of the supernal reality.

The saint's activity can be defined by these two conceptions. Rabbi Kook wrote:

The supreme contemplators,[1] who are girdled with constant lovingkindness,[2] are aware of the ugliness in evil more thoroughly than those whose spirit is ruled by anger and irritability. Due to their knowledge that evil cannot exist by itself in the world, they do not fear to stand against it with the greatness [*gedulah*] of their inner soul, and they draw from its inner essence all the good points within it. Since their eyes are always open to seek the good point, no hatred of people can rule them. For in every place they find the good point, they hold its value in greater esteem than any object, and in the brilliance of its greatness it covers all the ugliness in evil, to the extent that it cannot be seen by them to leave some impression of impatience and a paucity of love.[3] Accordingly, the great of soul are the righteous, the progenitors [or: prototypes] of lovingkindness in the world, and their love of every creature is endless. Specifically because of the great godly love in their hearts, they walk with all law,[4] and they are capable of fortifying the standing of the world, to manifest its points of goodness by the toil of their body and spirit; it is they who are the servants of the Lord, who are as the angels on high, who strive to do good and kind deeds,[5] peace and justice,[6] with all their heart and with all their soul. It is they who establish the world on the basis of righteousness and morality, directing to it the radiant countenance from on high[7] with all the force of their refinement.[8]

This passage seemingly offers a routine version of the labor of the extraction and elevation of the sparks, while presenting a few details regarding the saint and his activity.

First and foremost, the saint reacts to evil by contemplation. He is distinguished from other leaders in that they respond emotionally (irritation,

---

[1] Above (Chapter Six, n. 9) we discussed the value of the anticipation of salvation, and explained that, for Rabbi Kook, the anticipation is greater than the realization.

[2] See Isaiah 11:5; see also Rabbi Jacob Zevi Jolles, *Kehilat Yaakov* (Lemberg, 1870), fol. 7c.

[3] That is, evil completely vanishes, without leaving any trace.

[4] "*Mishpat,*" referring to the Kabbalistic concept of *din*.

[5] Following Proverbs 21:21.

[6] Following Zechariah 8:16.

[7] That is, the divine emanation comes down to the world by merit of the practice of justice and morality. See *Mekhilta, Vayisa* 2 (ed. Horovitz-Rabin, 162 l. 13).

[8] *Shemonah Kevatzim* 3:189 (vol. 2, 76-77).

anger), while the saint's response is cognitive. Rabbi Kook consequently elected to call the righteous one a "supreme contemplator [*mistakel elyon*]." The cognitive or contemplative response expresses the saint's tremendous self-control. This initial contemplation reveals the substantial dimension of evil, and the "contemplator" uncovers evil's hideous basis.

Second, the saint's response is cognitive and contemplative. He is aware that no substantial evil exists in the world. God created a world that is good, and any evil is merely accidental. And this is why the saint does not fear to face evil. Here, too, the saint's sentiment, that is, his courage, is fashioned in accordance with his worldview. Courage is needed in the face of the "hatred of people." Additionally, the routing of evil has a clearly cognitive factor: the uncovering of the good overshadows evil, so that it is so shunted aside and is no longer visible.

Third, the saint's response is flexible, according to the dialectical situation in which he finds himself. He is motivated by the endless lovingkindness and love that he emanates, but the result of his activity is strict judgment ("law"—*mishpat*). He channels the emanation of lovingkindness to the ways of strict judgment, in order to reveal the good and effect the disappearance of evil.

Once again, the saint is presented as the one who is responsible for the divine emanation in this world, and in this context his activity is of a dual nature: in the first stage, he is responsible for preparing to receive the emanation, this disposition consisting of establishing the values of justice and morality in the world. In the second phase, he brings down the emanation by means of his theurgic activity. In this manner, he routs the evil in the world.

Moral Knowledge

Morality is unquestionably the primary characteristic of the saint. One question that arises is: do the saint's moral criteria differ essentially from those of the ordinary person, or do they share the same basis, to which the saint, specifically, is totally loyal? Rabbi Kook did not answer this directly. Another question is whether the saint's sources of morality, and his moral authority, are the same as those of any other individual. An examination of Rabbi Kook's moral conception in relation to the saint emphasizes the superiority of revelation over cognition and moral intuition. The saint is characterized by heavenly inspiration and emanation, and it is only natural that the message he brings is that of godly morality, the foundations of which are described in revelation. Rabbi Kook writes:

> Philosophy, that attained the general moral law of the world—and this is the entire basis of its knowledge of the divine—cannot reach the individual depth, how all the moral quality and quantity in a person's soul is derived from this supernal law, which are intertwined with each other, like the beams [...] that come forth from the sun. The freedom of will and choice, and the aspects of necessity within it, regarding both man and the world, all are intertwined in the wonderful dispositions that are being revealed in their finest details in the counsel of the Lord for those who fear Him (Psalms 25:14). The wisdom of the fear of the Lord, that penetrates to all the depths of life, and the great light of the divine communion of the righteous, the mighty creatures[9] and the true servants of the Lord, in might and in holiness—He shows them these secrets in a manner that penetrates the profundities of the truth, which is unparalleled among all the intellective discoveries in the world, but is only in the counsel of the Lord for those who fear Him, but He is intimate with the straightforward (Proverbs 3:32).[10]

Rabbi Kook refers here to the Kantian and post-Kantian philosophies that based the conception of God on morality. For Kant, God is merely a "regulative idea" that develops from within the moral conception.[11] This Kantian approach also made a deep impression on Jewish thought in the nineteenth century, and Rabbi Kook was probably aware of it from the summaries present in Hebrew books, journals, and newspapers. Rabbi Kook maintained that these philosophical notions do not provide a complete explanation for the soul's moral activity. Philosophers are incapable of explicating moral principles ("quality") and their details and realization ("quantity"). In contrast, the righteous, who absorb the supernal inspiration, are capable of depicting the moral activity of the soul

9   See Psalms 103:20.
10 *Shemonah Kevatzim* 6:278 (vol. 3, 103).
11 The criticism that Rabbi Kook leveled at this conception in the continuation of this passage is not directly relevant to the topic of our discussion. On Rabbi Kook's conception of morality, see, e.g., N. Rotenstreich, *Studies in Jewish Philosophy in the Modern Period* (Tel Aviv, 1978), 41-55; on the righteous individual, see ibid., 53 [Hebrew].

in all its detail, and of deriving from the moral elements ("dispositions"—
konaniyyot) the balance between necessity and choice. They can follow the
application of the moral principles in man's mental structure. The moral
role of the righteous individual is an additional example of his contribution
to the public.

Creativity

We saw above that the genius is characterized by his creativity, a faculty
that is also a drive. "Whoever has the soul of a creator, must create ideas
and thoughts."[12] Creativity has an aesthetic dimension, and the imagination
is an important mental source of artistic creativity. Rabbi Kook stated that
"the righteous one's imaginative faculty is replete with true wisdom,[13] and
effects tangible actions in the world, for wisdom and might unite within
him."[14]

Additionally, the saint's creative faculty sets tasks for him. During the
period that Rabbi Kook served as rabbi in Bausk, he composed the poem
"*Mas'at Nafshi*" (My Soul's Yearning), in which he formulated his hope and
longing to author ramified and popular literary works. He portrayed the
creative process from the germination of the idea to the dissemination of
books. He truly believed that literary writing would aid in gathering the
exceptional individuals to him, to create a circle of outstanding Torah
scholars. He wrote:

> And from the points[15] of my thoughts
> That will be gathered into flocks,
> I will take[16] my letters
> and they will become articles [*ma'amarim*].

---

12 *Shemonah Kevatzim* 7:190 (vol. 3, 229). Rabbi Kook compared the creative faculty with
    "Talmud," that is concerned with repetition.
13 Rabbi Kook might be alluding to the mythical and symbolic nature of Kabbalah.
14 *Kevatzim*, vol. 2, 172.
15 Rabbi Kook alluded in the poem to the emanation from *Hokhmah* ("point") to *Yesod*, which is
    the righteous one ("letter," which appears with multifaceted meaning).
16 In the 1917 version: "[my letters] will be taken."

And the articles, joined together,[17]
Will become books,
And the books in every city
Will be scattered.
To them [my books] will be gathered
The remnants[18] from my people,
Who are very few,
Only individuals.[19]

We saw above that an important literary mission imposed on the "individuals" and "remnants" consists of addressing the masses by writing introductions, in understandable and detailed language, to literature that is thought to be complicated, especially the Kabbalistic literature. This task is both literary and social. Rabbi Kook believed that the elect are to engage in literary writing, in the sense of explaining complex matters in understandable and detailed language. He felt that such writing must relate to the experience. He wrote:

> In order to develop literature with original true and holy content, the thinkers whose ideas issue from the holy source must accustom themselves to detailed thought. The great flood with which the holy light inundates the soul causes the things that originate in the supernal emanation to be opaque; the literary expositions do not offer detail, and accordingly, the world remains and wonders, without knowing what is the content about which those who perceive the holy knowledge lecture. Consequently, all the influence remains based on the inner sentiment, that remains dormant for the entire masses, and based on the heavenly breadth of vision of the exceptional individuals, that is hidden from the entire congregation,[20] until they set this forth in detail bit by bit.[21]

That is, the saint experiences the descent of the heavenly emanation from the divine source ("the supernal emanation"—*atzilut elyonah*) and its

---

17 That is, the assembling of the articles into a collection; following Exodus 26:4, 10.
18 An appellation for the exceptional individuals; see above.
19 *Orot ha-Re'ayah*, 29.
20 Following Leviticus 4:13.
21 *Shemonah Kevatzim* 3:285 (vol. 2, 103-4). See BT Pesahim 39b, 111b; Avodah Zarah 30b.

absorption in his soul. The saint formulates his experiences in mystical language replete with interconnected symbols and contexts, but this language is not accessible to the masses. Accordingly, the perfect individual is tasked with translating the message of this experience for the broad public. He therefore needs a faculty for flowing, understandable, and detailed ("bit by bit") literary writing. Significantly, the aesthetic literary task is meant to bring the world of the perfect individual closer to the public at large. Before the literary detailing, the saint's connection with the public is intuitive and emotional ("the inner sentiment"); after this detailing, the two join together. This is one of the ways in which the saint elevates the entire world. Thus, according to Rabbi Kook, the moral and the aesthetic, either together or separately, adapt the image of the saint to the contemporary reality.

Chapter Eight

Antinomianism

The antinomian conception appears a number of times in Rabbi Kook's thought, especially in his personal, aphoristic passages. Such a conception naturally comes into play in the figure of the saint. One of religious law's important goals is to refine man, who possesses urges and deficiencies. A person on the level of the saint, who has achieved maximal equilibrium, seemingly would have no need for such a law.[1] At times, the law is even seen as limiting the saint's spirit of freedom. Rabbi Kook's thought advances additional considerations, such as the commandments that relate to details, while the saint has reached the level of generality. We will examine the system of considerations that leads to the attribution of antinomianism to the image of the saint in the thought of Rabbi Kook.

Principles

Antinomianism is generally based on a hierarchical perception of the religious act. According to this view, some religious mandates are of greater importance, and are not to be waived, while others, in certain circumstances, need not be fulfilled ("*aseh*"—positive commandments) or may be transgressed ("*lo ta'aseh*"—prohibitions). In a passage in *Shemonah Kevatzim*, Rabbi Kook based antinomianism on such a hierarchy:

> The special ones among men, who possess the inclination to knowledge of the Lord, must be immersed in this more than in all the disciplines of the Torah and wisdom in the world, and they

---

[1] On the types of antinomianism, see I. Twersky, "Concerning Maimonides' Rationalization of the Commandments; an Explication of *Hilkot Me'ilah*, VIII:8," in *Studies in the History of Jewish Society*, ed. I. Etkes and Y. Salmon (Jerusalem, 1980), 32-33 [Hebrew]; Schwartz, *Fourteenth Century Neoplatonic Circle*, 246-49; see also Cherlow, *The Tzaddiq*, 197-98.

must not regress from their level for any reason in the world, not even if it seems to them that by their absorption in knowledge of the Lord they lose several matters relating to the practice of the commandments and the knowledge of the Torah, or that they are not fulfilling their obligations regarding worldly occupation [*derekh eretz*]. For all the practical and Torah perfection is merely direction to bring a person to that supreme trait of seeking knowledge of the Lord; and when a person has already reached such an exalted level, far be it from him to abandon major holiness and occupy himself with minor holiness. It is certain that [by] the supernal illumination of his soul [*neshamah*], that is truly immersed in the light of the Lord, all the paths of knowledge will be expanded for him, and his heart will be filled with the light of righteousness and the welfare of humanity[2] until he will find blessing and the broadness of mind to be very successfully occupied with true holiness, also in the practical part of the Torah and worldly occupation, much more than those who are engrossed solely in the practical matters, who have not reached that attribute of true thirst for the knowledge of the Lord.[3]

In this passage Rabbi Kook discusses "the knowledge of God [*da'at Elohim*]" as intellectual pursuit and discipline, to which the perfect ones must devote their entire attention. What is the knowledge of God? Two passages earlier in *Shemonah Kevatzim*, Rabbi Kook explained that it is possible to extract and elevate the holy sparks from the depths of impurity by "communion with God and the knowledge of God."[4] He maintained that the praxis of the knowledge of God consists of surveying the general philosophical and theological methods and approaches, and deriving their positive elements. Such a process is patently intellectual, and relies on expertise and access to conceptual writings. As such, the knowledge of God is "higher than any knowledge."[5] It contains a religious, Jewish, and Kabbalistic critique of the sciences and ideas. We can easily understand that this is a task to which the perfect man must devote himself totally, as a sort of polymath who is

2   See BT Sanhedrin 24b; *Genesis Rabbah* 13:1. Rabbi Kook used these symbols to describe a process of emanation within the soul: *Da'at* ("knowledge of God"), *Tiferet* ("true holiness"), and *Malkhut* ("the light of righteousness"). Eventually, the process of Sefirotic emanation influences this world, as the end of the passage indicates.

3   *Shemonah Kevatzim* 1:80 (vol. 1, 25-26); see Garb, *Chosen Will Become Herds*, 77-78.

4   *Shemonah Kevatzim* 1:78 (vol. 1, 25).

5   Ibid., 1:79 (vol. 1, 25).

fluent in the range of knowledge of his time, from which he extracts the positive elements.[6] Additionally, this is refined knowledge that morally and religiously elevates the one occupied with it.

The ideal of the acquisition of knowledge and the extraction of its true content demands a person's full personality and time. Rabbi Kook undoubtedly relied on the process of the extraction of the sparks in Lurianic Kabbalah. He incorporated in this framework a rationalist Maimonidean outlook that speaks of the ideal of acquiring all the sciences and total dedication to this end. Maimonides accordingly adopted an ascetic worldview in which the perfect man undertakes a certain degree of abstinence in order to devote himself to the ideal of knowledge.[7] In this spirit, Rabbi Kook argued that the individual who devotes himself to the acquisition of knowledge does so while forgoing the observance of some commandments, or the study of certain halakhic topics, and the like. Rabbi Kook wrote in the beginning of the above passage that the perfect individual fears ("it seems"—*yitdameh*) lest his devotion to the study of ideas will cause him to miss "the practice of the commandments," "the knowledge of the Torah," or "worldly occupation"; while in the continuation of the passage, this concern becomes a fact. The perfect individual is occupied with "major holiness [*kodesh hamur*]," and has no time for "minor holiness [*kodesh kal*]." Here, antinomianism generates a hierarchy of the degrees of holiness.

In this passage, Rabbi Kook depicted the two stages of the process experienced by the perfect individual who has attained such an "exalted level [*midah elyonah*]":

(1) "major holiness": full occupation with the knowledge of God, namely, the clarification and extraction of general philosophical and theological ideas;

---

6   In the following passage Rabbi Kook states that the content of the knowledge of God includes "the great meditation of Torah and of wisdom, all the wisdom [i.e., science] of the world and the wisdom of life, all the natural uprightness of morality and of culture, and every disposition of the body's strength and the soul's might" (ibid., 1:80 [vol. 1, 26]). He thereby adapts the Maimonidean ideal to his time.

7   On the ascetic rationalist tradition, see D. Schwartz, "Ethics and Asceticism in the Neoplatonic School of the 14th Century," in *Between Religion and Ethics*, ed. A. Sagi and D. Statman (Ramat Gan, 1993), 185-208 [Hebrew].

(2) "minor holiness": the return to matters that had been perceived as insignificant, and the presentation of their profound meaning.

The experience of the perfect man can be compared to Plato's cave metaphor. The saint experiences a situation of ascent, in which he extracts ideas and disregards common norms. After being in the heights of this experience, he returns to the norms, in which he discovers profundities, that are so deep that they cannot be experienced by anyone has not gone on this intellectual journey.

An additional principle that Rabbi Kook adopted in an antinomian context is that the Torah addresses the collective.[8] At times, therefore, for some individual or other, "the observance of the Torah will weigh heavy upon him, and he must toil as a slave in order to mend the collective, for preventing separation from the collective builds it."[9] In the end, the result of the inner struggle within such an individual contributes to the collective's strength and empowerment. By the same coin, however, this principle provides an opening for antinomianism.

Double Behavior

Generally speaking, the saint seemingly leads a double life. On the one hand, he participates in active life, while on the other, his mind is in the upper worlds. Such tension is portrayed in the last chapters of Maimonides' *Guide*. At times there is severe dissonance between the saint's outer appearance and his deep inner consciousness.[10] Involvement in active life represses inspiration and sanctity. Sometimes, however, inspiration and sanctity come to dominate the perfect man, and then he lives a supernal life. In such a state, religious behavior assumes a completely different meaning. Rabbi Kook wrote about the value of the perfect man's Torah study and prayer:

---

[8]   See E. S. Rosenthal, "'For the Most Part,'" *P'raqim: Yearbook of the Schocken Institute ...* 1 (1967-1968): 183-224 [Hebrew]. A few responses to this classic essay have been written.

[9]   *Kevatzim*, vol. 1, 100.

[10] *Kevatzim*, vol. 1, 177.

At times the righteous one must learn much and pray much, while at other times a very small amount suffices, to express the veracity of the focus of his holy aspirations. At yet other times all he must do is think and feel, and then he ascends from every vocal expression and speech.[11]

Great righteous ones must know and be cognizant of the light of the Lord that dwells within them.[12] At times they cannot engage in Torah [study], nor in prayer or the commandments, because the supernal holiness that emanates upon them seeks to spread. All their talk then is truly Torah,[13] all their wants and propensity is prayer, and all their movement is a commandment. The supreme inner light, that is both concealed and revealed in all these, vivifies the entire Torah, all prayer, and all the commandments of their entire generation, and on occasion, of several generations, before and after them. Say of the righteous, that it shall be well with him (Isaiah 3:10).[14]

Rabbi Kook checkered the second passage with terms such as "appearance [hofa'ah]" and "spread [hitpashtut]." That is, the perfect individual draws down the divine emanation by his active divine service, namely, the observance of the commandments. At times, however, the emanation appears thanks to the saint's exceptional personality. Then he does not require Torah study or commandments—or, in other words, "magical" means for bringing down the emanation. The antinomian behavior of saints becomes a metaphor for the commandments. Their talk is Torah, their desire is prayer, and their movement is commandment. Furthermore, the value of the emanation of the saint at the time when he does not fulfill the commandments imparts significance to the normative behavior of the generation in the past, the present, and the future. Paradoxically, antinomianism becomes a source for the fulfillment of the law, to which it imparts meaning. The saint's breach of the law is its fulfillment by the public at large.

---

[11] *Kevatzim*, vol. 2, 172.

[12] See Leviticus 16:16; Numbers 5:3. The self-awareness of the righteous individual was discussed above, the end of Chapter Six.

[13] See BT Sukkah 21b; Avodah Zarah 19b.

[14] *Shemonah Kevatzim* 8:76 (vol. 3, 265-66). Cf. Cherlow, *The Tzaddiq*, 198, who bases the antinomian conception on "situations of spiritual tension."

134   Chapter Eight

Universality

We saw in the preceding discussions that generalization and generality are not only a distinct faculty of the saint, they also characterize his entire existence. Thus, in Rabbi Kook's thought, universality is, to some degree, an antinomian factor. The perfect man seeks to attain the infinite and inclusive light of the divine heights, and therefore limitation, allotment, and restriction are foreign to him. Rabbi Kook presented this general inclination of some saints:

> There are wise righteous ones such as these, whose mind and heart and all their vitality is always full of thoughts of and desires for the divine. Because of this, they are incapable of bringing anything limited into their soul [*nefesh*], nor to establish for themselves fixed studies, and the exclusive occupation with limited actions, even the most holy, is extremely difficult for them, because of the measure in things that are inherently bounded.[15]

The fulfillment of the halakhah and occupation with its ramifications are particularistic. If generalization is the true reality, and general cognitions are the whole ones, then occupation with details loses its importance. Rabbi Kook set forth the focus on detail as temptation: "There are those of clear cognition and great righteous ones who, out of their great desire for clear and abstract cognitions, and true communion with the Lord, may He be blessed, cannot fill [literally, expand] their thought with the details of halakhot and individual actions."[16] He took care not to discuss practice, and spoke only of the study of halakhah. There is, however, no reason to distinguish between the details of study and those of practice; Torah study is perceived as a commandment and as an act.

Temptation

Antinomianism is a temptation for the saint. The saint is portrayed as a vulnerable figure, who is constantly subject to temptations, dangers, and

---

[15] *Kevatzim*, vol. 1, 215.

[16] *Shemonah Kevatzim* 1:212 (vol. 1, 83). See C. Kohat, "The Distress of the Torah Lerner in Rav Kook's Philosophy," in *Iggud: Selected Essays in Jewish Studies* 1 (2008): 407-28 [Hebrew].

stumbling blocks. Ascent to the level of universality does not guarantee constancy, and greatness does not lessen vulnerability. On the contrary, the vast distance between the saint and sin requires his "superb guarding" of himself, since he is unaware of the great danger posed by sin.[17] At times the imagination and the bad qualities lie in wait for the saint's communion with God, and sometimes society weakens the saint and threatens his communion with the divine.[18] The saint, too, repents for the flaws in his soul, and does not always succeed in mending them.[19] From a certain view, the saint's life is one of repentance,[20] since he is a man of perfection. Even if his communion is not perfect, he repents. For example, if the saint experiences communion with God that is characterized solely by love, without the dimension of fear, or the reverse, he feels the need to repent; and even if the combination of love and fear was not balanced and precise, he repents for this "flaw."[21] Rabbi Kook thereby distinguished between complete righteous ones and those of a "repentant nature."[22] The ethos of "Ashkenazi Orthodoxy" (i.e., those opposed to Hasidism) is suitable for the former, and for the latter, the way of Hasidism, which is dynamic and lively.

Moreover, the more exalted the saint, the greater the temptations that face him. "When the general power of life is great and bold, so, too, is the bad part within it, as the inner content of everyone who is greater than his fellow: his inclination is greater than [that of] the other."[23] Worldliness, that is, involvement in worldly affairs, is a stumbling block in the path of the perfect individual.[24] It is only after he has sufficiently ascended that

[17] *Shemonah Kevatzim* 3:342 (vol. 2, 121).

[18] See, e.g., ibid., 1:257 (vol. 1, 96-97); 1:389 (vol. 1, 131). The standing of the imaginative faculty was discussed a few times above, mainly in reference to its negative aspect. This negative aspect, however, is anchored in its positive aspect: the exceptional individuals' imaginative power is great, and they therefore see visions. "The imaginative power of those of great cognition is very great and sublime, and it is connected with the most general visions in the reality" (ibid., 1:721 [vol. 1, 331]). The standing of the imagination, therefore, is dialectical: its great power is the source of its inherent danger.

[19] Ibid., 1:300 (vol. 1, 107-8). See also *Kevatzim*, vol. 1, 169.

[20] *Shemonah Kevatzim* 1:353 (vol. 1, 121); 3:191 (vol. 2, 77).

[21] Ibid., 6:169 (vol. 3, 59).

[22] Ibid., 5:62 (vol. 2, 218).

[23] BT Sukkah 52a; *Shemonah Kevatzim* 1:258 (vol. 1, 97).

[24] "The righteous must pass through a river of fire [*dinur*; see Daniel 7:10] in order to obliterate

he will succeed in transforming this worldliness into an expression of holiness. Rabbi Kook included, among the material temptations, the sexual temptation, which may be overcome by means of "the intellective mission [ha-teudah ha-sikhlit]"[25] and the elevation of "all the desires and all the cravings of the entire world."[26] Consequently, the life of the saint is dynamic and lively, and consists of overcoming temptations. The existence of the saint is characterized by ascents and descents.

Freedom

Rabbi Kook devoted much thought to the meaning of freedom.[27] Liberation from limits is a central characteristic of the perfect individual. Rabbi Kook frequently mentioned his own personal need not to be subject to the rules of reason, the laws of science, and so on. This writing is typically personal and revealing. "Do not close me up in any cage, neither material nor spiritual";[28] "Why should I afflict my soul [neshamah], that seeks freedom; if it feels itself to be a free agent, why should I place the bonds of affliction on its legs?"[29] Limitation of thought is "great cruelty" to the soul.[30] Generally speaking, the righteous are the "free ones in the world."[31]

One of the dimensions to which he constantly alludes in his writings is the contrast between the value of freedom, on the one hand, and religious institutionalization (that is, the theoretical study of the halakhah and its practical application), or, at the least, the friction between them, on the other. Rabbi Kook spoke of the study of halakhah in the following passages:

---

the images of this world" (*Shemonah Kevatzim* 6:27 [vol. 3, 12]). On the connection between the river of fire and the fire of Gehinnom, see, e.g., BT Hagigah 13b.

25 *Shemonah Kevatzim* 1:329 (vol. 1, 117).

26 Ibid., 8:114 (vol. 3, 279).

27 See Ish-Shalom, *Between Rationalism and Mysticism*, 100-8.

28 *Shemonah Kevatzim* 3:279 (vol. 2, 102).

29 Following Psalms 107:10; the passage is from ibid., 8:115 (vol. 3, 319). Rabbi Kook mentioned here the *neshamah*, which is the highest level of the soul. The relationship between the parts of the soul causes suffering.

30 *Shemonah Kevatzim* 6:98 (vol. 3, 35).

31 Ibid., 4:124 (vol. 2, 179).

At times the speculative sweep of vision, which is above any limited reason, and certainly [above] any fixed applied halakhah, arises within man, and then his heart aspires to the heights, and he in no wise is capable of binding his soul within designated studies.[32]

The great soul, by its nature, cannot be confined within details, whether the details of thought or those of deed, and feels great affliction under this yoke. At any rate, at times it must endure affliction and struggle to study Torah [i.e., in its details];[33] the details are inscribed within it, and afterwards it senses within them great freedom and very awesome general pleasantness.[34]

At times free initiative is curtailed by institutionalization. Rabbi Kook contrasted freedom with timidity out of conservative religious reasons. He wrote, in a personal tone:

My soul [neshamah] is broad, great, and mighty. I sense my magnificence [tifereti] and the majesty [hadar] of my soul within me,[35] I am filled with valor and freedom. The cowardice that dresses itself in the garb of fear of Heaven cannot deceive me.[36]

Rabbi Kook used the words "freedom," "magnificence," and "majesty" to express the emanation within the soul (Binah, Tiferet, and Malkhut, respectively). Emanation requiring preparation or a substrate in which it will be absorbed is a central Kabbalistic principle. At times this substrate is called a "vessel" (keli). The underlying meaning of this passage is that the soul's containment of the emanation is dependent on freedom, with its antiestablishment dimension. Following the establishment does not

---

[32] Ibid., 1:151 (vol. 1, 59). Here, the antinomian inclination is a consequence of freedom. Rabbi Kook, however, also attributed the objection to studying halakhah, or to the inclination to do so, to the nature of the saint. The halakhah is based on unyielding strict judgment, while the saint is all lovingkindness and love (see above). He wrote: "There are such great righteous ones who are above any root of strict judgment and therefore are incapable of studying any halakhic matter. When they overcome their nature and engage in the profundity of halakhah, they ascend to a great and unfathomable level, and they ameliorate judgments in their root" (Kevatzim, vol. 2, 174).

[33] The Hebrew ("li-lmod Torah be-af) follows Yalkut Shimoni, Ecclesiastes 2:968 and Midrash Zuta on Ecclesiastes: "Torah that I studied be-af endures for me."

[34] Kevatzim, vol. 2, 104.

[35] Tiferet and hadar appear together in Proverbs 20:29.

[36] Shemonah Kevatzim 1:295 (vol. 1, 106).

facilitate the absorption of the emanation. Whether this passage is given a prosaic or mystical reading, tension between freedom and conservatism is present in the soul of the saint.

To this point, we have seen that freedom borders on antinomianism. Rabbi Kook referred mainly to study and his wariness of the garb of "the fear of Heaven," while taking care not to call for the revocation of the law. Rabbi Kook slowly gravitated into actual antinomianism. He wrote:

> There are such righteous ones, who need to study or pray[37] only at times, as Rabbi Judah,[38] and they must not smash [i.e., fight against] their moral character [i.e., inclinations]. Rather, they allow their will and all their propensities to expand and spread; all they wish shall be done, they will decree and it will be fulfilled for them;[39] and the entire world lives by their power, and is nourished by their merit.[40]

Rabbi Judah, who would pray once every thirty days, is the paradigm of the righteous individual who does not limit himself. The hierarchy of values that he set for himself shunts aside prayer, or dictates that it is to be engaged in only rarely. According to the interpretation that Rabbi Kook gave the narrative of Rabbi Judah, freedom consists of breaching boundaries. The saint does not struggle with himself, he allows his soul and its powers to follow their inclinations. We saw above that the saint does not quarrel with his community and his people. The antinomian approach strengthens the equanimity of the saint. In a sense, the saint rises above struggles, just as he rises above contrasts.

The saint's freedom is expressed, not only in regard to halakhic norms, but also, as we might expect, in his attitude toward moral criteria. Rabbi Kook wrote:

> When the great soul, that encompasses expanses and soars to the lofty heights like a giant,[41] whose inner essence rises above the

---

37   The second edition added the words "according to their level."

38   Following BT Rosh Hashanah 35a.

39   Following Job 22:28.

40   Following BT Berakhot 17b; Hullin 86a. The passage is from *Shemonah Kevatzim* 2:34 (vol. 1, 305).

41   See Rashi, to BT Sotah 34b, s.v. *"Shehayu Ma'anikim et ha-Hamah be-Komatan."*

concept of morality and virtues, leaves its heights and contracts only into their [narrow] moral content, its strength fails, and it wanes, until it prevails in supreme repentance, and will drink from the supernal dew of *Hokhmah*, from which morality naturally extends.[42]

The saint rises above morality and "virtues"—which also refers to the divine attributes, the *Sefirot* (the Hebrew *midot* refers to both virtues and divine attributes). When the perfect person ascends to the degree of *Binah* (which is symbolized by "repentance") and *Hokhmah*, then moral conduct is natural for him. The saint cannot limit himself to the rules of morality. His perspective is inclusive, and is not limited to a specific realm. From the outset, the saint deports himself in a moral manner stemming from the divine emanation with which he is blessed, but Rabbi Kook appears to say that he eventually rises above the rules of morality. He most likely meant that the perfect individual's morality is natural. Such an individual has no need of moral education limited to the improvement of certain traits.

Halakhah and Kabbalah

To return to the value of Torah study: the value of Torah study is harmed by the preference of other realms of knowledge. Rabbi Kook highlighted the preference of certain "great ones," who are "masters of aggadah and poetry," for the inner dimension of the Torah.[43] The lively religious consciousness seeks communion, and also, the "inner" realms of knowledge and contemplation that lead to its attainment. We spoke above of Rabbi Kook's profound commitment to Kabbalah, and the practical and messianic meanings that his theoretical doctrine attributed to its dissemination. We learn that this commitment led to a neglect of Torah study. He wrote:

> My neglect of Torah study [*bittul Torah*] does not come from carelessness, but from inner longings for the goodness of the Lord in the secrets of the Torah, for supreme communion. My soul desires, in the shelter of Your hand, to know every secret of Your counsel.[44] Although much prevents me from actualizing the depth of the holy

---

42   *Shemonah Kevatzim* 8:141 (vol. 3, 288).
43   See ibid., 8:229 (vol. 3, 325).
44   From *Shir ha-Kavod*. See Habermann, *Shirei ha-Yihud ve-ha-Kavod*, 47 l. 2.

in my soul, it is not for this that I will abandon my way. The way of the holy calls to it, and the supernal Torah is the source of my delight,[45] and it brings me the blessing of Torah, the depth of piety, the humility of justice, fierce light and grandeur. My heart will open to truly attain the light of the Lord, to pray for whoever groans and is crushed,[46] for whoever needs compassion, for the entire world, for the generation, for the oppressed souls, for every suffering and lack.[47]

Thus, Rabbi Kook sinned by "neglecting Torah study" because he preferred to engage in the esoteric Torah. Occupation with the "supernal Torah" is fruitful for the one who studies the revealed Torah ("the blessing of Torah"), just as it is for the fountain of prayer and the mending of society ("the generation") and the world as a whole. This term (*Torah elyonah*) might be understood as expressing experiential communion, and it could also be interpreted as the *Sefirah* of *Hokhmah*, since in some texts, such as *Sefer ha-Temunah*, this *Sefirah* is called "supernal Torah."[48] Alternatively, this might refer to *Tiferet* and *Malkhut*, which are symbolized by the written Torah and the Oral Law, respectively. Kabbalah seemingly compensates for the neglect of Torah study. In another passage, Rabbi Kook observed that "intellective communion [*devekut sikhlit*]" causes the Torah of the righteous to be "blessed." Consequently, they need not set fixed times for Torah study.[49] Occupation with the abstract idea, whether philosophical or Kabbalistic, leads to both the neglect of Torah study and the inspiration and fructification that confer the benefits of Torah study.

Rabbi Kook related to his tremendous urge to study and disseminate Kabbalah as a temptation. Rabbi David Cohen ("the Nazir") attested that Rabbi Kook was struck by conscience pangs for spreading Kabbalah.[50]

---

45   Following Psalms 119:77, 102, 143, 174.

46   See Psalms 38:9-10.

47   *Shemonah Kevatzim* 6:6 (vol. 3, 5).

48   See *Sefer ha-Temunah* (Lemberg, 1892), Introduction to *Temunah* 3, fol. 26a. Rabbi Kook himself declared that "the pure and holy righteous one comes from the Torah to the source of the Torah" (*Shemonah Kevatzim* 6:100 [vol. 3, 35]).

49   *Shemonah Kevatzim* 3:16 (vol. 3, 9).

50   "When *Maran* [our teacher], the *Rav* [=Rabbi Kook], of blessed memory, incurred his last illness, from which he did not recover, and he lay in bed in his home before he was moved to the hospital, in Yemin Moshe [...] *Maran*, the *Rav*, began to cry, and he said, 'This is

Apparently, the latter was not at peace even with the study of Kabbalah. He wrote:

> My inner emotions regarding the parts of the Torah, as to which are more essential for me and are suitable for my soul's needs, although they are not to be followed totally, and at times one must fight with the emotions, as well; but I definitely must pay attention to them, for it is not for nothing that an inner spirit awakens to attract me to the hidden studies, including matters that are above my level and worth. A wise man's heart discerns time and judgment [Ecclesiastes 8:5], to know how to speak timely words to the weary [Isaiah 50:4].[51]

Rabbi Kook admitted that he was attracted to the study of Kabbalah. The secret, mysterious, and inner captivated him. He feared depression as a result of what he called "the paucity of my part in the revealed."[52] He assuaged his fears by claiming that some righteous ones need not forgo their familiarity with the revealed Torah in order to acquire comprehension of the esoteric teachings.[53] Two statements in what he wrote, however, attest to his lack of confidence in his intellectual propensities:

(1) Reservations: he notes that at times he must struggle against these predilections ("one must fight with the emotions, as well").

(2) A lack of boundaries: he admitted that he was drawn to study topics that are beyond his capabilities ("my level and worth").[54]

The saint struggles with a series of temptations, but the seemingly most challenging of them all is the attraction to forbidden spiritual realms. Such topics occupied Rabbi Kook mainly when he was in Europe, when in

---

a punishment for me, for my having revealed secrets'" (*Hug ha-Re'ayah: From the Collection of Classes in Orot ha-Kodesh by Maran, the Rav, R. Abraham Isaac ha-Kohen Kook* [Jerusalem, 1988], 20 [Hebrew]).

51 *Shemonah Kevatzim* 6:45 (vol. 3, 18).

52 Ibid., 6:69 (vol. 3, 25). A series of passages on Rabbi Kook's attraction to Kabbalah appears in *Hadarav*, 99-118.

53 *Shemonah Kevatzim* 6:114 (vol. 3, 40). Along with them, there are righteous ones "who disregard any revealed cognition, so that their mind will be unencumbered and clear for the hidden supreme spiritual insights, which, in regard to the revealed [cognitions], are as spirituality to materiality."

54 As he noted in *Shemonah Kevatzim* 6:106 (vol. 3, 37), this might be an expression of humility. Rabbi Kook, however, was very sincere and straightforward when writing about himself.

1915-1916 he wrote the sixth of the eight booklets of *Shemonah Kevatzim*, some passages of which relate to the enticements of Kabbalah.

Summation

Rabbi Kook was not deterred by the boundaries conservatism imposed. As is well-known, he was stringent regarding halakhic observance, and deemed stringency to be of worth.[55] Furthermore, he adopted the theurgic meanings of the observance of the commandments; consequently, the saints influence their social and national environments mainly by means of the commandments.[56] Nonetheless, the value of freedom clashes with the concept of commandment, resulting in a dialectic between conservatism and antinomianism. Freedom consists, primarily, of following one's inner mandate and proclivity. The movement between conservatism and antinomianism is already evident in Rabbi Kook's famous attitude toward the *halutzim* of the Second Aliyah. On the one hand, they were extreme secularists, while on the other, they were idealists, who were willing to give their lives for values, and as such were on a very high level, despite their secularism. In regard to antinomianism, a different sort of tension manifests itself: on the one hand, the righteous individual derives the maximum, in terms of commitment and obligation, from observance of the commandments, while on the other, at times his nature causes him to disregard, to a certain degree, the divine mandate. In summation, antinomianism is a major attribute of the saint. It reveals his freedom, his unique personality, and his individual ways. The lack of boundaries was almost always in the spiritual realms, and not in praxis. Thus, antinomianism is characteristic of the saint.

---

[55]   See M. Z. Nehorai, "Remarks on the Rabbinic Rulings of Rabbi Kook," *Tarbiz* 59 (1989-1990): 481-505 [Hebrew]. Rabbi Kook's halakhic conception has recently become of great scholarly interest. See, e.g., N. Guttel, *Innovation in Tradition: The Halakhic-Philosophical Teachings of Rabbi Kook* (Jerusalem, 2005), 56 [Hebrew]; Rozenak, *Prophetic Halakhah*; H. Ben-Artzi, *The New Shall Be Sacred: Rav Kook as an Innovative Posek* (Tel Aviv, 2010) [Hebrew].

[56]   See *Shemonah Kevatzim* 3:13 (vol. 2, 13), in which Rabbi Kook speaks of "the pleasantness of the qualities of the commandments."

Chapter Nine

RABBI KOOK AS RELIGIOUS GENIUS: DISCUSSION

In this chapter we will examine the extent to which the image of Rabbi Kook as saint conforms with the parameters that enable interreligious discourse. The discussion will follow the outline set forth in the position paper on religious genius and its implications written by Alon Goshen-Gottstein.[1] We will also clarify what Rabbi Kook added to the conception of the saint, and see what from these teachings provides a basis for the broadest possible discourse.

The Moral and Aesthetic Aspect

The study of saints teaches that the strongest position that facilitates interreligious discourse is the moral stance. The three main Western religions, for instance, ascribe altruistic qualities to exceptional individuals. Eastern religions, as well, present a common moral basis for the saint discourse. Discussions of the saint in the context of moral philosophy are based on the assumption that the saint can be emulated (the "logic of imitation"). Moral virtue, by definition, is subject to imitation. This assumption also underlies the interreligious dialogue about saints. In this respect, the image of Rabbi Kook represents a certain tension. On his part, Rabbi Kook was convinced that he represented a congenitally superior individual. Congenital faculty cannot be imitated. Nor does the distinction between exceptional individuals and the masses allow for emulation. On the other hand, the religious genius is perceived as an educator whose influence

---

[1] A. Goshen-Gottstein, *Religious Genius and the Interreligious Study of Saints: Constructing a Category, with Implications for Understanding Wisdom, Spiritual Information and Character Development* (The Elijah Institute, Jerusalem and Dallas, 2012). The article may be found at http://www.elijah-interfaith.org/fileadmin/religious%20genius%20concept%20paper.pdf.

does not have an exclusively mystical basis; it also has an effect in the social and religious realms. In other words, the saint is not one-dimensional. He possesses a dimension that can be emulated, and another that cannot.[2]

Rabbi Kook's inclusion of the aesthetic factor made an important contribution to the moral discourse on saints. According to him, altruism is not a single, stable value, expressed in diverse ways in the behavior of saints, but is subject to creativity. For Rabbi Kook, the saint is not measured solely by his endless dedication on behalf of the individual, the nation, humankind, and all existence. Nor is the saint epitomized by the voiding of his personality in the face of the missions that he takes upon himself. The saint is also a moral genius, characterized by moral creativity that results from outstanding intellectual inspiration. In the final analysis, the rational-aesthetic element present in Rabbi Kook's writings also impacts on the altruism of the saint. Others also mentioned the creativity of the saint,[3] but Rabbi Kook emphasized genius, that is, he situated the discussion within the aesthetic sphere. Thus, the discussion of saints extends to a new realm, one that allows for discourse.

The Personality of the Saint

Rabbi Kook presents a model of the saint who manifests exceptional abilities in various realms. He constantly stressed that the true saint absorbs all. For example, he cannot be limited to altruism; creativity, genius, intellectual cognition, music, theurgy, magic, and other such characteristics are all within his purview. In this respect, he corresponds to an expansion of Robert Neville's conception,[4] as Goshen-Gottstein already suggested in his position paper. The saint reflects the perfection of the will, the intellect, and the heart (and not only the last, as Neville sought to claim). Heavenly inspiration and intuition are central faculties, with the same degree of importance, of the experience of the saint; and, indeed, Rabbi Kook set forth important insights regarding both these faculties, as we have seen.

---

2   Cf. the position of P. Sorokin, *The Ways and Power of Love: Factors and Techniques of Moral Transformation* (Boston, 1954), 38.

3   E.g., J. Templeton, *Possibilities for Over Hundredfold More Spiritual Information* (Philadelphia, 2000), 45.

4   R. Neville, *Soldier, Sage, Saint* (New York, 1978).

For him, however, the character of the saint far exceeded intuition and inspiration. To mention a few examples:

(1) The saint is a productive figure.

(2) The saint possesses tremendous interpretive capabilities for historical events.

(3) The saint is characterized by self-confirmation (congenital faculty, ontological distinction between himself and the masses, and the like).

Additionally, Rabbi Kook presented the saint as having a dynamic and dialectic personality. He adopted the classic traits of the saint, while at the same time indicating this individual's constant wrestling with the opposite attributes. For example: the personality of the saint withdraws before the universe and the Godhead. He experiences a sort of self-voiding, and is thereby able to include and love all. Parallel to this, however, Rabbi Kook asserted that the saint is characterized by self-confirmation. He knows his worth and is cognizant of his special personality. Consequently, the saint is not a finished entity. He presents an ethos of endless movement. The saint's social power is similarly depicted: on the one hand, he devotes himself to elevating his surroundings from within, as is finely reflected in Rabbi Kook's life, while on the other, he substantially separates himself from this environment. Rabbi Kook presented a dynamic and oscillating model.

Rabbi Kook understood the saint as one who gives meaning to life, which is expressed not only in his personal qualities, but also in the tasks that he takes upon himself. Even when the saint gives his life in an act of martyrdom, this is planned in advance, considered, and serves his goals. An example of this is Rabbi Kook's discussion of Rabbi Akiva, whose self-sacrifice occurred within the context of his desire to preserve the standing of the Rabbis.

These observations suffice to indicate that Rabbi Kook significantly expanded the discussion of the personality of the saint. At this juncture we should raise the question of methodology and systematization: Rabbi Kook's thought shows that, at times, a lack of systematization is the proper tool for a discussion of the saint. He did not deal with questions such as whether the saint's moral inspiration precede his religious development, or whether his intellectual faculty blossoms together with his altruism. On the other hand, he enabled the reader of his works to understand that his concept of the saint emerged in tandem with the formation of his intuitions regarding the "spiritual reality" and the inner dimension of reality. Moreover, Rabbi Kook allowed the reader to understand that religious genius is not to be divorced from cosmic and spiritual insights. He did this by refraining from systematic analysis, and providing only a "local" description. The system of tensions and dilemmas that he included in the image of the saint allows for a broad and complex basis for the personality of the latter, one that is familiar to us, for instance, from the portrayals of Christian saints. Consequently, Rabbi Kook's image diverts the discussion, in large part, from "saint" to "religious genius," even though we have not distinguished between the two.

Our discussion has been mainly concerned with Rabbi Kook's philosophy. We could just as easily have analyzed his historical personality and its implications, as is frequently done by hagiographers and historians. It should be mentioned that, ideologically, Rabbi Kook supported the Zionist enterprise. His personality, however, included almost all the religious orientations, and he therefore refused to be politically identified. He sought a political identity his entire life, but in vain (he participated in the Assembly of the ultra-Orthodox Agudat Israel, sought to establish the Degel Yerushalayim federation,[5] refrained from active membership in the Mizrachi movement, etc.). He bravely withstood attacks by the ultra-Orthodox for his support of the Zionist undertaking. Love and altruism were undoubtedly important components of his personality.

The Discourse of Saints

Rabbi Kook's image and thought are a phenomenon of the religious world. From this aspect, the saint is part and parcel of institutionalized religion. We saw, however, that Rabbi Kook did not accept this affiliation as self-understood. He believed that the restrictions and commandments of the specific religion frequently burden the saint. In other words, the religious genius frequently emerges from within a certain religion, but his central aspiration consists of fulfilling his personality in accordance with its unique character traits, which are not fully realized within such a specific religion. The fulfillment of personality, as we learn, is universal.

---

5   See above, Chapter One.

We now can address the question: will Rabbi Kook's image as a saint provide a satisfactory foundation for interreligious discourse in a post-modern world? Is there a common denominator of saints, that also applies to religions that are not based on such individuals, or in which saints have no place?

The phenomenological approach regarding saints enables us to isolate the substantive components of the saint in Rabbi Kook's thought. The universal aspect of the saint compels us to rise above environment and historical context. It is doubtful, however, whether the saint as personified by Rabbi Kook can be subjected to a full phenomenological analysis, since his character cannot be divorced from his national conception and messianic interpretation of events in a given period.

We similarly would have difficulty in discussing Rabbi Kook's concept of the saint apart from his singular conception of faith, in which Kabbalistic models are blended. Theurgic activity is an element in the image of the saint; this activity could be seen as altruistic, since it is conducted for the public good, but it can be interpreted only on its mystical background. Notwithstanding this, we can speak of an important advantage in Rabbi Kook's notion of the saint, namely, channeling the exclusive focus on religion as theological doctrines or religious praxis and ethos toward personality. Again, the background of Habad Hasidism is obvious. Now, the religious genius is no less important, and perhaps more so, than abstract conceptions of religion for understanding the religious consciousness. Rabbi Kook fits into the Hasidic tradition of *tzaddikim*, for example, that positioned the religious genius alongside belief. Now, religion is no longer solely speculative. Furthermore, since the saint is the mirror of the reality and the Godhead, transcendence and personality unite.

To return to our fundamental question: does the character of Rabbi Kook facilitate a discourse of saints? The factors mitigating against this may be listed immediately: first, Rabbi Kook was a national thinker. He felt that the saint's life at that time could not be understood without the image of the Jewish saint; and such a saint lives according to a hierarchy, in which the ontological preference of the Jewish people has substantive pride of place. Second, Rabbi Kook advocated the unbridgeable chasm between the saint and the masses. A saint is not an attainable paradigm. His level is mainly congenital, and not acquired.

Taking into account his national thought, does Rabbi Kook's image as saint detract from universal love? Rabbi Kook himself thought that the hierarchy of the saint's consciousness is built of layer upon layer, each of which has independent value, and value that is anchored in the existential hierarchy. That is, for his part, he loved man as such; his soul absorbed all the ways of human existence. Love for all humanity is the primal layer in the character of Rabbi Kook. He believed that on such a layer an additional one could be laid, that of the special love for the Jewish soul, over which the layer of the saint is to be placed.

Several questions arise in this context. What is the actual connection between these layers? Can the primal layer, that spans all humankind, be isolated, and thereby establish a common basis for interreligious discourse? Common sense says no. The other Western religions, too, have such a two-layered structure, in which the member of the specific religion has a special place. Can the interreligious discourse focus on what is shared? If the answer is positive, then the image of Rabbi Kook as saint significantly contributes to such a discourse. A series of truly altruistic qualities, on the one hand, and on the other, those of universal religiosity, join together in this figure. Importantly, we should add a reservation here: Rabbi Kook's viewpoint is always anchored in his approach to the reality in its entirety: the love of man is anchored in love of nature, and love of nature, in love of the universe, which in turn is rooted in love of God and the aspiration for communion with Him. Such an approach will likely expand altruism, but it might also limit the love of man as such, and present it as a mere component of a religious system.

At any rate, the image of Rabbi Kook is a paradigm of the saint in a world without stable and defined values, as in Wyschogrod's central thesis.[6] Rabbi Kook had the stature of saint in the Jewish world of his time and later. He is seen as such by broad sectors of the Jewish religious public (albeit some of them, who are not Zionists, regard him as a "naive saint" or "erring saint"). He is not perceived, at the present time, as a "global saint," although he possesses the potential to express such an image.

The perception of the saint as the mirror of the Godhead and as a tangible expression of processes within the Godhead enables a return of

---

6   See Wyschogrod, *Saints and Postmodernism.*

metaphysics, as least as nostalgia. Rabbi Kook did not waive the imprints left in his soul by the philosophical, ethical, and aesthetic schools. For him, nationalism was not a limiting factor, but an inbuilt component within the cosmic and divine universality; he was convinced that nationalism does not dim universality. Was his viewpoint objective? Probably not. But, we might be able to say that it is an alternative in a postmodern world. Rabbi Kook challenged the model of the saint presented in recent research. On the one hand, he presents a complex model that does not accept the shared basis of the discourse of the saint as such, while on the other, he enables us to face the particular in the religious experience.

Chapter Ten

Rabbi Kook as Religious Genius: Summation

Rabbi Kook's writing repeatedly incorporates passages from the Jewish sources, and presents a plethora of meanings. At times, the implied motifs that are embedded in his writings express profound insights that in themselves create a conceptional framework. In this respect, an interpretive reading of his writings justifies the negation of the leitmotif in favor of a mosaic of meanings, each of which is no less legitimate and important than the others. Just as nationalism, for example, is a leitmotif, prayer is such as well, and to the same degree; and just as the Kabbalistic meaning is significant, the concrete social meaning is substantive to the same degree. The image of the saint is constructed from within a series of interpretive and meaningful horizons. I wish to raise a few last thoughts as we conclude our discussion of the image of the saint.

Hierarchy

I mentioned at the beginning of this book that Rabbi Kook did not strive for precise and hierarchical definitions of types of saints. At times, however, we find an implicit hierarchy of saints. We mentioned a number of broad hierarchical outlines:

(1) From a saint who is attracted to rationalism to one who follows emotion;

(2) From a saint who is attentive to details to one who is drawn to general principles;

(3) From a saint who is capable of approaching the masses to one who cannot descend to such a level;

(4) From a revealed saint to one who is concealed;

(5) From a saint who is gifted with heavenly inspiration to one who does not experience revelation;

(6) From the universal to the Jewish saint.

Rabbi Kook used various synonyms when referring to the saint, and he did not distinguish between his different types. This teaches that he did not attempt to create a classification of saints, just as he did not seek to systematize the other thoughts he advanced. Establishing hard and fast rules would limit the discussion, and for Rabbi Kook, freedom was of importance for the saint's activity.

Oscillations

Rabbi Kook continued a rich tradition of thinkers who referred to themselves in the third person.[1] Restraint and exteriorization of the personality of the saint, however, do not overshadow his self-image. The world and all the fullness thereof are dependent on the image and activity of the saint. Writing in the third person paved the way for Rabbi Kook's description of the religious genius, since he himself related to his persona as such, and never intended to conceal his thoughts about himself. It is on this basis that we are to understand Rabbi Kook's continuing the tradition of philosophers and mystics whose paths were characterized by paradox and dialectic. In most instances, Rabbi Kook did not experience existential tension in the senses that were highlighted in existentialist philosophy (finality-eternity, objectivity-subjectivity, and the like). The tensions he depicts are mainly those between the individual and the collective, and between freedom and religious and social frameworks. The tensions that Rabbi Kook expressed in the image of the saint are mainly the following:

(1) Psychological tensions: hesitancy versus decisiveness, introversion versus extroversion. The central classic oscillation in his writings and personality is activism versus passivity. On the one hand, the saint initiates. He unites the groups split asunder, he performs magical activity to draw down the divine emanation for the general good. In the intellectual realm, he definitely reveals his activism. On the other hand, the saint influences

---

[1] See Cherlow, *The Tzaddiq*, 47-48.

in a passive manner. His distance from the public and his exceptional and unique character influence indirectly.

(2) Experiential tensions: the classic tensions of the religious literature, such as the pendulum swing between self-confirmation and -negation, greatly occupied Rabbi Kook. He was concerned with the issue of the self-awareness of the saint. For him, the saint's self-image included the system of congenital faculties and acquired accomplishments. The righteous individual is also capable of classifying himself on the scale of perfection. At the same time, however, the saint negates himself before the source of divine emanation, and he is also dedicated to the public, especially in order to elevate all Israel and the entire world, to the extent that his personality loses its distinctness.

(3) Social tensions: on the one hand, Rabbi Kook portrayed the gap between the saint and the masses as an actual chasm. The masses cannot be understood by the saint, and the distinction between them is analogous to the distinction between man and other animate creatures. On the other hand, Rabbi Kook posited the gradual convergence of the saint and the masses, and even let the reader realize that the two would unite in the future.

The tensions described by Rabbi Kook are eventually resolved. Moreover, these tensions are perceived as stages in a preplanned process, and therefore have a clearly teleological dimension. Descent leads to eventual ascent, depression serves happiness, conceptualization leads to abstraction, the descent to the masses causes their elevation, the focus on details leads to generalization, and so forth.

Tensions do cause anguish, because the way to harmony is one of opposites. The saint, as perceived by Rabbi Kook, is a purposeful individual. At times he is indecisive, and experiences insecurity. His dominant feeling, however, is purposefulness. The saint knows that the opposites are transitory. He reads the map of events, and these opposites are the path that he must take in order to implement his program for these events.

Altruism

Rabbi Kook's perception of the saint is altruistic. In contrast, say, to the model of the perfect human being in medieval rationalist thought, who is primarily "egotistical" (communion with the Active Intellect and the immortality of the intellect are purely individualistic goals), Rabbi Kook's saint acts on behalf of his fellow. Such a saint dedicates his time and skills to radiate light and lovingkindness on the entire world. He struggles with evil in order to banish it from the cosmic life.

Notwithstanding this, the saint, in Rabbi Kook's version, is not purely altruistic. We can indicate at least two reasons for this:

(1) For Rabbi Kook, the dominant dimension of exceptional individuals is to be found in their dedication to all Israel more than to individuals. He famously ended manifestos and letters with the wording "servant of the holy people," thereby blurring the boundaries between altruism and nationalism.

(2) Rabbi Kook constantly emphasized that the intellectual and creative dimensions are inherent in the exceptional individual. For him, the saint acts mainly in the speculative and intellectual realm, which is a personal one. Rabbi Kook was too deeply enrooted in the rational and mystical traditions to be purely altruistic.

Rabbi Kook's altruism was mingled with a ramified system of national and messianic considerations. Moreover, he wanted to preserve the image of the saint who lives on behalf of society, and who sacrifices himself for all existence. There is a pronounced "ecological" dimension in Rabbi Kook's thought, one that usually does not appear in the classic depiction of saints. In Rabbi Kook's understanding, the saint is anxious for the fate of the universe as a harmonic framework. Human beings are an important element of the cosmos, but not the only one. Obviously, Rabbi Kook also adopted the theurgic model, in which the saint is responsible for the perfection of the divine world. The environmental aspect, however, is new. Rabbi Kook's altruism does not fully correspond to the image of the saint as it is presented in Western religious literature.

The Collective

We will continue to examine the national and theurgic activities of the saint. The main innovation in the discussion of Rabbi Kook as saint undoubtedly lies in his being anchored in the collective (the nation) and in history. In most instances, saints were concerned about other individuals or the community. Rabbi Kook himself wrote that the saint is engaged in the extraction of the sparks and the rectification of the souls of the entire nation.[2] Here, however, matters take a turn. In Rabbi Kook's thought, the saint is connected to the collective, not only as a collection of individuals, but rather as an independent entity. In the theosophical realm, the saint is connected with the divine emanation that rests over the entire world, and especially over the Jewish people. In the national sphere, the saint is rooted in the renewed Jewish nationalism, while before the rise of this nationalism, the saint had been seen as elevated above particularism and nationalism. Rabbi Kook maintained that all the branches of Jewish thought, from understanding regular divine activity to the definition of repentance, require revision in light of the national revival. Such an argument has direct implications for the saint and his attributes. It also secures his special standing in light of historical development, in which cracks appear in the mythological and perfect existence of the saint in the past, and the image of the saint now accords with a public whose level rises and improves.

Rabbi Kook provided a full and consistent explanation for the Jewish national renaissance. His explanation includes extensive interpretation of contemporary events. According to his explanation, the saint has a key function in the national sphere. The role of the saint does not consist solely of his being an object of emulation, or even of his very existence, despite the substantive weight of his passive influence. Behind the scenes, it is the saint who truly effects national change. This assumption is based on the clearly theurgic activity of the saint: he brings down the divine emanation, and thereby drives the historical process. The activism of the saint is not limited to his heading the camp (such as the establishment of the Degel Yerushalayim movement). Saints bring about the elevation of the worlds. Admittedly, they are not alone in this task; the interaction between them and the collective is essential. Their main activity, however, is far from the limelight. The saint draws down the divine emanation from the *Sefirot*, thereby elevating the surrounding world. The process of national renaissance cannot be understood without the presence of the perfect individuals.

---

2   The labor of the rectification of souls is "proper and required of the righteous of the generations" (*Igrot ha-Re'ayah*, vol. 1, 143). See, e.g., Cherlow, *The Tzaddiq*, 318-19.

From this perspective, Rabbi Kook's concept of saints corresponds to the traditional characteristic of performing miracles.

Saint and Prophet

We should take note of an intriguing fact. The restoration of prophecy is an important motif in Rabbi Kook's thought. He and the circle of his closest students regularly sought after heavenly revelations, using diverse techniques.[3] The image of the saint in Rabbi Kook's conception, however, is distant from that of the angry prophet who "reproaches in the gate." The saint generally effects the most substantive changes in passive and intimate fashion. That is, as previously stated, he is engaged in bringing down the emanation from its divine source, thereby succeeding in elevating the nation, and even the entire world. Rabbi Kook accordingly frequently used the motif of illumination to describe the effect of the saint. "Illumination" denotes passive influence, as distinguished from active involvement. Additionally, lovingkindness dominates the saint. Although he is capable of using strict judgment, and of engaging in harsh struggles, lovingkindness is the guiding principle of his personality.

Rabbi Kook constantly stressed that saints are not all stamped from the same die. There are different types of saints; and furthermore, the saint experiences a dialectic between forcefulness and passivity. He wavers between the image of the charismatic military leader and the introverted Torah scholar and intellectual. The truth, however, must be said: the saint who acts in a passive, inward manner, with endless goodness and love, is dominant in Rabbi Kook's thought.

---

3   See *Shemonah Kevatzim* 4:17 (vol. 2, 137); A. Ravitzky, *Messianism, Zionism, and Jewish Religious Radicalism*, trans. M. Swirsky and J. Chipman (Chicago, 1996), 119-20; E. Schweid, "Renewed Prophecy in the Face of the Beginning of Redemption," *Daat* 38 (1997): 83-103 [Hebrew]. Rabbi Harlap describes a climate of heavenly revelations; see Yaakov Moses Harlap, *Hed Harim: A Collection of Letters* (Elon Moreh, 1997), 75 [Hebrew]. On prophecy and charisma in the thought of Rabbi Kook and his disciple, Rabbi David Cohen ("the Nazir"), see Schwartz, *Religious Zionism*, 55-56, 191-97. On Rabbi Zevi Yehudah Kook, see G. Aran, "Jewish Zionist Fundamentalism: The Bloc of the Faithful in Israel (Gush Emunim)," in *Fundamentalisms Observed*, ed. M. Marty and S. Appleby (Chicago, 1991), 268, 299-300; idem, "The Father, the Son, and the Holy Land: The Spiritual Authorities of Jewish-Zionist Fundamentalism in Israel," in *Spokesmen for the Despised: Fundamentalist Leaders in the Middle East*, ed. S. Appleby (Chicago, 1997), 304, 315.

We can only assume that Rabbi Kook viewed the prophet in a manner different from what emerges from the biblical books of the prophets. The modern prophet elevates his surroundings out of love and consent. He wages the harsh and dialectic struggle with himself; reproach is reserved more for his personal idolatry, and less for his environment. Both ancient prophecy and the modern saint aspire to attain the spirit of divine inspiration (*ruah ha-kodesh*). Rabbi Kook devoted much attention to the question of charisma, that is, the modes of supernal revelations (voices, lights, and the like) that bring the holy closer to the prophet, which we have not examined in our discussion. This rounds out the prophetic dimension of the saint.

Limits

This work focused on the consciousness of the saint in Rabbi Kook's thought and actions. Rabbi Kook attracted a circle of students and admirers during his lifetime, and a complete study should discuss Rabbi Kook's consciousness as saint in their eyes. The mystical and philosophical aspects of the circle's consciousness has already been extensively explored by myself and other scholars such as Moshe Idel, Semadar Cherlow, Uriel Barak, and Jonathan Garb. As an example of interaction between Rabbi Kook and his circle, the saints' literature speaks of rebirth following revelation or some other charismatic event. A regular person undergoes a metamorphosis or conversion, and becomes a saint.[4] Rabbi Kook did not experience such an occurrence, but some of his students described events resembling a personality metamorphosis. This is a single example of the circle's enrichment of the conception of Rabbi Kook as saint. The circle's intervention in the editing of Rabbi Kook's writings has been examined by myself, Avinoam Rozenak, Udi Abramovich, and Meir Munitz. However, since I elected to conduct a phenomenological research of the image of the saint, and because Rabbi Kook himself left many writings that document his substantive experiences, we can discuss his self-image, that is, his consciousness as saint, as we showed above. In the current work I did not explore all the aspects of the saint. At times Rabbi Kook alluded to various

---

4   James devoted two lectures to conversion in his *The Varieties of Religious Experience*.

facets of the saint in his writings, one example of which is the cult of the saint. Rabbi Kook wrote of saints: "whoever receives them, it is as if he receives the actual Divine Presence."[5] Although the Rabbis frequently express similar thoughts, here it borders on encouraging the active adoration of the saint. Rabbi Kook, however, did not go beyond such allusions.

Clearly, Rabbi Kook created a new and rich type of saint in Jewish tradition. His innovativeness does not lie in its originality, but in diversity and open horizons in the image of the saint. The portrayal of the saint is built of one layer over another, and one tradition over another, without a single central leitmotif, which is the source of its force and contemporary relevance. Rabbi Kook hardly waived a single hue in the existence of the saint; nor, however, did he insist on necessary and unequivocal properties for such a figure. He evaded absolute statements. He (the writer) and the reader together build the stature of the saint. In practical, social, and political terms, the saint has a clear and purposeful agenda; of this there can be no doubt. The attainment, however, of the national and messianic goals was merely the lower chamber in a rich and variegated image, one that refused to fit into any standard mold or pattern.

---

5   *Shemonah Kevatzim* 3:163 (vol. 2, 68). In a similar vein, Rabbi Adin Steinsaltz used the adjective "saintly" when referring to Rabbi Menachem Mendel Schneerson (*My Rebbe* [Jerusalem, 2014], 1).

Appendix

ON RABBI KOOK
AND RELIGIOUS ZIONIST THOUGHT

Chapter Eleven

RABBI KOOK AND THE REVOLUTIONARY CONSCIOUSNESS OF RELIGIOUS ZIONISM

From the very inception of the movement (1902), the thinkers of religious Zionism were infused with a revolutionary spirit. This feeling was evidently well-founded. We must emphasize: while the revolutionary motivation of secular Zionism is well-known and has been documented and researched,[1] religious Zionism has not fared so well. The religious Zionist community was a partner to the Zionist revolution as a whole, and the degree and complexity of that revolutionary drive is even more impressive, given the conservative, traditionalist background within which it continued to exist.[2]

As far as the messianic and political idea in Judaism is concerned, the very appearance of a religious Zionist ideology was revolutionary: here, for the first time, human initiative took direct and surprisingly forceful action, explicitly rebelling against the passivity of the exiled Jewish people (that is, refusing to await redemption by divine means). Another aspect

---

[1] See, e.g., B. Harshav, "The Revival of Eretz Israel and the Modern Jewish Revolution: Reflections on the Current Situation," in *Observation Points: Culture and Society in Eretz Israel*, ed. N. Gertz (Tel Aviv, 1988), 10, 23 [Hebrew]. Thus, the Hebrew translators of David Vital's classical trilogy on the history of Zionism chose the title *Ha-Mahapekhah ha-Zionit* (*The Zionist Revolution*) (I-III, Tel Aviv, 1978-1991); J. Barnay, "On the Question of the Origin of Zionism," in *From Vision to Revision: A Hundred Years of Historiography of Zionism*, ed. Y. Weitz (Jerusalem, 1998), 136 [Hebrew].

[2] For an excellent summary of the revolutionary parallels between secular and religious Zionism, see J. Gorni, "On Social 'Manners' and National Interest: The Question of Religious-Secular Coexistence in the Zionist Movement," in *Priesthood and Monarchy: Studies in the Historical Relationships of Religion and State*, ed. I. Gafni and G. Motzkin (Jerusalem, 1987), 269-70 [Hebrew]. Cf. E. Schweid, *The Idea of Modern Jewish Culture*, trans. A. Hadary (Boston, 2008), 212-25.

of the revolutionary element was the desire to create a new religious type, a "redeemed person," who would respond to the demands posed by the need to construct a modern political entity and would reshape his or her religious faith in accordance with those demands. The entry into organized politics signaled by the founding of the Mizrachi movement (1902) was a major landmark in the emergent revolutionism and its institutionalization.

Rabbi Kook's Image

Rabbi Kook was not one of the founders of the Mizrachi movement, and his attitude toward it was quite ambivalent. At times he even disdained the movement. Rabbi Kook's political endeavor was the creation of a different religious Zionism (Degel Yerushalayim), theologically all-encompassing, and ideologically, politically, and halakhically uncompromising.[3]

Mizrachi, however, adopted Rabbi Kook as an important ideologist. As we have already seen in the previous chapters, Rabbi Kook's ideas may be characterized as innovative and revolutionary.[4] In this chapter I wish to set out the fundamentals of religious Zionist revolutionism.

Definition and Status

In regard to group self-definition, the religious Zionists rejected the exclusivity of the community cell as an expression of a religious (or rather, religiously observant) minority, sometimes well-organized but lacking national and sovereign features, subordinate to a non-Jewish majority with a social and religious leadership foreign to it.[5] The religious Zionist aimed to replace this status with a national status, where "nation" meant a politically and religiously independent entity with its own land, language, and other national characteristics. In other words, religious Zionism spurned the

3   See below.
4   See D. Schwartz, *Religious-Zionism: History and Ideology*, trans. B. Stein (Boston, 2009), chap. 4.
5   See D. J. Elazar, "The Community from Its Beginnings till the Threshold of the Modern Era," in *Kinship and Consent: The Jewish Political Tradition and Its Contemporary Uses*, ed. idem (Jerusalem, 1981), 174-207 [Hebrew].

existing status and sought another. "We have resolved to bring into being a new creation."[6]

One consequence of the desire to change status from community cell to nation was the negation of the *Galut*, the existence of the Jewish people in Exile, uprooted from its homeland: religious Zionism defined itself as "a movement built on the foundations of pure recognition of the concepts of Judaism and our historical spiritual values, free of any *Galut* influence."[7] Many of its spiritual mentors likened *Galut* to "the burial place of our national body."[8] For Rabbi Kook and other religious Zionist thinkers, *Galut* was an anomalous episode of the denial of the nation's real identity, while the return to the national homeland and language was the "return to ourselves, to the roots of our individuality";[9] *Galut* was landlessness, while the national renaissance meant "life in the bosom of nature";[10] *Galut* erected a barrier between the sacred and the profane, between Torah and

---

6   Yeshayahu Aviad (Wolfsberg), *Reflections on Judaism* (Jerusalem, 1955), 117 [Hebrew]. Aviad, a leader of religious Zionism in Germany, was speaking of the state as against *Galut*.

7   Samuel Hayyim Landau (one of the founders of Ha-Poel ha-Mizrachi, the socialist sector of the Mizrachi movement), *Ketavim* (Writings) (Warsaw 1935), 27 [Hebrew]. See also the quotation in the name of Rabbi Isaac Nussenbaum, a Zionist preacher who joined Mizrachi, in J. Tirosh, "Religious Zionism: Selected Writings of Religious-Zionist Thinkers," in *Mizpeh (Hazofeh Yearbook for 1953)*, 39 [Hebrew]. On various aspects of the negation of *Galut* in religious Zionist thought, see at length E. Don Yehiya, "The Negation of Galut in Religious Zionism," *Modern Judaism* 12 (1992): 129-55.

8   Rabbi Zevi Yehudah Kook, Rabbi Kook's son and the spiritual mentor of Gush Emunim, in: *Ha-Torah ha-Go'elet* (The Redemptive Torah), ed. H. A. Schwartz (Jerusalem, 1983), 80 [Hebrew]. Rabbi Eliezer Berkovits, an important religious Zionist philosopher who officiated as rabbi in Sidney and Boston, pointed out that *Galut* is considered an abnormal condition even though the Jewish people have lived longer in exile than in the Land of Israel; see his *Faith after the Holocaust* (New York, 1973), 120.

9   Yeshayahu Bernstein (an ideologue of Ha-Poel ha-Mizrachi), *Ye'ud va-Derekh* (Goal and Way) (Tel Aviv, 1956), 87 [Hebrew]. Elsewhere, Bernstein wrote that any spiritually and culturally rich nation jealously preserved its individuality and the special expressions of its identity, thus safeguarding its existence, its uniqueness, and its ability to maintain its creativity (101). Thus, *Galut* exposed the Jews to foreign influences and obscured its individuality.

10   Nehemiah Aminoah (an ideologue of Ha-Poel ha-Mizrachi), "Our Goals in the *Moshavei Ovdim*," in *Yalkut: Anthology of Articles on the Torah ve-Avodah Concept*, ed. N. Aminoah and Y. Bernstein (Jerusalem, 1931), 105 [Hebrew].

general knowledge, while the national renaissance meant a return to unity and total sanctity.[11]

Some Zionist thinkers, particularly those of religious Zionism, placed emphasis on the revival of the Jewish nation as a united people, in contrast to the plethora of movements characteristic of the Emancipation period.[12] National status became a dogma, a basic principle underpinning Judaism,[13] while the negation of "*Galut* negativity"[14] became an unquestioned goal. In addition, the very founding of Mizrachi as an independent faction in the Zionist Organization marked a profound change, from the participation and membership of observant individuals in organizations and movements (such as Hibbat Zion) to institutionalized political involvement. This change is highly significant as far as the tradition of political thought in traditional Judaism is concerned. In addition, quite a few in the religious Zionist camp were adherents of Marxist theory, which holds that the mere fact of organization is expressive of revolutionary consciousness.[15] In this respect, the suffering, exploited Jew was seen as parallel to the proletarian,

---

[11] Rabbi Moshe Zevi Neriah, in the name of Rabbi Kook, published in *The Seventh Conference of ha-Po'el ha-Mizrahi in Erez-Israel ... 1935*, ed. Y. Avneri (Ramat Gan, 1988), 64 (Hebrew).

[12] See Rabbi Judah Leib Maimon (Fishman, leader of Mizrachi for many years), *La-Sha'ah vela-Dor* (On the Hour and the Generation) (Jerusalem, 1965), 96 [Hebrew]. Cf. his statement: "Zionism, in its entirety and full extension, is not only a national movement, but it is national revival pure and simple, the revival of the Hebrew nation, of Hebrew emotion and language, and the revival of the Land of the Hebrews. Zionism strives to develop and strengthen the life force of the Hebrew nation in fulfilling its material and spiritual needs, and its program embraces everything that is capable of revitalizing the Hebrew nation, endowing it with life on earth and eternal life, in all countries of the Diaspora and in its historical land" (97).

[13] For example: "It is surely a great and awesome principle of faith that we will return to the land of our fathers, for only there, as a free nation in its own land, shall we be able to evolve and become a wise, intelligent people, a kingdom of priests and holy nation [...] It is clear, therefore, that whoever does not believe in the future of the Jewish people in its historical land divests the Torah of its meaning" (Rabbi Moshe Samuel Glasner [one of the first Hungarian rabbis to espouse Zionism], "Zionism in the Light of Faith," in *Torah and Kingdom: On the Place of the State in Judaism*, ed. S. Federbusch [Jerusalem, 1961], 67 [Hebrew]). See also Schwartz, *Faith at the Crossroads*, 8-9, 224; idem, *Land of Israel in Religious Zionist Thought* (Tel Aviv, 1997), 31-33 and passim [Hebrew].

[14] The term was coined by Moshe Unna, *On the Paths of Thought and Deed* (Tel Aviv, 1955), 63 [Hebrew].

[15] Cf. S. Avineri, *The Social and Political Thought of Karl Marx* (Cambridge, 1968), 141-43. Many young Jews, including Rabbi Kook's colleague and disciple Rabbi David Cohen ("the Nazir"), were involved in revolutionary activity in Russia at the turn of the century.

redeemed in an act of organization that highlighted his or her special status. Another aspect of the change in political status that religious Zionism brought to the traditional world was the very use of modern political terminology, indicative of future forms of government, even in a relatively early stage of Mizrachi.[16]

In sum: religious Zionism's total negation of *Galut* status and its desire to modify the nation's self-definition were unmistakable expressions of revolt and revolutionism. The revolutionism implicit in the mere fact of political organization is particularly evident in light of a well-known quip of Nahum Goldmann, to the effect that the only Jewish statesman in thousands of years of exile was the Messiah.[17]

Messianic-Theological Significance

Religious Zionism lent legitimacy to human efforts that aimed to shape divine and cosmic events, such as redemption and the revival of Jewish nationality. Even more: cosmic events owed their inception, at least, to human agency. Exclusively divine action was no longer the sole factor in shaping the fate of humankind and the world. What was revolutionary here was that a mortal, as it were, would take God's place in paving the road to redemption. Even the most apocalyptically-minded thinkers, such as Rabbi Kook, his students, and their students in turn (below: Rabbi Kook's

---

[16]   See, for example, the following declaration of Rabbi Mordecai Nurock: "We, who stand on the foundations of traditional Judaism, aspire to instruct and show everyone that 'Tradition and Freedom' are not two opposites, but a uniform whole, and that they can both be fulfilled: one can be a complete democrat in all the minutest details, a loyal lover of the broadest sectors of the nation, and at the same time be an observant Jew, devoted with all his heart and soul to the tradition of his ancestors, for whom his Torah and religion are part and parcel of himself. The foundations of the Torah are not only not opposed to the broad foundations of democracy, but these concepts are intertwined and interlinked as a flame is to the glowing coal" (*Zekher Mordekhai: Dedicated to the Life and Activity of Rabbi Mordecai Nurock*, ed. A. Tartakower et al. [Jerusalem 1967], 116 [Hebrew]. This declaration was first issued late in 1917, while the Bolshevik Revolution was still in progress in Russia). Nurock even proposed establishing an educational system that would combine religious and secular studies.

[17]   The fascination implicit in the idea of political organization before the advent of the Messiah may also be discerned in discussions of the status of the modern State of Israel relative to messianic fulfillment by Rabbi Shlomo Goren, formerly Chief Rabbi of Israel; see his *Torat ha-Medinah* (Jerusalem, 1996), 18-27 [Hebrew]. Cf. E. Belfer, *The Kingdom of Heaven and the State of Israel: The Political Dimension in Jewish Thought* (Ramat Gan, 1991), 58-71 [Hebrew].

circle), who defined the ultimate Redemption as an eminently miraculous situation—particularly in regard to the imminent resurrection of the dead—had to concede the natural character of the beginning of the process, which was entrusted to human hands.

Religious Zionism was quite aware of the theological revolution implicit in its self-perception as an active partner in the redemption, an awareness evident in the writings of its founding father, Rabbi Isaac Jacob Reines. Rabbi Reines declared that the Hibbat Zion movement "is strongly connected with Redemption," and "there is no greater manifestation of the Redemption."[18] God Himself, as it were, was waiting for mortals to initiate the redemptive process, and only then would He intervene. "[T]he unexpected fruits of human endeavor reveal themselves as the mysterious manifestation of divine guidance."[19]

The implications for the ideas of the Divine and of Divine Providence are fundamental and would exceed the purview of the current work.

At the same time, the Land of Israel was brought down, as it were, from heaven to earth, no longer a divine, spiritual realm, but a temporal, concrete land. Although its divine dimension as the Holy Land was preserved, even enhanced and expanded, the once-hidden temporal dimension came to light. The nation's attachment to its homeland, once an abstract, disembodied yearning, could now focus on a real land.[20] Two approaches developed with regard to this "descent" of the land from metaphysical heights to this world: some saw it as a shift from the divine interior to the divine exterior; while others believed that the land would also, as it were, drag God down with it, implying His presence in the very clods of its earth.[21] In any case, the abstract God was thus tied to the terrestrial soil—a revolutionary theological step in the context of traditional thought.

18   See the discussion and quotations in J. Shapira, "Thought and Halakhah in the Philosophy of Rabbi Isaac Jacob Reines" (PhD diss., Hebrew University, Jerusalem, 1997), 133-35 [Hebrew].

19   Berkovits, *Faith after the Holocaust*, 156.

20   "This primeval right of the Jewish people to its land is not abstract, and its validity is not confined to the realm of its special spiritual qualities [...] The Jewish people has possessed [the Land of Israel] since the time of the Patriarchs as a legally valid acquisition and inheritance" (Rabbi Shlomo Goren, *Torat ha-Mo'adim* [Jerusalem, 1996], 642 [Hebrew]).

21   For an account of these two approaches, see my *Land of Israel in Religious Zionist Thought*.

Anthropological Significance

Religious Zionism wished to create what was almost a new anthropological model, the religious type of the messianic world.[22] The earliest supporters of religious Zionism clearly distinguished between the religiosity of instinct and the religiosity of purposeful awareness. Rabbi Kook wrote:

> In the situation of the nation in Exile, the instinct of the national will to exist ruled each and every individual Jew, impelling him to preserve the religion and respect the faith in general—even though that particular individual had no clear consciousness of the value of Jewish religion and faith and the value of the sanctity of Israel—out of a hidden, instinctive feeling that any weakening of the unifying link of religion and faith would nullify national emotions and might lead to disintegration of the entire nation. Whereas it was not possible for the clear awareness of the nation's will to exist and its paths of renaissance to be actualized and be revealed in the nation as a whole [...] now that the light of the national movement has arisen, out of will and awareness, on a practical basis, with the strong ambition to assemble in the Land of Israel and renew the former life of the people as of old, the time has come for this clear awareness to be revealed in the nation as a whole. And when the process is complete, great things will take place for the existence of the Divine light, for the knowledge of the Lord that is unique to Israel, for faith and observance of the Torah, which constitutes the Jewish way of life much more than all the actions of natural, blind instinct.[23]

Those early supporters of religious Zionism distinguished as well between the *Galut* person, egotistical, wrapped up in oneself, and the new person, whose actions were conditioned by the needs of the community;[24] between

---

[22] There is a certain parallel here to the secular Zionist myth of the "new Jew"; see A. Shapira, *New Jews Old Jews* (Tel Aviv, 1997), 155-74 [Hebrew].

[23] Rabbi Abraham I. Kook, *Ma'amarei ha-Re'ayah* (Articles of Rabbi Kook) (Jerusalem, 1980), 30 (first published in 1911).

[24] "The *Galut* Jew cannot strive for anything but the selfish goal of his own good, and, as he is cut off from his land and never sure of his sustenance, his heart and mind are preoccupied with his profit and his own preference at the cost of others." By contrast, "the awareness of the simple farmer, whose diligent tending of his land does not serve him and his family alone, but the entire nation, elevated and refined his Jewish awareness and his character to such a degree that he had to come to the study house only on Sabbaths and festivals" (Glasner, "Zionism in the Light of Faith," 72).

a depressive psychological state of anxiety, fear, and self-denigration and
a state of mental health;[25] and between alienation from general culture
and involvement in it.[26] The religious Zionist would say: "The deeds and
achievements of Zionism are quite well-known: the metamorphosis process
that created the new people, the wonders of the awakening of the language,
the immigrations [to the Land of Israel] beginning with the Second
[Aliyah], the rebuilding of the land, the importance of agriculture and labor
as a whole, the establishment of the Hebrew school, the pioneering spirit—
all the deeds that stand before us as a historic achievement, which has
already struck roots in the soil of history, but nonetheless is not the legacy
of the past, but continues to exist and act. Let us not forget in this survey,
that is not complete, that there is one phenomenon that is entirely internal:
the new man, the liberated Jew—the resurrection of the individual within
a liberated nation."[27]

The transition to the new type of person could not be effected unless
the very state of *Galut* was shattered, so as to expose the new reality. To this
day, the national renaissance in the Land of Israel is understood as recovery

25   "The sojourn in the darkness of the lands of Exile, subservience to the Gentiles, determined
      to a unique degree the inner depression in the tents of Jacob, in the innermost parts of his
      soul and spirit [...] This spiritual and mental darkness and gloom hindered absorption of the
      sight of the light of dawn that was shining forth and rising, through the concealing mask of
      external and internal circumstances, while the Jewish spirit was awakening to reveal the force
      of its truth and the rebuilding of its perfect life" (Rabbi Zevi Yehudah Kook, *Li-Netivot Yisra'el*
      [Jerusalem, 1989], 136-37). "Just as fear belongs to Exile, and on the other hand courage is
      revealed in the era of redemption, so self-humbling before the Gentiles was fitting for Exile
      [...] as against the straightening of our public stature that is now being revealed in our
      midst" (Rabbi Shlomo Aviner, a contemporary religious Zionist rabbi, *Am ke-Lavi* [A People Like
      a Lion] [Jerusalem, 1983], vol. 2, 184-85 [Hebrew]).

26   Providence demands of us now, perhaps for the first time in Jewish history, to meet the outside
      world with pride and courage, with the *kippah* on the head and the tractate Yebamoth in the
      hand, and to sanctify it by conquest [...] Wherever we place our feet—be it in the laboratory
      or in the business office, in the university campus or in the factory—must be sanctified by us:
      that the young man who enters there subdues them and does not allow the secular to swallow
      up the holy" (Rabbi Joseph B. Soloveitchik, *The Rav Speaks: Five Addresses on Israel, History, and
      the Jewish People* [Brooklyn, NY, 2002], 154).

27   Yeshayahu Aviad (Wolfsberg), *Yahadut ve-Hoveh* (The Judaism of the Present) (Jerusalem,
      1962), 30 [Hebrew]. Aviad went on to assert that Zionism had created "a new, interesting and
      fascinating type of person," and to attribute the appearance of this multifaceted, flexible Jew
      to a combination of the tradition of Torah study, on the one hand, and the ability to survive in
      Exile, on the other (67). On religious Zionism as a rebellion and revolution, see further, 110-11.

from "the malady of *Galut*."[28] Formally speaking, indeed, the goal was to retrieve the ancient past, a time when Israel was living an autonomous life upon its own land. But religious Zionist thinkers were well aware that the rebuilding of the nation demanded new cultural orientations, hence also suitable educational preparation, in order to shape and stabilize the new type.[29]

Revolt against Rabbinical Authority

By taking the messianic initiative into their hands, the religious Zionists necessarily brought the movement to rebel against the rabbinical leadership. As a general rule, with individual exceptions, it seems clear that religious Zionism did not deliberately or willingly rebel against rabbinical authority; the revolt grew out of a given situation, in which most of the leaders of the Torah world were opposed to the Zionist movement and rejected it out of hand. The Mizrachi leaders confessed: "We left our mentors and went to the Land of Israel."[30] They knew that Zionist activity involved activism of a pioneering and political stamp that was foreign to the leadership of the existing Torah world. "For none in the study hall would succeed in this."[31] This was a notable, and emphatic, expression of the revolutionary element in religious Zionism. Through various conflicts and controversies, such as that over women's suffrage, which began toward the end of the 1920s, those in Mizrachi in the Land of Israel and in the Diaspora arrived at a position which limited the authority of the rabbis. "The question is cultural, and in no way religious";[32] or, as one Mizrachi leader put it in particularly blunt terms: "In matters of *issur ve-hetter* ["purely" religious matters] [...] we

---

28   Quoting Rabbi E. Jacob Dushinsky, a religious Zionist preacher who spent his last years in South Africa; see his *In the Wake of Festivals and Solemn Days: Thoughts of the Festivals and Solemn Days* (New York, 1982), 152 [Hebrew].

29   See Schwartz, *Faith at the Crossroads*, 140-51.

30   As stated, for example, by Rabbi Meir Bar-Ilan (Berlin), the most prominent leader of Mizrachi for many years, at the Seventh Conference of Ha-Po'el ha-Mizrachi in the Land of Israel (1935); see *Seventh Conference*, 32.

31   Rabbi David Zevi Katzburg, cited in I. Z. Zehavi, *From the Hatam Sofer to Herzl: The History of Hibbat Zion and the Beginnings of Zionism in Hungary* (Jerusalem, 1966), 336 [Hebrew].

32   Simon Menahem Lazer, *Al ha-Mizpeh: Selected Writings*, ed. G. Kressel (Jerusalem, 1969), 174 [Hebrew].

consult the rabbis, but in matters of life in the marketplace they must ask us."[33] Another case was the controversy over partition (1937), when certain rabbis insisted that political questions such as the partition of the Land of Israel were not halakhic issues.[34] This view is in sharp contrast to the idea of *Da'at Torah* (the view of the Torah) current today in the ultra-Orthodox community.

The rebellion went as far as rejecting the Hasidic leadership, and questioned the leadership ability of its *admorim* (leaders of Hasidic sects). In areas formerly under the exclusive sway of Hasidism, religious Zionists issued the call

> to release the followers and students of the Torah from the chains and yoke of *admorut*; this *admorut*, now empty both of its original content and its early nature, which has been so bold as to prohibit the Land of Israel and the Hebrew tongue; this *admorut*, so remote from worldly life and the life and desires of the nation, which is nothing but an instrument of wrath wielded by a few unknown and irresponsible persons.[35]

Even opponents of this view, who believed that "one could be a Hasid and man of good deeds and heed the counsel of the *admorim*, while relying in

---

[33]   Rabbi Judah Leib Maimon (Fishman), speaking in reference to women's suffrage; see M. Friedman, *Society and Religion: The Non-Zionist Orthodoxy in Eretz-Israel—1918-1936* (Jerusalem, 1978), 166 [Hebrew].

[34]   This was the view of Rabbi Reuben Margaliot; see I. Warhaftig, "Rabbinic Reaction to the 1937 Peale [*sic*] Partition Plan," *Tehumin* 9 (1988): 276 [Hebrew]. See also S. Dothan, *Partition of Eretz-Israel in Mandatory Period: The Jewish Controversy* (Jerusalem, 1980), 182 [Hebrew]. On the term "*Da'at Torah*," see G. Bakon, "Torah Opinion and Pangs of the Messiah," *Tarbiz* 52 (1983): 497-508 [Hebrew].

[35]   Rabbi Judah Leib Zlotnik (Avida), a Mizrachi rabbi in Poland, cited in A. Rubinstein, *A Movement in a Period of Transition* (Ramat Gan, 1981), 158 (Hebrew). Zlotnik bewailed the fact that "the ritual of *admorut*" still existed in Mizrachi circles, and was worried that certain people "might transfer this ritual to the Land of Israel, too." He went on to say: "Surely no one would dare suspect these *admorim* of hardening their hearts, of cruelty, but we see here people who are remote from life, for whom the matters of the people are foreign and strange, and who are not awake to the sorrow of the nation. For the time has come to explain to all ranks of the religious that these people, for all their greatness in Torah and observance, cannot direct the nation in its way of life and lead it to its renaissance" (164). Zlotnik's blunt appeal attracted others, such as I. Gruenwald (Opotchna); see 197.

political matters on Sokolow, Weizmann, and others," admitted quite freely that the *admorim* had no "knowledge of politics."[36]

Many prominent religious Zionist thinkers took pains to conceal the revolt against rabbinical authority; against these, however, many leaders of Mizrachi, particularly of various factions in the Torah ve-Avodah movement, were emphatic concerning their rejection of total rabbinical authority. "In no wise are we to accept the way of blind obedience as correct, regarding the rabbinate as it is today."[37] In many periods, indifference to rabbinical leadership was a fact of life. Professor Menahem Zevi Kaddari, a leader of the Bnei Akiva movement in Hungary during the years 1943-1946, and later Rector of Bar-Ilan University, surveying attitudes at the time, writes:

> It did not occur to anyone that rabbis were needed at the head of a political movement. There was nothing wrong if a member had achieved the rabbinical level in his studies: he could continue his activities in the leadership as well. But it would have been unwarranted to bring rabbis in from the outside to serve in the key positions in the movement.[38]

It is worth noting that many had given up the hope that the Chief Rabbinate heralded the reinstitution of the Sanhedrin.

Despite such differences in the nature of the reactions, from group to group and from place to place, it seems clear that this revolutionary aspect was the practical result of the three previous aspects. Many religious Zionists, including Rabbi Kook, found this aspect problematic. Rabbinical authority has been firmly rooted in the Jewish religious consciousness for hundreds of years.

---

[36]   Rabbi Katriel Fishel Tchorsh (a member of the Council of the Chief Rabbinate) (Rubinstein, *Movement*, 167).

[37]   Zuriel Admanit (a central idologue of the religious kibbutz movement), in *Be-Tokh Ha-Zerem ve-Negdo* (Within the Stream and Against It), ed. Y. Asher (Tel Aviv, 1977), 352 [Hebrew].

[38]   M. Z. Kaddari, "The Ideology of 'Bnei-Akiba' in Hungary," in *Hundred Years*, vol. 2, *Historical Aspects*, 351.

Rabbi Kook and Rabbinical Authority

Rabbi Kook strove to contend with this revolutionary aspect. He drew closer
to the ultra-Orthodox, either deliberately or due to the circumstances, when
he issued several stringent rulings that represented his halakhic views,[39]
obviously in opposition to Mizrachi. He pinned great hopes on Agudat
Israel, although this movement also included Mizrachi secessionists. He
even left in 1914 to participate in an Agudat Israel conference in Germany,
and remained stranded in Europe for the duration of the war. Only in
1918, when planning to establish his own movement, did Rabbi Kook
object to Agudat Israel's anti-Zionist stance, although even then he did not
completely cut ties with it. Members of Rabbi Kook's circle also drew closer
to Agudat Israel and even participated in its political bodies, as did Rabbi
David Cohen ("the Nazir"), who was an Agudat Israel representative.

At the end of World War I, Rabbi Kook felt that his fifteen years
of activity in the Land of Israel and abroad had prepared the ground for
a genuine alternative to Mizrachi. Rabbi Kook felt that Mizrachi's moderate
course was entirely wrong, and the Balfour Declaration reinforced his sense
of the impending Redemption. His persistent and longstanding critique of
Mizrachi flared up into an open political conflict. "Degel Yerushalayim"
was the name of the federation established by Rabbi Kook which aimed
to bring together all observant Jews who supported the building of the
land.[40] The movement was meant to operate in all the areas that had so far
concerned Mizrachi: political and cultural activities and the settlement of
the Land of Israel. As opposed to the minor and moderate role Mizrachi
had played, Rabbi Kook expected Degel Yerushalayim to launch a militant
struggle to impose religion on the Jewish national movement. He must have
known of Mizrachi's hard struggle at the time to collect a sufficient number
of signatures to enable it to change its status from faction to federation, but
did not hesitate to establish a competing body. For propaganda purposes,
he insisted on clarifying he had no wish to hinder the Zionist movement,
and especially not Mizrachi, but did not hide his hope that "Mizrachi

---

[39]   See M. Z. Nehorai, "Remarks on the Rabbinic Rulings of Rabbi Kook," *Tarbiz* 59 (1990): 481-505
[Hebrew]; Rosenak, *Prophetic Halakhah*.

[40]   See Y. Avneri, "Degel Yerushalayim," *Bi-Shvilei ha-Tehyiah (In the Paths of Renewal: Studies in
Religious Zionism)* 3 (1989): 39-58 [Hebrew].

will also join the federation [meaning Degel Yerushalayim]." Despite the open objections of his admirers from Mizrachi—Rabbis Maimon, Bar-Ilan, and others—Rabbi Kook proceeded along his new political course. His close disciples—Rabbis Jacob Moses Harlap, David Cohen, and his son Zevi Yehudah Kook—joined him in this endeavor, and branches were established in various countries (the Land of Israel, Switzerland, England, and others).

The new movement quickly declined and vanished. According to Rabbi Kook, the reasons for the decline were to be found in his own unique personality. Rabbi Kook had brilliant political insight, but leading an international movement required efforts beyond what he was willing to invest, and exacted a spiritual price he was unwilling to pay. The movement's success depended on Rabbi Kook's magnetic, charismatic personality, and to achieve results he would have had to remain in Europe (at least in Western Europe), as he was explicitly asked to do more than once. Rabbi Kook, however, longed for the Land of Israel and was unwilling to remain abroad. He also wrote less during his stay in London. His stormy personality sought spiritual heights, but an international movement demands engagement in routine, mundane tasks, far removed from the intellectual world. The movement, therefore, dwindled and died on its own. His affinity to the Old *Yishuv* was revealed also in his resolute opposition to the Mizrachi stance on the question of women's suffrage.[41]

In summation: the approach of Rabbi Kook sought to counter the revolt against rabbinic authority. In recent years, the militant position of religious Zionism *vis-à-vis* rabbinical authority has weakened, and many of its leaders have come to accept rabbinical discipline and to advocate obedience to rabbinical opinion. In addition, rabbis have penetrated leadership positions. This process is the outcome of a variety of factors, which require a separate interdisciplinary investigation.

---

[41]   See Z. Zohar, "Traditional Flexibility and Modern Strictness: Two Halakhic Positions on Women's Suffrage," in *Sephardi and Middle Eastern Jewries: History and Culture in the Modern Era*, ed. H. Goldberg (Bloomington, IN, 1996), 119-33; H. Boaz, "The Religious 'Status Quo' and the Generation of Social Categories: The Struggle for Female Suffrage in the Pre-State Period," *Theory and Criticism* 21 (2002):107-31 [Hebrew].

Conclusion

It is easily understood that these four aspects of revolutionism reveal basic characteristics of the religious Zionist revolution. One basic characteristic of revolutionism is the totality of social change.[42] This element, which is present in the major revolutions of both East and West, is also relatively valid for a national revolution, such as Zionism in general and religious Zionism in particular. The most cautious formulations of the founding fathers of religious Zionism at the end of the nineteenth and the beginning of the twentieth centuries reveal an uncompromising readiness to adopt the total change in social and religious order that followed from the Zionist enterprise. The desire for change and rebellion became manifest in various areas, as mentioned above. It is therefore clear that religious Zionists developed a strong revolutionary consciousness, expressed in their belief in their centrality in the messianic process and in their explanation of Zionist history (using the theology of Rabbi Kook), a fact that runs counter to the movement's exclusion from the power centers of the *Yishuv* and of the young State of Israel. This situation changed after the Six-Day War, and the new circumstances promoted practical expression of the revolutionary consciousness of religious Zionism—and it is not surprising that Rabbi Kook's disciples became the spiritual leaders of this movement. This development requires further research.

---

[42]   See S. N. Eisenstadt, *Revolution and the Transformation of Societies* (New York, 1978).

Chapter Twelve

MAIMONIDES IN RABBI KOOK'S
AND RELIGIOUS ZIONIST PHILOSOPHY:
UNITY VS. DUALITY

Calls for a return to the "Golden Age" of Spain have occasionally resonated in religious Zionism.[1] The open, broad-minded, and creative world of the Andalusian sages was significant for the movement's leaders and thinkers. Mossad Harav Kook, the publishing house that had previously been associated mostly with religious Zionist ideology, published a series of textbooks on Andalusian *piyyut*, exegesis, and philosophy.[2] The interesting question is: why did the movement's leadership seek to rely on Andalusian sages such as Abraham Ibn Ezra, Judah Halevi, and Maimonides? Religious Zionism had tried to create a new religious type, incorporating two mutually contradictory dispositions:

---

[1]   Such calls were voiced, for instance, by Zeev Jawitz (*Ya'avetz*), Isaiah Bernstein, and Samuel Abraham Poznanski. See Schwartz, *Faith at the Crossroads*, 151.

[2]   In 1967, Mossad Harav Kook published an anthology of medieval philosophy and ethical literature and another of medieval *piyyut* (religious poetry) and secular poetry. These two works were designed for "high school *yeshivot* and religious high schools, according to the new curriculum of the Religious Education Department of the Ministry of Education and Culture." See N. Ben-Menahem, *Books of Mossad Harav Kook Published during the Years 1937-1970* (Jerusalem, 1970), 148 [Hebrew]; H. Zohar, *Mossad Harav Kook: Its Beginnings, Founders, Leaders, the Mizrahi Movement, Their Contribution to the Study of Religious Zionism and the Land of Israel* (Jerusalem, 2005), 32 [Hebrew]. A trend to educate in light of medieval Hebrew literature was widespread in the Zionist movement in general. In 1959, Hayyim Hanani proposed a curriculum that included works by Andalusian sages such as Shmuel ha-Nagid, Solomon ibn Gabirol, and Judah Halevi. See T. Tadmor Shimony, "The Textbook as an Ideological Text: The Formation of the National Identity in National School Readers and in Religious National School Readers," in *Between Tradition and Innovation: Studies in Judaism, Zionism and the State of Israel—Yehoshua Kaniel: In Memoriam*, ed. E. Don Yehiya (Ramat Gan, 2005), 467-93 [Hebrew].

(1) Progress: a type integrating deep religiosity with modernity.

(2) Conservatism: a type operating in a world of redemption, and thus promoting a messianic process.

The cultural and creative ideal of Spanish Jewry in the eleventh and twelfth centuries offers a concrete historical example of the potential integration of cultural progress and religious conservatism. Progress was evident in such theoretical realms as secular poetry, sciences, and philosophy, and in political involvement in local government. Maimonides is a prominent figure in this context, a unique and wondrous product of Spanish Andalusian culture, who, although deeply and absolutely committed to halakhah, evinced great openness. The Maimonides of *Mishneh Torah* symbolized the primacy of religious law, whereas the Maimonides of the *Guide of the Perplexed* was a paragon of ideological and cultural openness. The two works together present a distinguished scholar who was also attentive to the needs of his contemporaries and directed his spiritual endeavor to provide solutions for their hardships. No wonder, then, that his figure was symbolically and substantially influential in religious Zionist thought. Leaders and activists such as Rabbi Judah Leib Maimon (Fishman) and Meir Orian wrote monographs on Maimonides.[3]

Maimonides' *Mishneh Torah* was not confined to the exilic period. His rulings deal also with the Temple and with the laws of the sabbatical and jubilee years. For religious Zionists, the return to the Land of Israel obviously conveyed a possibility of paving the way for full compliance with the Torah. For thinkers such as Rabbis Isaac Nissenbaum and Simon Federbusch, the *Mishneh Torah* expressed the restoration of perfect worship.[4]

A significant issue recurrently discussed in religious Zionist thought is Maimonides' conservatism and the harmony of his personality. The distinction between the *Mishneh Torah* and the *Guide of the Perplexed* led to increasing awareness of this question.

---

[3] Rabbi Judah Leib Maimon (Fishman), *R. Moses b. Maimon: His Biography and Literary Oeuvre* (Jerusalem, 1960) [Hebrew]; Meir Orian, *The Guide for the Generations: R. Moses b. Maimon* (Jerusalem, 1956) [Hebrew].

[4] Schwartz, *Faith at the Crossroads*, 171.

The main purpose of the present chapter is to present various images of Maimonides that developed in religious Zionism and, in particular, to clarify the attitude of its thinkers toward the *Guide*. From the perspective of the history of ideas, however, the significant question can be formulated as: is there a religious Zionist reading of Maimonides? Was Maimonides interpreted in a particular or even unique way in religious Zionist thought? Unquestionably, Maimonides was an important symbol in the weaving of religious Zionist doctrine. At the same time, the interpretation of Maimonides' writings often draws on the interpreter's specific worldview. The question that will concern us below, then, is whether religious Zionist thought offers a unique interpretation of Maimonides' endeavor.

Split or Harmony?

The harmony within Maimonides' figure had concerned the rabbinic world in the past and is now of interest also to scholars. Given that religious Zionism has defined the contemporary period as an era of national renaissance and redemption, the characteristics and the stature of the "ideal man" has been one of its foremost concerns. Maimonides was obviously a paragon of this kind of renaissance. For religious Zionism, however, the "ideal man" possessed originality and self-respect, and Maimonides had relied extensively on foreign sources in his philosophical essay, particularly on Greek philosophical sources in Arab translation. Confusion increases even further because Maimonides was certainly not an ordinary figure or an amorphous personality. He displayed great originality and inspiration in his halakhic work, *Mishneh Torah*, which draws mainly on internal Jewish sources. As Isadore Twersky has excellently clarified,[5] the *Mishneh Torah* is unparalleled in its editing, its language, its style, and its scope. How, then, should we relate to these two contradictory elements in Maimonides? Are they integrated into a new paradigm or do they hint at a lamentable split?

These are the issues in the controversy between Zeev Jawitz and Rabbi Kook. Jawitz drew a sharp distinction between the Maimonides of the *Mishneh Torah* and the Maimonides of the *Guide*. In his comprehensive

---

[5] I. Twersky, *Introduction to the Code of Maimonides (Mishneh Torah)* (New Haven, 1980).

historical treatise, *Toledot Israel*, which is strongly imbued with a religious
Zionist spirit, he formulated a sharp and detailed critique of the *Guide*.[6]
He viewed this work as definitely a product of Greek culture, which he
counterposed to Judaism.[7] Jawitz relied on the following assumptions:

(1) Maimonides adopted a "Hebrew method" ("internal") in the
Mishneh Torah and a "Greek method" ("external") in the *Guide*.[8]

(2) Maimonides is a product of Andalusian culture, whose thinkers
and leaders were involved in Torah study, on the one hand, and in pursuit
of an "alien" philosophy, on the other.[9]

The second assumption justifies the first. Maimonides, as it were,
surrendered to Andalusian fashion and thus engaged in "external"
philosophical writing. Jawitz's historical sense led him to judge Maimonides'
endeavor in the context of his *Sitz im Leben*.

When assessing Maimonides, Jawitz sought to separate sharply
between the *Guide* and Maimonides' halakhic writings, particularly the
Mishneh Torah. He stressed that issues featuring in both treatises also differ
in value: holy in one (*Mishneh Torah*) and profane in the other (*Guide*), one
wheat and the other chaff:

> The reader of the *Mishneh Torah*, written by our master Moshe b.
> Maimon, may at times find it is inspired by the holy spirit of the
> Torah given by our master Moshe b. Amram. The Laws of Ethical
> Character (*De'ot*) and the Laws of Repentance in the *Book of
> Knowledge* will, even more strongly, affect the soul as if they had
> been given by Moses at Sinai. If the *Mishneh Torah* is all holy, the
> *Book of Knowledge* is the Holy of Holies, the spring of life to the spirit
> of the Torah of Israel.[10]

---

6   R. Michael, *Jewish Historiography from the Renaissance to the Modern Time* (Jerusalem, 1993),
    454-56 [Hebrew].

7   See D. Schwartz, *Challenge and Crisis*, 226-28.

8   Zeev Jawitz, *Sefer Toledot Israel*, vol. 12 (Tel Aviv, 1935), 42, 46-47. Jawitz focused his anger on
    the presentation of the prophets "as philosophers busy discussing the methods of Greek and
    Arab philosophy" (33). He is referring mainly to the chapters on prophecy and to the discussion
    about Job in the *Guide*.

9   Jawitz, *Toledot Israel*, 40-41. Jawitz mentioned Bahya ibn Pakuda, Solomon ibn Gabirol,
    Abraham ibn Daud, and, obviously, "the spirit of the witty sage R. Abraham b. Ezra, which
    ['philosophy'] sullied even more than all others" (41).

10 Jawitz, *Toledot Israel*, 48. In a footnote, Jawitz added: "And if they used the same yardstick
    to measure the Book of Knowledge [in *Mishneh Torah*] and the *Guide of the Perplexed*, what

Elsewhere, he claimed that the reasons for the commandments in the *Mishneh Torah* atone, as it were, for the reasons for the commandments in the *Guide*.[11]

Scholars have often noted differences between Maimonides' halakhic and philosophical writings. Unquestionably, however, a scrupulous reading of Maimonides' introductions to the Mishnah, and to the Laws of the Foundations of the Torah, the Laws of Ethical Character, and the Laws of Repentance in the *Mishneh Torah* reveal that the halakhic man was not far removed from the author of the *Guide*. Jawitz does not agree, and focuses his attack on the view that the *vita contemplativa* represents the apex of human perfection on two grounds:

(1) Underlying this outlook is the assumption that contemplation is superior to action, a distinctively Greek approach that views action as lacking intrinsic value. Judaism, by contrast, supports the intrinsic value of action and ascribes no importance to abstract theological inquiry.[12]

(2) This outlook is an expression of Maimonidean elitism, a typical feature of the *Guide*, "which pays no attention to the thousands whose spirit is incapable of fathoming these depths."[13] The elitist style also supports the superiority of Greek over prophetic wisdom, given that the Greeks had formulated the mysteries clearly, whereas the prophets had resorted to a vague allegorical style.[14]

Later on in his work, Jawitz ascribed the idea of contemplative perfection and its social and eschatological implications to the *Guide*:

---

they had in mind are chapters 2, 3, and 4 [of the Laws of the Foundations of the Torah], where he briefly outlines the Aristotelian method." These are cosmological chapters describing the foundations of reality.

[11] Jawitz, *Toledot Israel*, 46.

[12] Given that theological inquiry is not effective ("because human reason is unable to contain such sublime views" [Jawitz, *Toledot Israel*, 35]).

[13] Jawitz, *Toledot Israel*, 32.

[14] Jawitz deliberately resorts here to the glass metaphor in BT Yevamot 49b stressing the uniqueness of Moses' prophecy, an issue discussed at length in Maimonides' writings in general, and in the *Guide* in particular: "Hence, according to this view, foreign philosophy is superior to the Torah of the God of Israel, as a clear glass is preferable to a dim glass" (ibid., 39-40). Philosophy is actually parallel to Moses' prophecy.

This Greek inclination, which turns [philosophical] ideas into the key principle and makes moral virtues marginal, was also the inspiration for the *Guide of the Perplexed*, which defines "moral perfection" as "only a means, but not as an end in itself [...] [True perfection] consists in the acquisition of the rational virtues" (*Guide* 3:54).[15] And the righteous, pure, and innocent, who will not know how to engage in wisdom, that is, in the "alien" philosophy, none of his righteous deeds will be remembered and he will share the fate of the ignorant louts. And the righteousness of such a man will only bring him honor in the eyes of the uncouth mass that, in its folly, thinks that money and physical power, too, are an honor and an advantage.[16]

Was Jawitz correct when isolating the *Guide* from the rest of the Maimonidean oeuvre? A cursory examination will reveal that Maimonides formulates his elitist approach in his discussion about the final cause of human life in the general introduction to the *Commentary to the Mishnah*, and in his introduction to Chapter Eleven of Tractate Sanhedrin. The first presents the intellectual as the final end of humankind, and the second presents the immortality of intelligence according to the acquisition of wisdom in material life.[17] Chapter Eight of the Laws of Repentance clearly states that only intelligence is immortal ("that form of soul which is identical with the intelligence which apprehends the Creator as far as it is able"),[18] and that its immortality is contingent on the knowledge acquired in the course of material life. Although the *Mishneh Torah* is devoted to halakhah as the law incumbent on all segments of the people, its elitism is essentially no different from that of the *Guide*.

According to Jawitz, the weak points of the *Guide* are:

15 All quotations are from *The Guide of the Perplexed*, trans. S. Pines (Chicago, 1963).

16 Jawitz, *Toledot Israel*, 33.

17 D. Schwartz, "Avicenna and Maimonides on Immortality: A Comparative Study," in *Medieval and Modern Perspectives on Muslim-Jewish Relations*, ed. R. L. Nettler (Chur, Switzerland, 1995), 185-97.

18 Maimonides, *Mishneh Torah, The Book of Knowledge*, trans. M. Hyamson (Jerusalem, 1962), Laws of Repentance 8:6.

(1) Its cosmological and theological discussions. The *Guide* hardly deals with anthropology, and focuses instead on the cosmic order and on theology.[19]

(2) Its universal character. The *Guide* hardly addresses the special standing of the people of Israel.

Jawitz contrasted the cosmological and theological concerns of the *Guide* with other Andalusian works intensely concerned with anthropological and Jewish issues.[20] In an attempt to disclose Maimonides' "pure heart," Jawitz also points to a letter noting prophecy's superiority over philosophy that, although ascribed to Maimonides, is probably apocryphal.[21]

Jawitz took pains to devalue the *Guide*. In his strong opposition to Maimonides' view that the human creature is not the purpose of reality, he argued that the writings of Saadia Gaon and Bahya ibn Pakuda, who make the human being the purpose of creation, "are not inferior to the *Guide* even in their wide knowledge of Greek philosophy."[22] Maimonides, then, showed no special expertise in the philosophical sources, as it were, a claim that can only be understood as reflecting Jawitz's anti-Maimonidean intentions. Jawitz also dealt at length with the theory of the spheres to present the *Guide* as an archaic work irrelevant to modern Jews.

Jawitz discusses at length the exceptional nature of the *Guide* in the context of Maimonides' oeuvre. *Mishneh Torah* is a book of revelation, and Maimonides was, as it were, divinely inspired when writing it. Indeed, it is equivalent to the Mishnah ("the Mishnah of our holy teacher, R. Judah ha-Nasi").[23] The *Guide*, by contrast, is a one-time slip, the isolated mistake of a great man. In this book, Maimonides strayed after a passing trend,

---

[19]   Jawitz, *Toledot Israel*, 38. A prominent instance of the *Guide*'s neglect of anthropological concerns is its "loathing of the body" (45), referring to the ascetic outlook formulated in several places. See, for instance, Schwartz, "Ethics and Asceticism." Another indication of this approach is the view that man is not the final end of Creation (*Guide* 3:13).

[20]   Jawitz mentions Saadia Gaon, Bahya ibn Pakuda, and Judah Halevi (*Toledot Israel*, 38).

[21]   *Toledot Israel*, 41-42. This is a letter by Rabbi Hasdai Halevi, and Isaac Shailat has already pointed out its ascription to Maimonides as dubious. See I. Shailat, *Letters and Essays of Moses Maimonides*, vol. 2 (Maaleh Adumim, 1998), 673-76 [Hebrew].

[22]   Jawitz, *Toledot Israel*, 37. Under duress, Jawitz admitted that the *Guide* influenced Christian scholastics and Moslem culture (48).

[23]   *Toledot Israel*, 37.

which now lacks any value. Jawitz finds no merit in this book, except for its defense of Creation and Providence. The *Guide* presents Maimonides as a split personality, torn between sublime inner content and the appeal of a transient external fashion.

Although *Toledot Israel* is a comprehensive historical treatise written in the spirit of religious Zionism, Rabbi Kook was quite critical of it.[24] He objected to the classification of the *Guide* as "Greek wisdom" or "spirit of the Greek people," thus rejecting its exclusion. Rabbi Kook opposed setting dogmatic criteria for membership in the religious community. In his view, intra-national and intra-cultural controversies are legitimate, and he could see no difference between halakhic and theological disputes ("rules of beliefs and opinions")—all derive from "one shepherd."[25] This dialectical approach has a practical moral dimension as well—just as the philosophy of Maimonides, a spiritual giant, had helped him in his own religious progression, so will these views certainly be of assistance to many other Jews. Rabbi Kook's perception of the culture of dispute in general is also valid for a dispute on beliefs and opinions, and this issue has already been widely discussed.[26] Hence, the fact that Maimonides' views can be located within the framework of Judaism does not compel their acceptance. Rabbi Kook wrote:

> Even if many find that they are unable to connect their own spiritual values and beliefs to all the views stated in the *Guide*, they are free to connect the thoughts of their hearts to the views of sages of Israel who have paved other ways.[27]

---

[24] See Yaron, *Philosophy*, 176. This matter is discussed in greater detail in the original Hebrew version of this work, published in 1974, 208.

[25] According to Ecclesiastes 12:1. "*Ma'amar Meyuhad*," in *Ma'marei ha-Re'ayah* (Jerusalem, 1980), 105. This essay was published in 1935 in *Toledot Israel*, vol. 12, and appeared also in *Ha-Hed* under the title "On the Unity of Maimonides" (Hebrew), item 325 in the bibliography published by Y. Werfel (Raphael) in *Writings of the G[aon] R. A[braham] I[saac] Kook, of Blessed Memory* (Jerusalem, 1938), 42 [Hebrew].

[26] These questions have usually emerged in the context of discussions about tolerance and pluralism in Rabbi Kook's writings. See, e.g., Ish-Shalom, "Tolerance"; Ross, *Metaphysical and Liberal Pluralism*, 66-110.

[27] "*Ma'amar Meyuhad*," 106.

Rabbi Kook, then, vehemently rejects the view of the *Guide* as an "external," "alien," and "Greek" work. The discourse on the positions expressed in the *Guide* should be internal to the Jewish community, and the fundamental assumption of such a discourse is that opinions expressed in its course are legitimate.

Rabbi Kook went beyond the formulation of the dialectic principle stating that a theological controversy leaves room for all views, going into details to show that the *Guide* is not an "external" book. In order to ascribe to Maimonides the view that prophecy is superior to reason, Jawitz resorted to a letter of highly dubious provenance (attributed to Hisdai Halevi). He thereby asserted that he had revealed Maimonides' "pure heart," his genuine view. Rabbi Kook, by contrast, relied on the prophecy chapters in the *Guide*. The superiority of prophecy is one of the foundations "from which no reader of the *Guide* could be swayed."[28] Moreover, claimed Rabbi Kook, Jawitz had played down the controversy between Maimonides and the philosophers. The distinction between essence and existence, Creation and Providence, all reflect an abysmal, unbridgeable gap between the *Guide* and Aristotle. The profound difference between Maimonides and the philosophers makes any similarity between them superficial ("external").[29] Finally, contrary to Jawitz's claim of the superiority of contemplation over action and the disregard of "anthropology" [*torat ha-adam*], Rabbi Kook refers the reader to the final chapters of the *Guide*, which deal with the way those who "apprehend the true realities" worship God.[30]

Whereas Jawitz took pains to dismiss the value of the *Guide*, Rabbi Kook invested efforts in pointing out the breadth of this philosophical treatise. His tactic was to point to the *Guide*'s success in anticipating later and even modern viewpoints, as follows:

(1) The claim that the theory of the spheres is archaic is unsupported. Rabbi Kook relied on the discovery of bacteria to side with vitalism,[31] and

---

[28]   *"Ma'amar Meyuhad,"* 107.

[29]   *"Ma'amar Meyuhad,"* 107-8.

[30]   *"Ma'amar Meyuhad,"* 108-9. See E. Goldman, "The Worship Peculiar to Those Who Have Apprehended True Reality," *Bar-Ilan: Annual of Bar-Ilan University* 6 (1968): 287-313.

[31]   Jawitz, *Toledot Israel*, 110.

argued that an explanation of planetary movement through vital forces is not implausible.

(2) The repudiation of an approach negating that the human creature is the final end of Creation reflects narrow-mindedness. Through this claim, Maimonides actually prevented heresy from spreading at a later stage, since heresy in modernity relied on astronomical discoveries that dwarf planet Earth *vis-à-vis* the cosmos. Maimonides had already noted that the centrality of the human world is not the foundation upon which religion rests.[32] Furthermore, argued Rabbi Kook, echoes of this approach are also found in the Kabbalah, which is most certainly an "internal" text.

Ostensibly, the controversy between Rabbi Kook and Jawitz was definitely theological and entirely focused on the question of internal and external borders in Jewish faith. In this sense, this is a classic dispute dealing with the question of membership in the community of faith or exclusion from it.[33] Rabbi Kook, however, seems to have had additional reasons, bearing on the reality then current in the Jewish community in the Land of Israel:

> All the objections that the author [Jawitz], may he rest in peace, raises against our master for embracing Aristotelian philosophy and Arab wisdom had already been raised by his opponents and shaken the world when the book [the *Guide*] first appeared. Indeed, they do not deserve further discussion in our sacred literature, since we know that he did not follow Aristotle or his Arab exegetes blindly. We know that he inquired, and examined, and chose according to all the scientific resources available in his time and even beyond their limits. After clarifying that they did not contradict the foundations of the Torah and being himself inclined to accept them, he did not lie by saying that these had been his own ideas, and found it appropriate to interpret passages from the Written and the Oral Torah according to them.[34]

---

[32]   Ibid., 110-11.

[33]   See, e.g., G. Leff, *Heresy in the Later Middle Ages: The Relation of Heterodoxy to Dissent c. 1250–c. 1450* (Manchester, 1967); J. B. Henderson, *The Construction of Orthodoxy and Heresy* (Albany, 1998).

[34]   "*Ma'amar Meyuhad*," 106.

Rabbi Kook endorsed the view of many rationalists in the Maimonidean controversy that spread at the end of the twelfth to the thirteenth century. He argued that Maimonides had adopted only the philosophical views that do not contradict the foundations of Judaism. In his claim, however, he conveyed his suspicion that the controversy could reawaken. Rabbi Kook was aware that, in the past, the disputes between supporters and opponents of Maimonides had rocked Jewish communities ("shaken the world"), and well knew that the Jewish community in the Land of Israel was in a precarious situation concerning the relationship between Zionism and religion. Beyond their harm to the image of Zionism, new disputes could weaken the stance of the religious Zionist public and its stability, both inward (the Old *Yishuv* vs. the New *Yishuv*) and outward (the Zionist movement). This is an additional consideration to the dialectic perception of dispute, whereby the different views are integrated into a broader, uniform mosaic.

The following table presents the distinctions between them:

	Jawitz	Rabbi Kook
general evaluation of the *Guide*	"external," Greek model	"internal," Hebrew model
the book's concern	cosmological, ignoring human and Jewish issues	---------
standard of science and philosophy	as that in other Andalusian writings	----------
target audience of the *Guide*	elitist	a wide public will be assisted by the book
attitude toward religious action	contemplation is superior to action	the goal of wisdom is action, as evident from the final chapters
theory of spheres	archaic, of no value	fits with vitalism

	Jawitz	Rabbi Kook
the purpose of existence is not man	wrong, and disputed by Andalusian sages	important claim, which shielded the Jewish people from later heresy
prophecy	superior to reason	superior to reason

Rabbi Kook did not address the claim that Maimonides had ignored Jews, that is, the uniqueness of the Jewish people, since this issue is indeed not prominent in the *Guide*. Hence, Rabbi Kook emphasized that Jewish thought offers a variety of paths enabling individuals to choose according to their own inclinations. He did, however, contend with the other issues. Generally, Rabbi Kook strongly objected to Jawitz's perception of the *Guide*, accusing him of "extreme fanaticism."[35] From Rabbi Kook's perspective, the *Guide* does not endorse any philosophical outlook uncritically and without clarifying its contents. Furthermore, he considered that the positive influence of the *Guide* on the propagation of faith among Jews and Gentiles had been decisive. We may therefore conclude that Rabbi Kook drew no distinction between Maimonides in *Mishneh Torah* and Maimonides in the *Guide*.

Jawitz's critique was to some extent supported by Rabbi Joseph B. Soloveitchik in his mid-1940s writings. In *The Halakhic Mind*, Rabbi Soloveitchik claimed that Maimonides had failed in his attempt to offer reasons for the commandments in the *Guide*, but had succeeded in the *Mishneh Torah*. By contrast, in *Halakhic Man*, Rabbi Soloveitchik related to these two works as mutually corresponding and complementary.[36] Rabbi Soloveitchik, then, wavered between Jawitz's and Rabbi Kook's positions.

Maimonides as One

The previous section focused on discussions about unity in Maimonides' oeuvre. This section will focus on a view that is sometimes direct and

---

[35]   Ibid., 111.

[36]   See Schwartz, *Religion or Halakha*, chap. 3.

intuitive and sometimes the product of deeper scrutiny, dealing with the obvious complementarity between the two works. Various thinkers, who formed their attitude toward Maimonides a priori, determined that his corpus is characterized by unity.

This approach has been adopted by many religious Zionist thinkers, such as Rabbi Kook and his circle (including Rabbi Zevi Yehudah Kook and Rabbi David Cohen, "the Nazir"), Rabbi Ben Zion Meir Hai Uzziel, and many others. Relying on these views, I will present an approach that locates philosophy in general and the *Guide* in particular within the spiritual confines of Jewish creativity.

Isaiah Aviad (Wolfsberg) studied in Heidelberg and was one of the Mizrachi leaders in Germany. His writings deal at length with the meaning of history in philosophy in general and within Jewish thought in particular. "The fate of philosophy in Judaism has been strange," he wrote, "it has never been accepted by the majority."[37] Aviad ascribed great importance to the study of philosophy as leading to contact and mutual relationships between cultures, and claimed that the world of ideas leads to "fraternity among nations"[38] and to the realization of the messianic idea, no less (!). Whereas Jawitz drew a distinction between Saadia Gaon the thinker and Maimonides the philosopher, Aviad saw both as thinkers "bearing up with honor in the spiritual battle."[39] For Aviad, Maimonides is a paradigm of the idea that Jewish philosophy maintained mutual relationships with the surrounding culture without renouncing the special character of Jewish religion. Maimonides, then, is a typical instance of this mutuality, being the greatest Jewish philosopher as well as the greatest halakhist:

> Although no perfect system has been formulated, the fact is that the greatest of the philosophers and architects of halakhah was also the greatest builder of Jewish philosophy. This fact attests to an internal need, to the legitimacy of the trend, to the organic fit between these two directions. Philosophy must take into account that, in Judaism, primacy is given to halakhah, but halakhah is not alone in a vacuum, either. It too has a framework and bears a golden

---

[37] Aviad, *Reflections on Judaism*, 45.

[38] Ibid., 46.

[39] Ibid., 47.

crown[40] of thought, as we see in the *Mishneh Torah*. The *Mishneh Torah*, which establishes halakhah on metaphysical principles and concludes with a philosophy of history framed as a vision of the End of Days, introduces several connections to philosophy in order to strengthen the various links.[41]

As halakhah and aggadah complement one another, so do halakhah and philosophy. The structure of the *Mishneh Torah*, which opens and closes with philosophical reflections, confirms this statement. Despite the problematic place of philosophy and the struggle it wages for its role within Judaism, Maimonides succeeded in integrating philosophy and halakhah, creating an organic structure from both realms. Aviad did hint that Maimonides' halakhic endeavor was more systematic than his philosophical one. Aviad himself placed a high premium on systematic and clear formulations.[42] In any event, he saw no essential difference between Maimonides the halakhist and Maimonides the philosopher.

The Interest in the *Guide of the Perplexed*

The *Guide* was definitely involved in disputing with the science of its time and, as such, it has historical value. At the same time, the book is clearly a model of contending with the *Zeitgeist*. How was the *Guide* interpreted in religious Zionist thought? How can Maimonides' philosophical treatise be adapted to deal with current problems? Did the *Guide* play an important role in religious Zionist thought? These matters will concern us in the following sections.

Several religious Zionist thinkers wrote books whose titles were inspired by the *Guide* (*For the Perplexed of Our Time* by Moshe Avigdor Amiel and *A New Guide* by Rabbi Kook, still in manuscript). Research, however, has recently begun to focus on one of religious Zionism's more

---

[40]   According to Exodus 25:25, 37:11, and elsewhere.

[41]   Aviad, *Reflections on Judaism*, 48.

[42]   Aviad criticized Rabbi Kook for his lack of systematization and vague wording: "He [Rabbi Kook] sees sublime issues through a clear glass, but his readers do not usually merit such a clear view." See Yeshayahu Aviad (Wolfsberg), *Gateways to Philosophical Problems of Our Time* (Jerusalem, 1948), 91 [Hebrew]. On Maimonides' systematic approach in his halakhic work, see idem, *Reflections on the Philosophy of History* (Jerusalem, 1958), 150 [Hebrew].

interesting thinkers, Hayyim Hirschensohn, who devoted special efforts to the exegesis of the *Guide*.

Hirschensohn was a dynamic and enthusiastic religious Zionist activist. In his late forties he emigrated to the United States and became the rabbi of a small New Jersey city (Hoboken). When at a crossroads upon his arrival, he wrote and edited a series of discussions on the first chapters of the *Guide*. He later published these comments in a volume of twenty chapters entitled *Penei Hammah* (following BT Bava Batra 95a), which he printed together with his book *Musagei Shav ve-Emet* (On the Falsity and Truth of Some Concepts). Basically, this small volume is devoted to a sequential commentary on the *Guide*. Critical comments were embedded into chapters ostensibly meant as summaries. Often, Hirschensohn develops his exegesis while engaged in a dialogue with the work of Rabbi Aaron b. Eliyahu, *Etz ha-Hayyim*, and with the commentary of Solomon Maimon, *Giv'at ha-Moreh*.[43] Hirschensohn also wrote eighteen hermeneutical commentaries on the introduction of the *Guide* and several other glosses, and published them immediately after *Penei Hammah*. Hirschensohn was not fluent in Arabic, and his work, even more than providing an understanding of the *Guide*, served to clarify his own attitudes and his personal worldview.

Hirschensohn represents the most radical instance of the openness characterizing religious Zionism. His view fully realizes the notion of adapting conservative religion to modernity.[44] *Penei Hammah* expresses the

---

[43]   On this commentary, see G. Freudenthal and S. Klein-Braslavy, "Solomon Maimon Reads Moses ben Maimon: On Ambiguous Names," *Tarbiz* 72 (2002-3): 581-613 [Hebrew]. Hirschensohn was aware of the poor image of his commentary: "It is not my way in this book to offer many objections and explanations, or cite commentators and dismiss them, but only to explain our master's views. I do not care if the reader were to think that I have not innovated anything and only poured from one vessel to another in the same language. I know that whoever reads the book of our master and his commentators will understand the many innovations I have offered, and he who reads only my book, to him I have contributed by summarizing the views of our master, even without bringing him anything new." See his *Penei Hammah*, in "Five Selections of Religious Philosophy," in *Musagei Shav ve-Emet* (Jerusalem, 1932), 26 [Hebrew]. Hirschensohn's library on this topic was rather limited. He clarifies there that he quotes Samuel ibn Tibbon's book, *Ma'mar Yikavu ha-Mayim*, too, from *Etz ha-Hayyim*.

[44]   See E. Schweid, *Democracy and Halakhah: Studies in the Thought of Rabbi Hayyim Hirschensohn* (Jerusalem, 1978) [Hebrew]; Schwartz, *Faith at the Crossroads*, Index, s.v. "Hirschensohn"; D. Zohar, *Jewish Commitment in a Modern World: R. Hayyim Hirschensohn and His Attitude towards the Moderna* (Jerusalem and Ramat Gan, 2003).

principle of openness in the critical view that Hirschensohn consistently
displays toward the *Guide*, and concerning a number of specific issues
discussed in it. On the one hand, Hirschensohn valued the *Guide* as an
important work justifying independent discussion and, on the other, his
attitude toward it is critical and, to some extent, even sober. At times,
Hirschensohn also defended the *Guide* against accusations of heresy.[45]

Hirschensohn stated that Maimonides lacked appropriate historical
perspective ("for his interest in history was minimal").[46] This view is
particularly interesting in light of Maimonides' historicist explanations
of certain commandments, such as the sacrifices. Furthermore, although
Maimonides adduces reasons for the commandments, Hirschensohn's
critique is that he fails to explain in historical terms the community of
the Sabians[47] ("he did not look at it through a 'historical perspective'").
According to Hirschensohn, the lack of historicist thought in Maimonides
is evident in his disregard of the stylistic influences exerted by the
surrounding mythological environment of the Ancient East.

Hirschensohn assumed it was self-evident that the Bible had been
influenced by mythological language. The author of the Creation story
"couches the ideas of development in mythological metaphors."[48] How did
Hirschensohn explain these mythological stories? He separated paganism
from the "original" mythology. In his view, the mythological stories had
been, from the start, a description of a class struggle for which the narrators
resorted to symbolic language, just as the Bible refers to the sons of God and
the daughters of men (Genesis 6:2). Only later, then, did their deference
and their fear of their ancestors lead the Greeks to literal interpretations
of their mythology: "But before philosophy became dominant there, the
later Greeks had mistakenly revered their ancestors and thought of them

---

[45] One instance is his rejection of those who anchor the belief in the eternity of the world in *Guide*
1:9 (*Penei Hammah*, chapter 11).

[46] Hirschensohn, *Penei Hammah*, 4.

[47] See, e.g., S. Stroumsa, "The Sabians of Harran and the Sabians of Maimonides: On Maimonides
Theory of the History of Religions," *Sefunot* 22 (1999): 277-95 [Hebrew]; H. Mazuz, "The
Identity of the Sabians: Some Insights," in *Jewish Philosophy: Perspectives and Retrospectives*,
ed. R. Jospe and D. Schwartz (Boston, 2012), 233-54.

[48] Hirschensohn, *Penei Hammah*, 6.

as gods."[49] The Bible, then, uses a mythological style, but its messages are social and ideological.

The mythological style is at the focus of the discussion in the chapter Hirschensohn called "*Elohim*." Following the Rabbis, Maimonides stated that this term refers to judges, leading to its metaphorical usage to refer to the angels and to God:

> It did not occur to him [Maimonides] at all that the words of the serpent "you shall be as *Elohim*, knowing good and evil" (Genesis 3:5) was intended to mean the sons of gods and the demigods known in every mythology. The Onkelos translation, "you shall be as *ravrevaiya* [great men]" makes no sense. What did Eve know about great judges and leaders?! When using the term *ravrevaiya*, however, Onkelos, too, intended these gods, because this is also how he translated the verse about the sons of *Elohim* who desired the daughters of men (Genesis 6:2).[50]

According to Hirschensohn, "*Elohim*" is a distinctively mythological term, merely a stylistic remnant of the ancient world. The denotation of judges and political leaders was assigned to the term by Maimonides, who followed Onkelos.[51] Hirschensohn claimed that Maimonides had lacked historical perspective in his thought. The serpent, according to Hirschensohn, supported a developmental-dialectic method. The divine command (not to eat from the Tree of Knowledge) had a priori been meant to be disobeyed, because human development unfolds through the disclosure of good and evil by means of deeds that lead to good and evil ("inclinations").[52] Only after deceit and evil are actually committed do they become distinct acts

---

[49]   Ibid., 36. Hirschensohn ascribed the same mistake to Christianity ("the early Christians"), namely, the claim that Jesus was born from a union between a divine and a human partner.

[50]   "Sons of *ravrevaiya*." Cited from Hirschensohn, *Penei Hammah*, 4.

[51]   Hirschensohn explicitly noted that its source was "accepted interpretations in the Oral Law." By contrast, Hirschensohn noted that in the discussion about "*makom*" [place] in *Guide* 1:8, no mention is made of the denotation identifying *makom* with God, and argued that the reason is that the first part of the *Guide* is intended to explain only biblical terms, whereas this identification is Rabbinic (*Penei Hammah*, 24-25).

[52]   Hirschensohn defined Maimonidean "*muskalot*" as rational and aesthetic truths, and "*mefursamot*" as their realization in the concrete world. He used the terminology of "potentiality" (*be-koah*) and "actuality" (*be-fo'al*) to denote them, respectively (*Penei Hammah*, 5-6).

of which we can beware. Original sin is a stage in the development and maturation of humanity through experiences of failure ("there is no building without destruction/no seed without uprooting").[53] By contrast, the biblical approach negates rebellion against the divine command as a condition for development. Hirschensohn also explained *Guide* 1:2 in similar terms. He did understand that he was ascribing to Maimonides a (stylistically) mythological and anthropological-developmental explanation in claiming that the serpent was indirectly presented as a mythical entity possessing a personality. And yet, "although Maimonides was far removed from such [mythological] views, he sometimes could not refrain from feeling them 'instinctively.' Nevertheless, he did object to them."[54]

Despite Hirschensohn's critique of Maimonides, then, he still sought historicist intuitions in his personality. Hirschensohn also highlighted instances in the *Guide that* strive to preserve the literal meaning of the Bible. According to Maimonides, Moses shied away from the burning bush mainly because he understood the need for gradual acquisition of knowledge in the various sciences (logic, physics, and metaphysics, in that order) in order to engage in the apprehension of God. Moses feared apprehending God without suitable intellectual preparation. Hirschensohn comments on this exegesis:

> Indeed, Maimonides did not wish to disregard the literal reading of the Bible altogether and ignore that Moses hid his face because he was afraid to look upon the manifest light, so he said that Moses had been afraid to contemplate his thoughts about God. Had he been afraid to look upon the manifest light, he would have been all the more afraid to contemplate his thoughts about God, "who is greatly exalted above every deficiency." The Bible literally means that "Moses hid his face" (Exodus 3:6) and did not wish to look upon the manifest light, and this indicates that "he was afraid to look upon God" (loc. cit.), meaning that he was afraid to look upon his thoughts about the essence of God. The terminology of our master here is slightly inaccurate. Possibly the translation from the Arabic required this, or some words are missing from *safra batzira*,[55] and it should read from his fear to look upon the manifest light "and all the

---

[53]   Ibid., 10.

[54]   Ibid., 6.

[55]   Meaning "from the flawed book," referring to Hirschensohn's copy.

more so upon God, who cannot be apprehended by the eyes and is
greatly exalted above every deficiency."[56]

Hirschensohn was referring to the following formulation of Maimonides
in *Guide* 1:5:

> It is in this sense that it is said, "And Moses hid his face, for he was
> afraid to look upon God,"[57] this being an additional meaning of the
> verse over and above its external meaning that indicates that he hid
> his face because of his being afraid to look upon the light manifesting
> itself[58]—and not that the Deity, who is greatly exalted above every
> deficiency, can be apprehended by the eyes.

Hirschensohn stressed Maimonides' adherence to the literal reading: Moses feared the fire that erupted in the bush as well as the "destruction,"
meaning the apprehension of God (without preparation). According to
Hirschensohn's understanding, this is a case of "all the more so": Moses
feared the fire, and all the more so the apprehension. The fear of the flames
and the fear of apprehending God are a faithful description of the concrete
event—Moses feared both simultaneously. Hirschensohn attacked Solomon Maimon, who held that the apprehension is the deep meaning of the
fear.[59] In actual fact, Moses feared both the fire and the apprehension of

---

56   Ibid., 18.

57   That is, it is said concerning the need for gradual study of the sciences and abstention from
     engaging in metaphysics without any preparation in the introductory sciences.

58   Maimonides writes here (rendered from Michael Schwarz's Hebrew translation of the *Guide* [Tel
     Aviv, 2002], 38): "Besides the denotation suggested by the literal reading, that is, his fear of
     looking at the manifest light."

59   "It is not the case that our master thought that there were two exegeses for this verse, one
     literal and one of second order, as the author of *Giv'at ha-Moreh* thought. Our master has only
     seldomly endorsed such an approach, and [especially] not when the second meaning contradicts
     the first. Indeed, his [Maimonides'] view is that the first meaning of the verse is that he hid
     his face without looking at the manifest light, because he was afraid of contemplating God in
     his intellect before he had refined his views through the required introductory sciences. When
     he [Maimonides] says 'who is greatly exalted above every deficiency,' he means that, for this
     reason, the danger of a mistaken decision is great" (*Penei Hammah*, 18). Maimon presented the
     fear of the fire as an "open exegesis" and the fear of the apprehension as a "concealed exegesis"
     (Solomon Maimon, *Giv'at ha-Moreh*, ed. S. H. Bergman and N. Rotenstreich [Jerusalem, 1965],
     40-41 [Hebrew]). Maimon did not deny the concrete explanation, as is evident from the ending
     of his exegesis: "and the open exegesis is also true" (41). Hirschensohn, as shown below,
     objected to this attempt to undermine the literal interpretation by establishing a hierarchy.

God. The Arab original ("*la*") does not support the correction suggested by Hirschensohn ("all the more so"). This thought-provoking religious Zionist thinker, however, does not contribute to our philological understanding of the *Guide*, but rather to its ideological image and its exegetical trends.

Hirschensohn set up the literal reading of the Bible as one of the aims of the *Guide*. Moreover, in Chapter 13, Hirschensohn criticized Maimonides' attempts to explain verses on the basis of philosophical issues unsuited to a literal reading and not reflecting a genuine hermeneutical requirement. Maimonides thereby followed the "path of all medieval Jewish theologians."[60] Although "our master did not endorse the strange and crooked ways of other sophists [*mitpalsefim*] of his time,"[61] he still endorsed the allegorical interpretation that assumes the Torah has an inner layer. Loyalty to the literal reading suits Hirschensohn's efforts to present Maimonides' historicist consciousness as limited ("instinct").

Hirschensohn flinches from exaggerated allegories, as evident in his objection to the presentation of matter through an image of the female and of form through an image of the male. These terms originate in Aristotle's theory of nature and were the foundation of medieval science. These images were also at the focus of the controversy about the sciences at the end of the thirteenth century.[62] Hirschensohn ascribed these images to the "ramblings of Jewish medieval philosophers." Accordingly, he rejected the interpretation of Solomon Maimon, who had claimed that the discussion in *Guide* 1:6 about the names of man and woman referred to these symbols. In the course of these remarks, he was also critical of Kabbalah:

> Generally, this entire concept lacks any Jewish spirit, and Jews only received it through the Alexandrian Platonists. This concept was then newly recast by Christians and Gnostics, who turned form into the source of emanation [*mashpi'a*], and matter into its receptacle [*mekabel*], and then hallowed with divine sanctity by the Kabbalists,

---

60 Hirschensohn, *Penei Hammah*, 29. Hirschensohn argued that Maimonides had improperly argued the immutability of God (*Guide* 1: 11).

61 Hirschensohn, *Penei Hammah*, 39.

62 See, e.g., A. S. Halkin, "The Ban on the Study of Philosophy," *P'raqim* 1 (1967-1968): 35-55 [Hebrew].

who fought with their own weapons [...] Maimonides, of blessed memory, was far removed from these ramblings.[63]

Hirschensohn opposed a perception of Maimonides as an exegete who abided by medieval science. "Aristotelian ramblings have been dismissed, and our holy Torah lives and prevails forever and ever."[64] In his view, Maimonides did not symbolize the female through matter as a scientific concept, but rather the situation of materiality in general. Maimonides' intention in the various chapters was moral and, accordingly, he symbolized the material situation as female. *Guide* 3:8 (the harlot parable in Proverbs) should also be understood in similar terms, as a moral warning to be wary of materialism, and it is on these grounds that mainly the female is mentioned rather than the male. Hirschensohn senses the problematic nature of his interpretation of Maimonides:

> Indeed, here too [*Guide* 3:8], we see that medieval ramblings attempting to force Greek philosophy into biblical literature are dominant. Yet, the straight thinking of our master did not allow him to follow this spirit, although it did touch him, but he knew that the writer of the Book of Proverbs had not been concerned with the nature and essence of matter, only with its morality.[65]

---

[63]   Hirschensohn, *Penei Hammah*, 20. See also Maimon, *Giv'at ha-Moreh*, 42. For Hirschensohn's critique of Kabbalah, see Schwartz, *Faith at the Crossroads*, 112. The Kabbalists' mistake was their thinking from cause to effect, meaning their a priori assumptions. Such an approach is characterized by "faith rather than wisdom, study, and proof" (*Penei Hammah*, 40). Hirschensohn also highlighted the contrast between Maimonides and Kabbalah in his exegesis of the *Guide* 1:19 (*male*—to fill). Maimonides explained it as fullness, meaning a body entering and filling another body, and as the completion of a certain period of time ("And her days were fulfilled" [Genesis 25:24]). The meaning of completion, not necessarily of time, is also present in the verse "full with the blessing of the Lord" (Deuteronomy 33:23), implying that the blessed attain completion through the divine blessing. Hirschensohn claimed that Maimonides took pains not to ascribe the first meaning (of bodily presence) to this text, thereby rejecting Kabbalistic pantheism: "His particular concern seems to have been to tell the exegetes, who were influenced [by Gnosticism], not to rely on the first meaning of fullness, which refers also to a spiritual realm, as I explained. They, however, took this metaphor too far and explained the Divinity as well through this meaning, which is the foundation of all Kabbalistic wisdom. Our master did not want this, and he therefore explained this metaphor through the second meaning of completion" (48).

[64]   Hirschensohn, *Penei Hammah*, 32 (following PT Sanhedrin 6:10, 24a; BT Bekhorot 32a, 33a, and so forth).

[65]   Hirschensohn, *Penei Hammah*, 20. Hirschensohn admitted that, at least in his exegesis of

This is an interesting phenomenon: Hirschensohn the historicist, who was not reluctant to ascribe mythological meanings to the literal biblical text, fell into his own trap. Maimonides certainly supported the medieval scientific interpretation of the biblical text, although he did not hesitate to criticize the underpinnings of this science. The presentation of male and female as scientific images is an element of Maimonidean hermeneutics. To Hirschensohn, however, the implication that Maimonides had incorporated an archaic science into his exegesis of the sources was unbearable; hence his emphasis upon literalistic trends in the *Guide*.

A kind of counterreaction to the application of medieval science to biblical sources is discernible in the Kantian style that Hirschensohn ascribed to Maimonides' statements. Chapter 18 of *Penei Hammah* is devoted to a clarification of the "principles": matter, form, and privation.[66] Privation is the reason for the disappearance of one form and its substitution by another. However, privation cannot eliminate all forms:

> Matter, however, cannot be deprived of the form of expansion and calculation[67] intrinsic to it or, in other words, place and time, because there is no form without them that could replace them, since there is no form without these two substantial attributes. Matter must inevitably hold these two forms, unless God, the Lord of all matter and all forms and their Creator, were to create a new form that would not require these two. Matter could then exist in the absence of these two set forms and assume a new one.[68]

Although Hirschensohn presented space and time as forms and substantial attributes, this is a flimsy construct. Common to Aristotelian space and time is that they are not independent: space is the encompassing limit of the body, and time is a characteristic of movement. In a rather contrived formulation, one might say that space is form in relation to geometrical constructs. Since form and matter are relative concepts in Aristotelian theory, they can also be used in geometry. Why did Hirschensohn mention

Rabbinic texts, Maimonides did follow the scientific interpretation of matter and form and other similar notions (39).

[66] See, e.g., T. Irwin, *Aristotle's First Principles* (Oxford, 1988). These statements are formulated in a discussion of the *Guide* 1:17.

[67] A reference to time.

[68] Hirschensohn, *Penei Hammah*, 42.

space and time rather than other characteristics that the body cannot survive without (such as color, resilience, or impenetrability)? Probably because Hirschensohn was influenced here by the Kantian style that presents space and time as forms of sensibility and, as such, modes of knowledge. In any event, Hirschensohn explained through space and time the principle that bodies operate under certain necessary conditions. Only in another world could we think about existence without the conditions of space and time. Divine omnipotence allows such a world to exist. In our world, however, only God as necessarily existent is not contingent on space and time.

Maimonides' *Guide* was interpreted according to Hirschensohn's needs and expectations. He distanced Maimonides from a scientific interpretation of the biblical text and strove for a separation between archaic science and the Bible. The Bible should indeed be interpreted literally, and this literal reading should also take the Ancient East surroundings into account. However, the Bible should not be presumed to rest on scientific fashions that appear as vain ramblings to a modern thinker. Hirschensohn took the lexicographic chapters of the *Guide*, which are merely an attempt to preclude anthropomorphism, and invested them with an image of Maimonides tailored to his needs. Hirschensohn's sharpness and originality affect his style, leading to a wondrously open philosophy. His tendentiousness, however, diverted Hirschensohn more than once from the original intention of the *Guide*. What is definitely clear is that such an interpretation of the *Guide*, coming directly from Orthodox ranks, could only have been written by a religious Zionist such as Hirschensohn.

Summary

The considerations that shaped the image of Maimonides in religious Zionist thought create the following process:

(1) The importance of the Maimonidean figure: the personality and endeavor of Maimonides suited the aims of religious Zionist thought. Maimonides was the paragon of a leader open to his surroundings, an original thinker attentive to general culture, and a halakhist encompassing many realms. Religious Zionist thought, therefore, presented Maimonides as a model for imitation and a paradigmatic figure.

(2) The threat of the *Guide*: the writers of the religious-national renaissance, however, were suspicious of the *Guide*. Religious Zionism, as noted, strove to create a redemptive religious type. As such, this type must certainly engage with the surrounding culture, but must also preserve his self-respect and his originality. The *Guide*, however, is perceived as somewhat obsequious. Its commitment to medieval science in general and to Aristotle in particular threatened the goal of self-respect.

(3) Toward a solution: most religious Zionist thinkers reconciled the *Mishneh Torah* and the *Guide*, and thereby "returned" the philosophical treatise to the bosom of Judaism. Only activists and individualists (Jawitz, and Rabbi Soloveitchik in his 1940s writings) found it hard to resolve the *Guide* with Maimonides' figure.

Note that many religious Zionist thinkers preferred Judah Halevi's approach to that of Maimonides. These include, for instance, the circle that gathered around Rabbis Abraham and Zevi Yehudah Kook, who hallowed the *Kuzari* and called for it to be treated with awe, and Isaiah Aviad (Wolfsberg), who remained faithful to Halevi's approach in his articles. Maimonides' figure thus became a symbol, an intersection of several qualities: leadership, halakhic greatness, creativity, as well as philosophical and cultural openness. This figure suited the mold of the new (religious) man of the generation promoting a religious-national revival. As far as content is concerned, most religious Zionists found other thinkers far more appealing than Maimonides. As an expression of an overpowering, ideal religious pattern, however, there was no alternative to the Maimonidean figure.

We can hardly claim that religious Zionism as a movement developed a special interpretation of Maimonides' personality and endeavor. His figure, however, was a focus of identification or resistance, since his essential role in a movement of religious revival was obvious to all. Hence, the passionate controversy between Rabbi Kook and Jawitz and, indirectly, also Rabbi Soloveitchik, is not merely a historical but a current matter. Maimonides was an icon in the controversy over the acceptable level of openness to general culture and the depth of the mutual relationship between the Jewish heritage, on the one hand, and Western culture and its philosophical foundations, on the other. Religious Zionism, as noted, voluntarily endorsed the openness warranted by the adoption of the national ideal. Maimonides' figure symbolizes the borders of openness in light of the conservatism warranted by the religious dimension.

The current study should also have considered Maimonidean scholarship in Israel and abroad. Most of the second generation of scholars of the *Guide* in Israeli universities are identified with the religious Zionist idea (Warren Zev Harvey, Steven Harvey, Raphael Jospe, Yaakov Levinger, Daniel J. Lasker, Michael Zevi Nehorai, Avraham Nuriel, Howard Kreisel, Menahem M. Kellner, Aviezer Ravitzky, and others). Despite the ideological differences between these scholars, which are at times profound, all are Orthodox and all support Zionism. Many of them were educated in foreign universities and even attained high-ranking positions there, but they immigrated to Israel for ideological reasons.

The harsh struggle between supporters and opponents of Maimonidean esotericism among these scholars owes its passion partly to religious-national ideology and the adaptation of Maimonides' image to it. In this essay, I confined my research to Mizrachi ideologues, because their religious Zionist motivations are easily traceable, whereas scholars take pains to conduct their research according to "objective" criteria. It can easily be shown that the unity that David Hartman discerns in Maimonides,[69] for instance, fits his philosophical approach. But can we also say so about the other scholars mentioned above? The very admittance of ideological underpinnings could impair scholarly objectivity, a question that is occasionally discussed.

The relationship between Maimonides, Israeli academics, and religious Zionism is a complex issue, but the existence of this triple association is unquestionable. Indeed, this association sheds further light on the significant place of Maimonides' image in religious Zionism.

---

[69]   D. Hartman, *Maimonides: Torah and Philosophic Quest* (Philadelphia, 1976).

BIBLIOGRAPHY[1]

Cited Works of Rabbi Kook[2]

Eder ha-Yakar = *Eder ha-Yakar ve-Ikvei ha-Tzon* ("The Noble Sum" [see Zechariah 11:13; also a reference to the Aderet, an appellation for Rabbi Kook's father-in-law Rabbi Elijah David Rabinowitz-Teomim] and "The Tracks of the Sheep" [see Song of Songs 1:8]). Jerusalem, 1967.

Ein Ayah (The Eye of Abraham Isaac ha-Kohen) = *Ein Ayah on the Rabbinic Aggadot in Ein Yaakov*, Berakhot. Jerusalem, 1987.

"*Eitzot me-Rahok* [Counsels from Afar]." *Ha-Peles* 2 (1902): 457-64, 530-32.

Hadarav (His Chambers) = *Hadarav: Personal Chapters Collected from the Writings of Rabbi Abraham Isaac ha-Kohen Kook*. Edited by R. Sarid. Mevaseret Ziyyon, 2002.

Hug ha-Re'ayah: From the Collection of Classes in Orot ha-Kodesh by Maran, the Rav, R. Abraham Isaac ha-Kohen Kook. Jerusalem, 1988.

Igrot ha-Re'ayah (Letters of Rabbi Kook). Four volumes. Jerusalem, 1962.

Kevatzim mi-Khtav Yad Kodsho (Collections from His Holy Handwriting) = *Kevatzim mi-Ktav Yad Kodsho: The Writings of R. Abraham Isaac ha-Kohen Kook, May the Memory of the Righteous Be for a Blessing*, vols. 1-2. Jerusalem, 2006-2008. (In the footnotes: *Kevatzim*)

Ma'amarei ha-Re'ayah (Articles of Rabbi Kook). Jerusalem, 1962.

Mussar Avikha ("The Discipline of Your Father" [see Proverbs 1:8]) = *Mussar Avikha ve-Middot ha-Re'ayah*. Jerusalem, 1975.

Olat Re'ayah (wordplay based on the acronym for Rabbi Kook's full name and the burnt-offering for the pilgrimage festivals). Two volumes. Jerusalem, 1963.

Orot ha-Re'ayah (Lights of Rabbi Kook). Jerusalem, 1970.

Otzrot ha-Re'ayah (Treasures of Rabbi Kook). Edited by M. Y. Zuriel. Five volumes. Shalabim, 2002.

Shemonah Kevatzim (Eight Collections). Three volumes. Jerusalem, 1999.

---

[1]   Standard bibliographical format is frequently unsuitable for Jewish primary sources, and they appear in the Bibliography in the format in which they appear in the footnotes. If reference is not made to a specific edition, primary sources do not appear in the Bibliography. Similarly, authors of scholarly works who are historically important in their own right have their first names given in full.

[2]   All in Hebrew.

Primary Sources

Admanit, Zuriel. *Be-Tokh Ha-Zerem ve-Negdo* (Within the Stream and Against It). Edited by Y. Asher. Tel Aviv, 1977. [Hebrew]

Albo, Joseph. *Sefer ha-'Ikkarim; Book of Principles.* Edited by I. Husik. Philadelphia, 1946.

Aminoah, Nehemiah. "Our Goals in the *Moshavei Ovdim.*" In *Yalkut: Anthology of Articles on the Torah ve-Avodah Concept.* Edited by N. Aminoah and Y. Bernstein, 104-9. Jerusalem, 1931. [Hebrew]

Aviad (Wolfsberg), Yeshayahu. *Gateways to Philosophical Problems of Our Time.* Jerusalem, 1948. [Hebrew]

------. *Reflections on Judaism.* Jerusalem, 1955. [Hebrew]

------. *Reflections on the Philosophy of History.* Jerusalem, 1958. [Hebrew]

------. *Yahadut ve-Hoveh* (The Judaism of the Present). Jerusalem, 1962. [Hebrew]

Aviner, Shlomo. *Am ke-Lavi* (A People Like a Lion). Jerusalem, 1983. [Hebrew]

Berkovits, Eliezer. *Faith after the Holocaust.* New York, 1973.

Bernstein, Yeshayahu. *Ye'ud va-Derekh* (Goal and Way). Tel Aviv, 1956. [Hebrew]

Cordovero, Moses. *Or Ne'erav.* Vilna, 1899.

Dushinsky, E. Jacob. *In the Wake of Festivals and Solemn Days: Thoughts of the Festivals and Solemn Days.* New York, 1982. [Hebrew]

Goren, Shlomo. *Torat ha-Medinah.* Jerusalem, 1996. [Hebrew]

------. *Torat ha-Mo'adim.* Jerusalem, 1996. [Hebrew]

Harlap, Jacob Moses. *Hed Harim: A Collection of Letters.* Elon Moreh, 1997. [Hebrew]

Horowitz, Isaiah. *Shnei Luhot ha-Berit.* Warsaw, 1930.

Israel, the Maggid of Koznitz. *Avodat Yisrael.* Munkacs, 1929.

Jedaiah ha-Penini Bedersi. *Behinat Olam.* Premishla, 1872.

Jolles, Jacob Zevi. *Kehilat Yaakov.* Lemberg, 1870.

Joshua Heschel of Apta. *Ohev Israel.* Zhitomer, 1863.

Kook, Zevi Yehudah. *Ha-Torah ha-Go'elet* (The Redemptive Torah). Edited by H. A. Schwartz. Jerusalem, 1983.

------. *Li-Netivot Yisra'el.* Jerusalem, 1989.

Landau, Samuel Hayyim. *Ketavim* (Writings). Warsaw, 1935. [Hebrew]

Lazer, Simon Menahem. *Al ha-Mizpeh: Selected Writings.* Edited by G. Kressel. Jerusalem, 1969. [Hebrew]

Maimon (Fishman), Judah Leib. *La-Sha'ah vela-Dor* (On the Hour and the Generation). Jerusalem, 1965. [Hebrew]

Maimon, Solomon. *Giv'at ha-Moreh.* Edited by S. H. Bergman and N. Rotenstreich. Jerusalem, 1965. [Hebrew]

Maimonides. *The Guide of the Perplexed.* Translated by S. Pines. Chicago, 1963.

------. *The Guide of the Perplexed.* Translated by M. Schwarz. Tel Aviv, 2002. [Hebrew]

------. *Mishneh Torah, The Book of Knowledge.* Translated by M. Hyamson. Jerusalem, 1962.

Nahmanides. *Ramban (Nahmanides): Writings and Discourses*. Translated by
    C. B. Chavel. New York, 1978.
Saadia Gaon. *The Book of Beliefs and Opinions*. Translated by S. Rosenblatt. New
    Haven, 1948.
Sefer ha-Temunah. Lemberg, 1892.
Soloveitchik, Joseph B. *The Rav Speaks: Five Addresses on Israel, History, and the
    Jewish People*. Brooklyn, 2002.
Toledot Yeshu = Sefer Toldos Jeschu: A Jewish Life of Jesus. Edited and introduction
    by M. Krupp. Jerusalem, 2001; text: facsimile of ed. Altdorf 1681.
Unna, Moshe. *On the Paths of Thought and Deed*. Tel Aviv, 1955. [Hebrew]
The Zohar. Translated and with commentary by D. C. Matt. Stanford, 2004-.

Scholarly Literature

Altmann, A. *Studies in Religious Philosophy and Mysticism*. London, 1969.
Ambrose, D., and T. Cross, eds. *Morality, Ethics, and Gifted Minds*. New York, 2009.
Aran, G. "The Father, the Son, and the Holy Land: The Spiritual Authorities of
    Jewish-Zionist Fundamentalism in Israel." In *Spokesmen for the Despised:
    Fundamentalist Leaders in the Middle East*, edited by S. Appleby, 294-327.
    Chicago, 1997.
------. "Jewish Zionist Fundamentalism: The Bloc of the Faithful in Israel (Gush
    Emunim)." In *Fundamentalisms Observed*, edited by M. Marty and
    S. Appleby, 265-344. Chicago, 1991.
Avineri, S. *The Social and Political Thought of Karl Marx*. Cambridge, 1968.
Avivi, J. "History as a Divine Prescription." In *Rabbi Mordechai Breuer Festschrift:
    Collected Papers in Jewish Studies*, edited by M Bar-Asher et al., 709-71.
    Jerusalem, 1992. [Hebrew]
------. "The Source of Light: Rabbi Abraham Isaac Hakohen Kook's *Shemonah
    Kevatzim*." *Zohar* 1 (2000): 93-111. [Hebrew]
Avneri, Y. "Degel Yerushalayim." *Bi-Shvilei ha-Tehyiah (In the Paths of Renewal:
    Studies in Religious Zionism)* 3 (1989): 39-58. [Hebrew]
Avneri, Y., ed. *The Seventh Conference of ha-Poel ha-Mizrahi in Erez-Israel … 1935*.
    Ramat Gan, 1988. [Hebrew]
Bakon, G. "Torah Opinion and Pangs of the Messiah." *Tarbiz* 52 (1983): 497-508.
    [Hebrew]
Barak, U. "Can Amalek Be Redeemed? A Comparative Study of the Views of Rabbi
    Abraham Isaac Kook and Rabbi Jacob Moses Harlap." *Daat* 73 (2012): xxix-
    lxix.
------. "The Formative Influence of the Description of the First Degree of Prophecy
    in the *Guide* on the Perception of 'The Beginning of the Redemption' by
    Rabbi A. I. Kook's Circle." *Daat* 64-66 (2009): 361-415. [Hebrew]
------. "New Perspective on Rabbi Kook and His Circle." PhD dissertation, Bar-Ilan
    University, 2009. [Hebrew]

Barnay, J. "On the Question of the Origin of Zionism." In *From Vision to Revision: A Hundred Years of Historiography of Zionism*, edited by Y. Weitz, 135-42. Jerusalem, 1998. [Hebrew]

Belfer, E. *The Kingdom of Heaven and the State of Israel: The Political Dimension in Jewish Thought*. Ramat Gan, 1991. [Hebrew]

Ben-Artzi, H. *The New Shall Be Sacred: Rav Kook as an Innovative Posek*. Tel Aviv, 2010. [Hebrew]

Ben-Menahem, N. *Books of Mossad Harav Kook Published during the Years 1937-1970*. Jerusalem, 1970. [Hebrew]

Ben-Shlomo, J. "Perfection and Perfectibility in Rabbi Kook's Thought." *Iyyun* 33 (1984): 289-309. [Hebrew]

Bland, K. P. *The Artless Jew: Medieval and Modern Affirmations and Denials of the Visual*. Princeton, 2001.

Boaz, H. "The Religious 'Status Quo' and the Generation of Social Categories: The Struggle for Female Suffrage in the Pre-State Period." *Theory and Criticism* 21 (2002): 107-31. [Hebrew]

Brown, P. *The Cult of the Saints: Its Rise and Function in Latin Christianity*. Chicago, 1981.

Cherlow, S. "The Circle of Rav Kook as a Mystical Fraternity." *Tarbiz* 74 (2005): 261-303. [Hebrew]

------. "Messianism and the Messiah in the Circle of Rav Kook." *Moreshet Israel* 2 (2006): 42-87. [Hebrew]

------. *The Tzaddiq Is the Foundation of the World: Rav Kook's Esoteric Mission and Mystical Experience*. Ramat Gan, 2012. [Hebrew]

Cherlow, Y. "On Modesty and Regeneration: An Exchange of Letters between R. Kook and R. David Cohen." *Iyyun* 46 (1998): 441-50. [Hebrew]

------. *The Torah of the Land of Israel in Light of the Teachings of R. Abraham Isaac Hakohen Kook*. Hispin, 1998. [Hebrew]

Cornell, V. *Realm of the Saint: Power and Authority in Moroccan Sufism*. Austin, TX, 1998.

Don Yehiya, E. "The Negation of Galut in Religious Zionism." *Modern Judaism* 12 (1992): 129-55.

Dothan, S. *Partition of Eretz-Israel in Mandatory Period: The Jewish Controversy*. Jerusalem, 1980. [Hebrew]

Efros, I. *Philosophical Terms in the Moreh Nebukim*. New York, 1924.

Eisenstadt, S. N. *Revolution and the Transformation of Societies*. New York, 1978.

Elazar, D. J. "The Community from Its Beginnings till the Threshold of the Modern Era." In *Kinship and Consent: The Jewish Political Tradition and Its Contemporary Uses*, edited by D. J. Elazar, 174-207. Jerusalem, 1981. [Hebrew]

Engell, J. *The Creative Imagination: Enlightenment to Romanticism*. Cambridge, MA, 1981.

Ernst, C. *Manifestations of Sainthood in Islam*. Istanbul, 1993.

------. *Ruzbihan Baqli: Mysticism and the Rhetoric of Sainthood in Persian Sufism.* Richmond, Surrey, 1996.

Freudenthal, G., and S. Klein-Braslavy. "Solomon Maimon Reads Moses ben Maimon: On Ambiguous Names." *Tarbiz* 72 (2002-2003): 581-613. [Hebrew]

Friedman, M. *Society and Religion: The Non-Zionist Orthodoxy in Eretz-Israel—1918-1936.* Jerusalem, 1978. [Hebrew]

Garb, J. "'Alien' Culture in the Circle of Rabbi Kook." In *Study and Knowledge in Jewish Thought,* edited by H. Kreisel. Beersheva, 2006

------. *The Chosen Will Become Herds: Studies in Twentieth-Century Kabbalah.* Translated by Y. Berkovits-Murciano. New Haven, 2009.

------. "Rabbi Kook: National Thinker or a Mystic Poet." *Daat* 54 (2004): 69-96. [Hebrew]

------. "Rabbi Kook: Working out as Divine Work." In *Sport and Physical Education in Jewish History,* edited by G. Eisen, 7-14. Netanyah, 2003.

Glasner, M. S. "Zionism in the Light of Faith." In *Torah and Kingdom: On the Place of the State in Judaism,* edited by S. Federbusch. Jerusalem, 1961. [Hebrew]

Goldman, E. "The Worship Peculiar to Those Who Have Apprehended True Reality." *Bar-Ilan: Annual of Bar-Ilan University* 6 (1968): 287-313. [Hebrew]

Gorni, J. "On Social 'Manners' and National Interest: The Question of Religious-Secular Coexistence in the Zionist Movement." In *Priesthood and Monarchy: Studies in the Historical Relationships of Religion and State,* edited by I. Gafni and G. Motzkin, 269-276. Jerusalem, 1987. [Hebrew]

Goshen-Gottstein, A. *Religious Genius and the Interreligious Study of Saints: Constructing a Category, with Implications for Understanding Wisdom, Spiritual Information and Character Development.* Elijah Interfaith Institute concept paper, 2013.

Gurevitz, D. *Postmodernism: Culture and Literature at the End of the 20th Century.* Tel Aviv, 1997. [Hebrew]

Guttel, N. *Innovation in Tradition: The Halakhic-Philosophical Teachings of Rabbi Kook.* Jerusalem, 2005. [Hebrew]

------. *Mekhutavei Re'ayah: The Circles of R. Avraham Itzhak HaCohen Kook's Correspondents.* Jerusalem, 2000. [Hebrew]

Habermann, A. M. *Shirei ha-Yihud ve-ha-Kavod.* Jerusalem, 1948. [Hebrew]

Halkin, A. S. "The Ban on the Study of Philosophy." *P'raqim: Yearbook of the Schocken Institute ...* 1 (1967-1968): 35-55. [Hebrew]

Harpham, G. G. *The Ascetic Imperative in Culture and Criticism.* Chicago, 1993.

Harshav, B. "The Revival of Eretz Israel and the Modern Jewish Revolution: Reflections on the Current Situation." In *Observation Points: Culture and Society in Eretz Israel,* edited by N. Gertz, 7-31. Tel Aviv, 1988. [Hebrew]

Hartman, D. *Maimonides: Torah and Philosophic Quest.* Philadelphia, 1976.

Harvey, Z. "Maimonides and Spinoza on the Knowledge of Good and Evil." *Binah* 2 (1989): 131-46.

Henderson, J. B. *The Construction of Orthodoxy and Heresy*. Albany, 1998.

Hirschenson, Hayyim. *Penei Hammah*, in "Five Selections of Religious Philosophy." In *Musagei Shav ve-Emet*. Jerusalem, 1932. [Hebrew]

Horne, J. "Saintliness and Moral Perfection." *Religious Studies* 27 (1991): 463-71.

Idel, M. "On the History of the Interdiction against the Study of Kabbalah before the Age of Forty." *AJS Review* 5 (1980): i-xx. [Hebrew]

------. "Rabbi Abraham Abulafia, Gershom Scholem and Rabbi David Ha-Kohen (Ha-Nazir)." In *The Path of the Spirit: The Eliezer Schweid Jubilee Volume* (*Jerusalem Studies in Jewish Thought*) 19, edited by Y. Amir, 819-34. Jerusalem, 2005. [Hebrew]

Inge, W. R. *Christian Mysticism*. London, 1899.

Irwin, T. *Aristotle's First Principles*. Oxford, 1988.

Ish-Shalom, B. *Rav Avraham Itzhak HaCohen Kook: Between Rationalism and Mysticism*. Translated by O. Wiskind-Elper. Albany, 1993.

------. "Tolerance and Its Theoretical Basis in the Teaching of Rabbi Kook." *Daat* 20 (1988): 151-68. [Hebrew]

Jawitz, Z. *Sefer Toledot Israel*, vol. 12. Tel Aviv, 1935. [Hebrew]

Kaddari, M. Z. "The Ideology of 'Bnei-Akiba' in Hungary." In *A Hundred Years of Religious Zionism* vol. 2: *Historical Aspects*, edited by A. Sagi and D. Schwartz, 339-56. Ramat Gan, 2003.

------. "Introduction to an Analysis of the Language of Rabbi Avraham Yitzhak Hacohen Kook." In *A Hundred Years of Religious Zionism*, vol. 1: *Figures and Thought*, edited by A. Sagi and D. Schwartz, 255-60. Ramat Gan, 2003. [Hebrew]

Kant, I. *Critique of the Power of Judgment*. Translated by P. Guyer and E. Matthews. Cambridge, 2000.

Kellner, M. M. *Maimonides on the "Decline of the Generations" and the Nature of Rabbinic Authority*. Albany, NY, 1996.

Kepnes, S. "Introduction." In *Interpreting Judaism in a Postmodern Age*, edited by S. Kepnes. New York, 1996.

Kohat, C. "The Distress of the Torah Lerner in Rav Kook's Philosophy." *Iggud: Selected Essays in Jewish Studies* 1 (2008): 407-28. [Hebrew]

Kollender, A. *Transcendental Beauty*. Jerusalem, 2001. [Hebrew]

Leff, G. *Heresy in the Later Middle Ages: The Relation of Heterodoxy to Dissent c. 1250–c. 1450*. Manchester, 1967.

Lifshitz, H. *Shivhei ha-Re'ayah: What Was Related about Rabbi Abraham Isaac ha-Kohen Kook*. Jerusalem, 1979. [Hebrew]

Maimon (Fishman), Judah Leib. *R. Moses b. Maimon: His Biography and Literary Oeuvre*. Jerusalem, 1960. [Hebrew]

------. *Rabbi Abraham Isaac ha-Kohen Kook*. Jerusalem, 1965. [Hebrew]

Mazuz, H. "The Identity of the Sabans: Some Insights." In *Jewish Philosophy: Perspectives and Retrospectives*, edited by R. Jospe and D. Schwartz, 233-54. Boston, 2012.

Melamed, A. *On the Shoulders of Giants.* Ramat Gan, 2003. [Hebrew]

Michael, R. *Jewish Historiography from the Renaissance to the Modern Time.* Jerusalem, 1993. [Hebrew]

Nehorai, M. Z. "Remarks on the Rabbinic Rulings of Rabbi Kook." *Tarbiz* 59 (1990): 481-505. [Hebrew]

Neumann, B. *Land and Desire in Early Zionism.* Translated by H. Watzman. Waltham, MA, 2011.

Neville, R. *Soldier, Sage, Saint.* New York, 1978.

Orian, Meir. *The Guide for the Generations: R. Moses b. Maimon.* Jerusalem, 1956. [Hebrew]

Pike, N. *Mystic Union: An Essay in the Phenomenology of Mysticism.* Ithaca, NY, 1992.

Ravitzky, A. *Messianism, Zionism, and Jewish Religious Radicalism.* Translated by M. Swirsky and J. Chipman. Chicago, 1996.

Rosenberg, S. "Introduction to the Thought of Rabbi Kook." In *Yovel Orot: The Thought of Rabbi Abraham Isaac ha-Kohen Kook, of blessed memory,* edited by B. Ish-Shalom and S. Rosenberg. Jerusalem, 1985. [Hebrew]

------. "R. Abraham Isaac Hakohen Kook and the Blind Crocodile (*Orot ha-Kodesh* and the Philosophy of Schopenhauer)." In *Beoro: Studies in the Teachings of R. Abraham Isaac Hakohen Kook and the Ways of Teaching It,* edited by H. Hamiel, 317-52. Jerusalem, 1986. [Hebrew]

Rosenthal, E. S. "'For the Most Part.'" *P'raqim: Yearbook of the Schocken Institute ...* 1 (1967-1968): 183-224. [Hebrew]

Ross, T. "Between Metaphysical and Liberal Pluralism: A Reappraisal of Rabbi A. I. Kook's Espousal of Toleration." *AJS Review* 21 (1996): 61-110.

------. "The Elite and the Masses in the Prism of Metaphysics and History: Harav Kook on the Nature of Religious Belief." *Journal of Jewish Thought and Philosophy* 8 (1999): 355-67.

Rotenstreich, N. "On Prophetic Consciousness." *Journal of Religion* 54 (1974): 185-98.

------. *Studies in Jewish Philosophy in the Modern Period.* Tel Aviv: Am Oved, 1978. [Hebrew]

Rozenak, A. "Halakhah, Aggadah and Prophecy in Torat Eretz Israel through the Prism of 'the Unification of Opposites' in the Writings of Rabbi A.I.H. Kook." In *A Hundred Years of Religious Zionism,* vol. 1: *Figures and Thought,* edited by A. Sagi and D. Schwartz, 261-85. Ramat Gan, 2003. [Hebrew]

------. *Prophetic Halakhah: Rabbi A. I. H. Kook's Philosophy of Halakhah.* Jerusalem, 2007. [Hebrew]

------. *Rabbi A. I. Kook.* Jerusalem, 2007. [Hebrew]

Rubinstein, A. *A Movement in a Period of Transition.* Ramat Gan, 1981. [Hebrew]

Salmon, Y., "The 'New Jew' in the Perception of Religious Zionism." *Israel: Studies in Zionism and the State of Israel* 17 (2010): 239-57. [Hebrew]

Schlegel, F. von. *Philosophical Fragments.* Translated by F. Firchow. Minneapolis, 1991.

Scholem, G. G. *Major Trends in Jewish Mysticism*. New York, 1969.

Schwartz, D. *Aggadah in the Prism of Phenomenology: A Reexamination of "Heavenly Torah."* Forthcoming. [Hebrew]

------. "Avicenna and Maimonides on Immortality: A Comparative Study." In *Medieval and Modern Perspectives on Muslim-Jewish Relations*, edited by R. L. Nettler, 185-97. Chur, Switzerland, 1995.

------. *Challenge and Crisis in Rabbi Kook's Circle*. Tel Aviv, 2001. [Hebrew]

------. *Contradiction and Concealment in Medieval Jewish Thought*. Ramat Gan, 2002. [Hebrew]

------. "The Debate over the Maimonidean Theory of Providence in Thirteenth-Century Jewish Philosophy." *Jewish Studies Quarterly* 2 (1995): 185-96.

------. "Epigrams ('Siyyurin') of R. David Ibn Bilia." *Kiryat Sefer* 63 (1990-1991): 637-54. [Hebrew]

------. "Ethics and Asceticism in the Neoplatonic School of the 14th Century." In *Between Religion and Ethics*, edited by A. Sagi and D. Statman, 185-208. Ramat Gan, 1993. [Hebrew]

------. *Faith at the Crossroads: A Theological Profile of Religious Zionism*. Translated by B. Stein. Leiden, 2002.

------. "From First Blossoming to Realization: The History of the Religious Zionist Movement and Its Ideas." In *The Religious Zionism: An Era of Changes; Studies in Memory of Zvulun Hammer*, edited by A. Cohen and Y. Harel, 40-51. Jerusalem, 2004. [Hebrew]

------. *Habad's Thought from Beginning to End*. Ramat Gan, 2011. [Hebrew]

------. *Land of Israel in Religious Zionist Thought*. Tel Aviv, 1997. [Hebrew]

------. *Messianism in Medieval Jewish Thought*. Second edition. Ramat Gan, 2006. [Hebrew]

------. *Music in Jewish Thought*. Ramat Gan, 2013. [Hebrew]

------. "On Religious Zionist Extremism: Education and Ideology." In *Dor le Dor: Studies in the History of Jewish Education in Israel and the Diaspora*. Forthcoming. [Hebrew]

------. *Philosophy of a Fourteenth-Century Jewish Neoplatonic Circle*. Jerusalem, 1996. [Hebrew]

------. *The Philosophy of Rabbi Joseph B. Soloveitchik*. Translated by B. Stein. Vol. 1: *Religion or Halakha*. Leiden, 2007; vol. 2: *From Phenomenology to Existentialism*. Leiden, 2012.

------. *Religious-Zionism: History and Ideology*. Translated by B. Stein. Boston, 2009.

------. "Religious Zionism and the Idea of the New Person." *Israel: Studies in Zionism and the State of Israel* 16 (2009): 143-64. [Hebrew]

------. *Religious Zionism between Logic and Messianism*. Tel Aviv, 1999. [Hebrew]

Schwebel, M. "Moral Creativity as Artistic Transformation." *Creativity Research Journal* 6 (1993): 65-81.

Schweid, E. *Democracy and Halakhah: Studies in the Thought of Rabbi Hayyim Hirschensohn*. Jerusalem, 1978. [Hebrew]

------. *The Idea of Modern Jewish Culture*. Translated by A. Hadary. Boston, 2008.

------. "Renewed Prophecy in the Face of the Beginning of Redemption." *Daat* 38 (1997): 83-103. [Hebrew]

Shailat, I. *Letters and Essays of Moses Maimonides*. Vol. 2. Maaleh Adumim, 1998. [Hebrew]

Shapira, A. *New Jews Old Jews*. Tel Aviv, 1997. [Hebrew]

Shapira, J. "Thought and Halakhah in the Philosophy of Rabbi Isaac Jacob Reines." PhD dissertation, Hebrew University, 1997. [Hebrew]

Shatzmiller, J. "Jews, Pilgrimage, and the Christian Cult of Saints: Benjamin of Tudela and His Contemporaries." In *After Rome's Fall: Narrators and Sources of Early Medieval History*, edited by A. Collander Murray, 337-47. Toronto, 1998.

Sole, M. Z. "The Monotheistic Worldview in His Teachings." In *Ha-Re'ayah: Collected Articles from the Teachings of Our Master, Rabbi Abraham Isaac Hakohen Kook ...*, edited by Y. Raphael, 85-91. Jerusalem, 1966. [Hebrew]

Sorokin, P. *The Ways and Power of Love: Factors and Techniques of Moral Transformation*. Boston, 1954.

Steinsaltz, A. *My Rebbe*. Jerusalem, 2014.

Stroumsa, S. "The Sabians of Harran and the Sabians of Maimonides: On Maimonides Theory of the History of Religions." *Sefunot* 22 (1999): 277-95.

Summers, D. "Why Did Kant Call Taste a 'Common Sense'?" In *Eighteenth-Century Aesthetics and the Reconstruction of Art*, edited by P. Mattick, Jr., 120-51. Cambridge, 1993.

Tadmor Shimony, T. "The Textbook as an Ideological Text: The Formation of the National Identity in National School Readers and in Religious National School Readers." In *Between Tradition and Innovation: Studies in Judaism, Zionism and the State of Israel—Yehoshua Kaniel: In Memoriam*, edited by E. Don Yehiya, 467-93. Ramat Gan, 2005. [Hebrew]

Tartakower, A., et al., eds. *Zekher Mordekhai: Dedicated to the Life and Activity of Rabbi Mordecai Nurock*. Jerusalem, 1967. [Hebrew]

Templeton, J. *Possibilities for Over One Hundredfold More Spiritual Information*. Philadelphia, 2000.

Tester, K. *The Life and Times of Post-modernity*. London, 1993.

Tirosh, J. "Religious Zionism: Selected Writings of Religious-Zionist Thinkers." In *Mizpeh (Hazofeh Yearbook for 1953)*, 35-68. [Hebrew]

Tishby, I. *The Doctrine of Evil and the "Kelippah" in Lurianic Kabbalism*. Jerusalem, 1984. [Hebrew]

Twersky, I. "Concerning Maimonides' Rationalization of the Commandments; an Explication of *Hilkot Me'ilah*, VIII:8." In *Studies in the History of Jewish Society*, edited by I. Etkes and Y. Salmon, 25-33. Jerusalem, 1980. [Hebrew]

------. *Introduction to the Code of Maimonides (Mishneh Torah)*. New Haven, 1980.

Vauchez, A. *Sainthood in the Later Middle Ages*. Translated by J. Birrell. Cambridge, 1997.

Vital, D. *Ha-Mahapekhah ha-Zionit* (*The Zionist Revolution*), I-III. Tel Aviv, 1978-1991. [Hebrew]

Wall, J. "Phronesis as Poetic: Moral Creativity in Contemporary Aristotelianism." *The Review of Metaphysics* 59 (2005): 313-31.

Warhaftig, I. "Rabbinic Reaction to the 1937 Peale [*sic*] Partition Plan." *Tehumin* 9 (1988): 269-300. [Hebrew]

Werfel (Raphael), Y. *Writings of the G[aon] R. A[braham] I[saac] Kook, of Blessed Memory*. Jerusalem, 1938. [Hebrew]

Wertheimer, S. A. *Batei Midrashot*. Vol. 2: *Midrash Temurah ha-Shalem*. Jerusalem, 1953.

Wyschogrod, E. *Saints and Postmodernism: Revisioning Moral Philosophy*. Chicago, 1990.

Yaron, Z. *The Philosophy of Rabbi Kook*. Translated by A. Tomaschoff. Jerusalem, 1991.

Zaehner, R. C. *Mysticism Sacred and Profane*. Oxford, 1957.

Zehavi, I. Z. *From the Hatam Sofer to Herzl: The History of Hibbat Zion and the Beginnings of Zionism in Hungary*. Jerusalem, 1966. [Hebrew]

Zemach, S. *On the Beautiful: Methods to Explain Beauty and Its Sources*. Tel Aviv, 1939. [Hebrew]

Zohar, D. *Jewish Commitment in a Modern World: R. Hayyim Hirschensohn and His Attitude towards the Moderna*. Jerusalem and Ramat Gan, 2003. [Hebrew]

Zohar, H. *Mossad Harav Kook: Its Beginnings, Founders, Leaders, the Mizrahi Movement, Their Contribution to the Study of Religious Zionism and the Land of Israel*. Jerusalem, 2005. [Hebrew]

Zohar, Z. "Traditional Flexibility and Modern Strictness: Two Halakhic Positions on Women's Suffrage." In *Sephardi and Middle Eastern Jewries: History and Culture in the Modern Era*, edited by H. Goldberg, 119-33. Bloomington, IN, 1996.

Index of Names

INDEX OF SUBJECTS

emanation to *Tiferet* and *Malkhut*
        101 n. 11
Higayon 82
Hod 43, 45 and n. 57, 87
Holiness 67-68, 75 n. 10, 98 n. 2, 116,
        121, 125, 130, 133, 135
    majestic in holiness 14, 45-46 and n. 60
    supreme 57
    sparks 69
    of the soul 76
    divine 105-106
    increase holiness 119
    major (*kodesh hamur*) 131
    minor (*kodesh kal*) 131-132
    see also Saint, *Tiferet*
Holy 11, 33, 71, 120 125, 130, 134,
        139-140, 176
    "holy" sentiment (*regesh*) 15
    kadosh , kodesh, kedoshim meaning
        "holy" 29, 33 and n. 17
    in the writing of Rabbi Kook 34-36,
        43, 57
    the righteous and angels 37, 54, 64-65,
        140 n. 48
    genius perceives the holy 40
    holy people 51 n. 80, 153, 162 n. 13
    holy sparks 55 n. 5, 67-68, 69 and
        n. 72, 70, 86, 88, 98, 130
    holy light 58, 108, 127
    holy soul 64-65
    holy frame 67-68
    mission of 74 n. 4
    holy flesh of the Israelite body 76
    eating 98
    Holy One, Blessed be He 102, 104
    inner 102-103
    sentiment 103
    divine 105-106
    of the Second Aliyah 105-106, 118-119
    supernal 110
    supernal holy height 111
    laying a hand on 112
    holy life 113

holy of holies 113, 176
    spirit of the nation 116
    princes 116 n. 80
    extraction of 118
    wicked people increase holiness 119
    in the messianic era 121
    holy content of literature 127
    holy aspirations 133
    Holy Land 155 n. 3, 164
    and the prophet 156
    Mishneh Torah 176
    R. Judah ha-Nasi 179
    Holy Torah 193
    see also Music, Poetry, Secularization
Humility
    and the new man 27 and n. 21
    should be feared 65 n. 58
    body closeness to soul 76
    act of the genius 89
    and saint 89
    of justice 140
    Rabbi Kook expression of 141 n. 54
    see also Humility, New man, Perfect
        man, Righteous individual,
        Saint

                    I
Impertinence
    power of 67 and n. 66, 68
    at the beginning of Redemption 68
    saint must act impertinently 68
Inclusion 51, 61, 63, 91 and n. 72, 81,
        92-93
    saint 59
    perfect man 89
    act of 92
Individual see Righteous individual
Intellective mission 136
Intellective communion
        see Devekut sikhlit
Intellectual genius 40, 42 n. 47
Intelligence *see Binah*
Intuition 41

CPSIA information can be obtained
at www.ICGtesting.com
Printed in the USA
FFOW03n2256241115
18994FF